Word Dynamics

Word Dynamics

◆

Insights For Successful Living

Jerry Smith

iUniverse, Inc.
New York Lincoln Shanghai

Word Dynamics
Insights For Successful Living

All Rights Reserved © 2004 by Jerry Smith

No part of this book may be reproduced or transmitted in any form or by any means, graphic, electronic, or mechanical, including photocopying, recording, taping, or by any information storage retrieval system, without the written permission of the publisher.

iUniverse, Inc.

For information address:
iUniverse, Inc.
2021 Pine Lake Road, Suite 100
Lincoln, NE 68512
www.iuniverse.com

Unless otherwise noted, Scripture quotations are from the King James Version of the Bible.
Notations indicated by *NIV* refer to Scripture taken from the HOLY BIBLE, NEW INTERNATIONAL VERSION, Copyright © 1973, 1978, 1984 International Bible Society.
Used by permission of Zondervan Bible Publishers.
Notations indicated by *NKJV* refer to Scripture taken from the New King James Version. Copyright © 1979, 1980, 1982 by Thomas Nelson, Inc. Used by permission. All rights reserved.

ISBN: 0-595-30931-3

Printed in the United States of America

Contents

Preface vii

Chapter 1	Everything Hangs On A Word 1
Chapter 2	The Negative Power of Words. 11
Chapter 3	The Heart—The Place Where Words Work 21
Chapter 4	The Mysterious Nature Of Your Heart 28
Chapter 5	The Tin Man's Search 36
Chapter 6	Faith—The Activator Of Words 43
Chapter 7	Every Farmer's Struggle 51
Chapter 8	The Internal Operation Of Word Dynamics 61
Chapter 9	Your Heart—The Golden "Mercy Seat" 71
Chapter 10	Prayer And The Power Of Word Dynamics 79
Chapter 11	The Power Of Positive Word Dynamics 88
Chapter 12	The Practical Use of Positive Word Dynamics. 96
Chapter 13	Learning To Use Positive Word Dynamics 104
Chapter 14	Repairing The Damage Of Negative Word Dynamics 114
Chapter 15	Power Principles And Positive Word Dynamics 125
Chapter 16	Using Powerwords For Personal Success And Blessing 135

Chapter 17	Using Powerwords For Personal Success And Blessing (continued)	142
Chapter 18	Word Dynamics And Family Concerns	150
Chapter 19	Word Dynamics And Family Concerns (continued)	157
Chapter 20	Word Dynamics And Church-State Issues	165
Chapter 21	Word Dynamics And Important Life Decisions	173
Chapter 22	Word Dynamics And The Believer's Unique Relationship To God	181
Chapter 23	Word Dynamics And The Believer's Unique Relationship To God (continued)	190
Word Dynamics Summary Points		201
A Word Dynamics Action Inventory		205
About The Author		207

Preface

Everything in life hangs upon some word from some source producing success and blessing or defeat and curse. We cannot get around it. We operate by words every day of our life. We give forth words and receive words. The worlds were formed by the words of God and our world is formed by words as well. How we receive words or give forth words determines what happens in our life.

The principles, truths, and concepts contained in this work are put forth as an effort to identify words, become aware of them, combat negative harmful words, and use positive words for success and blessing. Our world is being affected by words, usually harmful words, this very moment. It is incumbent upon us all, especially believers in Jesus Christ, to examine the word our life is built upon and the words we use every day.

Examine the concepts in this material carefully and put them up alongside what you have always thought or believed. Approach this material with a determination to "think" and to seek out the truth. Jesus said, "If you hold to my teaching, you are really my disciples. Then you will know the truth, and the truth will set you free" (John 8:31,32, NIV).

We act upon words every day of our life. Words, like seeds, implanted on our heart produce good fruit or bad fruit. This material is designed to help you understand and use some of the most dynamic concepts in the universe for good and abundant fruit. My prayer for you is that God will enable you to learn the truths and put them into action so that you can stake a claim for the true riches of this life and the life to come.

Jerry Smith

1

Everything Hangs On A Word

The dictionary describes a *word* as a sound or a combination of sounds, or its representation in writing or printing, that symbolizes and communicates a meaning—an utterance, remark, or comment—the text of a vocal musical composition—an assurance or promise—a command or direction—a verbal signal—a password or watchword—news—remarks—the logos—the Scriptures or the Gospel. In our view it is also an agreement or covenant between two parties—an expression whether verbal, written, or physical—body language—a constitution—a law—a party platform—impressions—thought—a dramatic presentation—a picture—the theme of a movie—any thing communicated. A word can be a lie or a truth—government propaganda—"trash talk" in a ball game—a speech by a famous personality—Hollywood gossip. My point is that one should understand that a word is not just a written substance with vowels, consonants, and relative meaning. A word can be an involved communication in an abstract setting or subjective form. It can be in a single form or a composite of many words. It can even be an image that is impressed upon us. A word can be plain and visible or subliminal and veiled. It can be the word of a thing (outward statement) or the word in a thing (the real meaning).

The real meaning of a word must be made clear. Was it a matter of word interpretation when former President, Bill Clinton, looked into the reporter's cameras, pointed his finger at us and said, "I did not have sex with that woman"? Or maybe it was his veiled word interpretation when, before the impeachment committee, he casually answered, "It depends on what the meaning of *is* is." Possibly, his actions had no substance at all but were, in the words of Mrs. Clinton, a "Vast right-wing conspiracy."

How we interpret words or the intent of words is vitally important in regard to their true impact. A child may look up from his math homework and say, "Mommy, I have a problem." Or the Houston control station can receive a word from the space capsule, Apollo 13, "Houston, we have a problem." Yes there is a problem and then there is a problem! Words and how they are interpreted make a world of difference.

Words are important because they convey a *word*. When former President George H. Bush responded in a televised debate, "Read my lips—no new taxes," he was stating a plank in his platform. But then taxes were raised and it did not set well with the voting public who had endorsed the platform and believed the statement.

In seminary studies, and particularly in classes that deal with interpreting the Scriptures, we are taught the difference between *exigesis* and *eisegesis*. To exegete a passage is to get the true meaning out of it, taking into consideration things such as geography, social customs of the day, the context, grammar, and word-order emphasis, the author's intent, the audience, the setting, and the time period in which it was written. Eisegisis refers to reading into the text something that was not intended or not there in the original intent. The Bible says, "And Judas went out and hanged himself." It also says in another context, "Go, and do thou likewise." To combine these is to do grave injustice to the Scripture, theology, the Bible text, and the true meaning. Yet, people through history, have created their own theology and philosophies by reading into a text a meaning that is not really there.

I am going to spend a good deal of print here in the next few paragraphs to press home the definition of a *word*. I think we know, in a surface sort of way, the idea of a word. But the way we operate says that, if we understand, we are not applying the dynamics of it in a positive and prosperous way. We are, instead, allowing negative word dynamics to impress us and depress us in all kinds of areas.

A second emphasis that I want to make is that what we are about here cuts through *all of life*—all theologies, religions, philosophies, politics, and human experience. I have been trained in theology and have pastoral experience. I have a Scriptural, Biblical, and Christian bias that one will notice, weaves itself through this entire material. And I will approach this subject from that bias without timidity or embarrassment. Yet, I came to see quite early in my studies of this idea that it pervades all of human experience. It is not just for the conservative, Biblically-oriented, church-going, American. In fact, as I will point out, there are some common universals here that even the so-called atheist and agnostic can use. What may shock some, is that Jesus was the one to point out these universal truths. Wicked Caesar in the philosophies of the Greco-Roman empire could use these word dynamics. Jesus and the Apostle Paul used them. Adolf Hitler used them. The television evangelist and faith healer uses them. But the child in kindergarten, junior high, high school, or college uses them. The poor dirt farmer uses them as well as the physics teacher in the school for aerospace science. You use them—or they are used on you.

I am so confident of the truths in this book, that if you understand and apply what is being said, your whole life will be changed. Yes, that is a big statement but it is no bigger than the very statements regarding our abilities that were voiced by Jesus Christ, himself. Word dynamics are powerful and pervasive. In fact we use them or have them used on us every single day. You are what you are today because of either positive or negative word dynamics that have affected your life. But before I get ahead of myself, let us consider again, the bedrock definition of a *word*. We must first understand a *word* before we can understand how it works for us or against us.

The Word Of God

One of the first things that we need to learn is that everything in life hinges upon, or hangs upon, or is derived from a word. The Bible says that the worlds were formed by God speaking forth words. "By faith we understand that the universe was formed at God's command, so that what is seen was not made out of what was visible" (Hebrews 11:3, NIV).

Jesus Christ is called the "Word" (logos) from God in John's gospel. Then in Paul's letter to the Colossians, he writes that by this "Word," called Jesus, everything holds together. "He is before all things, and in him all things hold together"(Colossians 1:17, NIV). The literal Greek word translated *consist* in the King James Version and *hold together* in the New International Version means to *stick together* like glue. Not only is God's very nature and person a *word* to us but His entire body of rules and regulations form a *word* to us by which we know life and blessing.

According to the Bible (Romans 10: 9-10), the believer's salvation is dependent upon a word. First the word of the Gospel approaches. Then the recipient confesses this *word* and salvation comes. Everything hangs upon some word.

Our Government Operates By A Word

Our country holds together on the basis of a word we call the *Constitution Of The United States Of America*. Our government makes laws for us to live by which are nothing more than a *word* to us. The *Bill Of Rights* is a more defined word to the citizens of the United States. The state and local governments have constitutions, rules, and regulations that form a *word*. The courts, in turn, interpret that *word* in particular cases with an applicable ruling.

In our court system, we have a judge who seeks to apply the law to the situation at hand. The law is a *word* to go by. There is a defense attorney and a prosecutor who seeks to get at the true word of the conflict. The witnesses are asked to swear on the Bible to speak the truth, the whole, truth, and nothing but the truth. Why? It is because we are trying to get at the *word* of the situation. The jury then listens to the words being battered back and forth. Then they go away into their closed jury room to try to arrive at a verdict. A verdict is a *word* for the conflict. They return to the courtroom and give forth their word on the matter. Then the judge issues the sentence—which is a *word* to the one on trial.

Social Customs And Actions Are A Result Of A Word

In our country, a marriage is based upon a *word* we call a *marriage license*. It is further enhanced by the *engagement word* which preceded it. Then it is validated again before witnesses in a ceremony where *vows* or public *words* are voiced.

Violent gangs form around some word. Even their name is suggestive of their *word* or message; *Crips, Bloods, Hell's Angels, Gangster Disciples*. To join sometimes requires that the initiate perform according to the leader's *word*.

The posters and music in a teenager's room are words that the teen listens to, lives by, and patterns after. Body piercing nose rings and tattoos didn't just happen. A *rock singer* or a *Hollywood star* put forth that word. Everything hangs on a word.

Hollywood movies and life-styles sends forth a word that we can live in promiscuity and sexual freedom without having to pay a price. The true word is that sexually transmitted disease is a growing blight in our land. Scientists clamor to find a cure for *Aids* and other sexually transmitted diseases. Following after a wrong word is always devastating. Everything hangs on a word!

Our Economy Functions By A Word

Americans spend 110% of their income because they have first bought into an advertiser's slick *word* presentation we call an advertisement. A budget may be an answer. It is a *word*. Violate the word of the budget and you get into trouble. Listen to a wrong word about where and how to spend your money and financial bondage and drought will come. Many experts say that the number one cause of problems in marriages has to do with money, or the lack of it, or the misuse of it.

Abide by a good word about spending and saving, and your bad financial situation will turn around. Savings and abundance will come. Everything hangs upon some word from some source.

The Chairman of the Federal Reserve can go before Congress to give an economic report and the stock market will respond dramatically to his words. In fact, the news often shows a graph of the market while his report is being given. If he gives a positive word the market goes up. If he is negative the chart shows a dramatic down turn. The market is not responding to anything but a man's words. Everything hangs on a word!

Our Education System Is A Highly Charged Word Factory

Our public education system does not always teach or build good words into our students. Sometimes the system sends forth confusing words by which it expects our children to live. For instance, one year the school system is teaching phonics. Then they exchange this method for the *whole word* or *sight* method of learning to read. Then they change back when they see that a wrong *word* has been sent about learning. Children end up operating from an inferior method and do poorly on college entrance exams. They have been given a wrong *word*. Everything hangs on a word.

In many of our colleges, the professors who teach our young people have been exposed as socialists, Marxists, homosexuals, feminists, agnostics, atheists, and the like. This might be somewhat tolerable if they would stick to the discipline of what they have been hired to teach but their bias nearly always comes out and is a *word* to the students. Thus, the students graduate with a culture consciousness devoid of Scripture truth, and often, an attitude that is atheistic. The teacher's word of belief is imbedded in their heart. It will come out eventually. This is one reason that the Bible says that a teacher will come under greater judgment.

What happens when our government replaces the Word of God (Ten Commandments, Bible, prayer, creationism) in our school classrooms with a secularistic, humanistic, relativistic, evolutionary, historically revised, "politically correct" word? What happens when our society promotes sexual immorality, rebellion against parents, disdain for authority, and violence? What happens when the Word of God and its precepts are taken out of the home and replaced with the vile word of Hollywood coming through the cable television or computer? What happens when children are allowed to be bombarded by violent video movies and video games?

The answer has been very graphically self-evident. The children march confidently back into the classroom or into the work place not only armed with the wrong word but with assault rifles and bombs. After much bloodshed and the outcry of parents around the country, the Legislature decides that we have to find a solution to school killings. The Federal Government can even pass an amendment (a word) that would allow the states and the public schools to post the Ten Commandments to try to put a fix on the massacres. But, too little, too late, I say. A word has already been formulated, received, and fruit is being produced. When will we learn that everything is based on some word!

Recently, our nation was riveted on the stand-off situation that developed in Montgomery, Alabama. The controversy was over a granite block with the Ten Commandments chiseled into it and placed in a courthouse. The ACLU and others protested against Judge Roy Moore. Another judge ruled that it had to be moved. Thousands of people gathered around the monument to try to block the removal. It created quite a national and international stir. Why? Because it represented a *word*—a powerful word that some did not like. It was just a granite stone with words engraved into it. What was the big deal? The big deal was precisely what we are talking about—a word dynamic that affects lives. Those words on that rock stood for something—a powerful word dynamic. Words are powerful.

Our Physical Health Is Based On A Word

Our physical well-being is dependent upon us following a good word about diet and nutrition. The word from the media and advertising experts would have one believe that carbonated colas, candy, sugar-coated cereal, beer, double-layer hamburgers and fries are the way to go. Our growing population of over-weight children and couch potato parents are revealing the results of a generation who bought into the wrong word. Social observers are calling the overweight children issue an "epidemic." Everything hangs on a word!

The Laws Of Science Are A Word To Live By

Even what we call the *Laws of Nature* and *Newton's Laws Of Physics* are a word to us. If we violate the law of gravity we will pay a smashing price because the results are directly tied to this particular *word*. If we, who are mammals, try to breathe under water for any sustained length of time, we will die because there is a *word* attached to that realm and we have violated it.

Every area of life, whether it be religion, government, society, child-rearing, economics, commerce, finances, education, health, or science, demands that we abide by a word. Thus, life is filled with choices about which word to choose. Many wrecked lives, economies, and societies indicate that a wrong choice has been made about a philosophy of living. And again, a philosophy is a *word*.

Even The Antichrist Will Be A Word Master

The Bible prophecies, which are unique words in themselves, predict that the world dictator, called *The Antichrist*, will begin his rule during the Tribulation time by giving forth a false word about peace. The people who follow his diabolical *word* will experience the most horrible time in human history. He will rule the world by his *word*. His *mark,* or *word*, will be forced on every person's forehead and hand. Those who do not receive his *word* on their forehead and hand will perish. For everything, absolutely everything, functions on the basis of some word!

History Shows Us The Importance Of A Word

The history of the world says that mankind has struggled to operate from the right word. God gave Adam and Eve a good and right word in the Garden of Eden. Instead, they listened to the devil's lie and followed a wrong word. We have been struggling with thorns and thistles ever since.

The *Dark Ages* were a result of mankind following a wrong *word*, both from Pope and King, politician and pastor. When the *Enlightenment* came, it was because men decided to loose themselves from the shackles of a wrong word and attach themselves to a liberating and rejuvenating word. In fact, whenever major revivals of religion have swept across the land, it has been because of a *word*.

Christianity has spread throughout the world from the first century because the adherents shared the *gospel*. This word, of course, means the proclamation of *good news* and is a word in itself about the finished work of Christ. Christianity is based on a *word* in more ways than one. Everything hangs on a word!

But other words have also prevailed in our world. The attacks on the World Trade Center and on the Pentagon on September 11, 2001 by Muslim terrorists were the result of a word. The suicide bombers believed in the word that they had received from their teachers based in the word of the Koran. I heard one authority say that male suicide bombers would often lay awake at night thinking about the perpetual harem of virgins they would have in Paradise along with other luxuries. Many of them couldn't wait to die for Allah! And it was all because of a *word*.

All religions are based upon a *word*. Christianity is based upon the Bible. Judaism is based upon the Torah. Islam is based upon the Koran. But the question one must answer is—are all these word bases truth? Truth is an accurate word. What is the true word?

Choosing The Truth

There are many reasons why we do not choose a good word on which to build our lives. This material addresses those cobwebs and seeks to clean them out for practical revitalization. Just as in the *Age of Enlightenment*, or revival, or rebirth experience, you can experience newness, vitality, success, and blessings by choosing the right words on which to hang your life. Choose a right word about money and your financial condition will turn around. Choose a right word about marriage communication and your marriage can be saved. Choose a right word for your children and they can grow up strong and confident. Choose a right word about salvation and you can enjoy eternal life. Choose a right word about yourself and you can change your personality. Change your personality and you can change your habits. Change your habits and you can change your future. And it is all the result of choosing the right *word* and acting upon it. Everything hangs upon a word!

The Bible gives us a success formula in the very first Psalm. Notice the consistency and prolific use of the *word* concept. One cannot help but see the connection between *blessing* and *word*. It is definitely there.

"Blessed is the man who does not walk in the counsel (word) of the wicked or stand in the way (word) of sinners or sit in the seat (word) of mockers. But his delight is in the law (word) of the Lord and on his law (word) he meditates day and night. He is like a tree planted by streams of water, which yields its fruit (the result of choosing a right word) in season and whose leaf does not wither. Whatever he does prospers" (Psalm 1: 1-3, NIV, parentheses mine).

The Power Of Words

Is the pen mightier than the sword? Can words spoken change lives, rebuild cities, create happiness in people, or create wars among nations? Do the words we speak make a difference?

My wife has said of our children on numerous occasions, "They haven't listened to a word I have said!"

But have they heard? Will those often repeated admonitions somehow find their way deep down into the heart? Will they take root and one day sprout forth in new growth and budding fruitfulness? The Bible says to train up a child in the way that he should go and when he is old he will not depart from it. The secret is in the training. The secret of the training is getting a word to stick deep down inside.

What we think affects how we speak. How we speak affects how we think. And how we speak and think affects our life and the lives of others. That is why it is vital to have the proper words to think and speak. God has blessed us with a variety of word helps. They are found in the Bible. We call it His "Word."

Dawson Trotman, the man instrumental in starting the Navigators (a Bible-memory, discipleship group) would often say, "His Word, the last word."

His reference was to his practice of reading, thinking, praying, and meditating on the Word of God just before going to sleep each night. Dawson Trotman was a successful man of God whose influence and works continue to this very day.

Other thinkers and mind developers have spoken of the influence and power of words. One of these mind scientists taught that words have the ability to manipulate the subconscious to perform unbelievable feats. His famous saying is still being quoted—"You are what you think about all day long."

The Bible has said,

"For as he thinketh in his heart, so is he" (Proverbs 23:7).

The Psalmist also knew the power of heart words when he wrote,

"Let the words of my mouth, and the meditation of my heart, be acceptable in thy sight, O Lord, my strength, and my redeemer" (Psalm 19:14).

Whose Words?

Man's natural tendency is sin-ward, down-ward, and death-ward. If you are like most people you fight against the encroachments of negativism and fear. You struggle to be positive and operate in faith.

The Apostle Paul reflected this in his letter to the Romans when he cried:

"For that which I do I allow not: for what I would, that do I not; but what I hate, that do I.... For I delight in the law of God after the inward man: but I see another law in my members, warring against the law of my mind, and bringing me into captivity to the law of sin which is in my members" (Romans 7:15,22).

So I ask you, are you conscious of words? Our lives are built upon our words, other people's words, the devil's words, or God's words. But are you aware of the affect of words upon your life?

Maybe, just maybe, you have allowed wrong words from bad sources to enter into your heart. If those wrong words from bad sources have gotten down on your heart, you may have a problem or problems that a whole team of psychiatrists could not unravel. Certainly, you know of adults who are carrying childhood baggage that is nothing more than wrong words by bad sources that have taken root.

I started a lawn service for my three sons so that they could maintain a profit-making business of their own. When they started out I went over every detail of the machinery that involved safety. But, as I turned the work and the equipment over to them, I discovered that things were not always carried out as safely as I demanded. I knew that this machinery could cut off a foot, a hand, or put out an eye, or cause deafness.

One day I observed some unconcerned attitudes about safety and some youthful reasoning to excuse the attention to safety details. So I addressed the issue in a very strong way, attempting to implant my word upon their youthful consciousness.

It was so very important that my words of caution and respect for machinery from a historical and experiential perspective, replace their infantile and inexperienced *reasonings*. The same type of philosophy is applied in army boot camp.

God tells us that His Word is vital for our spiritual health and success. But, we often neglect it, choosing rather to *reason out* why we don't have to obey certain rules. Our life is a life-long effort of reprogramming with proper words. This is difficult when we are bombarded from birth by a powerful societal reprogramming effort from questionable or wrong word sources.

The message of this material you have in your hand is a *word*. It is presented in hopes of doing three things: awakening you to the concept, informing you as to how it works, and helping you choose the right *word* in your life for success and blessing. For if the concept is true that everything hangs upon some word, then we need to have both a defensive posture for protection and an offensive posture for provision.

2

The Negative Power of Words

One of the worst lies we inherit from childhood is the taunting refrain, "Sticks and stones may break my bones, but words will never hurt me." What a lie! Words, like an atomic bomb, will not only destroy you and those around you, but will leave a radioactive residue of death that will last for years. The truth should be—"Sticks and stones break bones—words kill!'

Any observer of societal behavior can discern that our world has bought into a negative and wrong word by which to live. Instead of getting better and better we are getting progressively worse. The seeds of loose morals and personal liberty of the 60's, 70's, 80's, and 90's have borne fruit in the start-up of the twenty-first century for all of us.

A California study compared the major discipline problems between the 1950s and today. Fifty years ago, the major complaints of teachers concerned talking, chewing gum, making noise and running in the hallways. Today, our schools are beset with drug and alcohol abuse, teen pregnancy, school shootings, and suicide.

In 1963, the national SAT scores began what would be a 16-year decline, finally leveling off at the combined verbal and math score of 890 to 900—far below its former level. Twenty years later, statistics showed that 13 percent of all 17 year-olds in the United States were considered functionally illiterate. This development prompted the U.S. National Commission for Excellence in Education to conclude in a 1983 report:

"If an unfriendly power had attempted to impose on America the mediocre educational performance that exists today, we might well have viewed it as an act of war." [*Psychiatry Eradicating Justice* (Los Angeles, CA 90028: Citizens Commission on Human Rights, 1997), p. 11].

Any casual observer of societal norms in the United States since World War II can see and read that crime has increased, illegitimate births have gone up, drug use is paramount, loose morals abound, divorce has increased, unmarried couples are increasing, and Biblical virtues are attacked.

There have been concerted efforts to suppress any reference to the Judaeo-Christian ethic, the Ten Commandments, and references to "God" in the Pledge of Allegiance or prayer in public gatherings. It is this author's opinion that we have, as a society bought into a faulty word. And the devastating affects of basing life decisions on a faulty word are obvious. When a society purposely redirects itself away from the *Word of Life* given by the *Author of Life* and creates its own humanist, logical, self-reasoning basis for life decisions, the results are less than satisfactory and far-reaching. Was it just coincidence that the school test scores began a sixteen year plummet the same year that our government leaders said that prayer and Bible reading in the public school was unconstitutional? Think about it.

The Diabolical Attempt To Supplant The Good Word

From the Garden of Eden to the Middle Ages and up to today there has been a diabolical attempt to usurp and supplant the Word of God; the *true word* by which we are to live. It is obvious in America's young history, and in spite of the efforts of historical revisionists, that the Pilgrims and founding fathers were about the business of planting a new word for the new country. The Word of God abounded from the halls of Congress to the one-room schoolhouse. But the relentless pursuit to diminish the Word of God has never ceased. Even in my lifetime, I have seen the effective removal of prayer and Bible reading from the public schools, and law suits to ban religious observance. Although there were many *words* in play during the last few decades, there was one that seemed to be a dynamic seed—possibly the genetic component of the social fruit we observe today. It had to do with the crystallization of worldliness, atheism, socialism, humanism, and evolution flavored by an anti-God sentiment. Its power was man-centered and its incubation and grow-bed was the public education system we know today.

After World War II a growing interest continued in the area of psychiatry, psychology, education, and human mind expansion. Some have called it a time of fear and pessimism when poison could masquerade as promise. John Dewey, a proponent of psychologist Wilhelm Wundt, and the man who would later influence America's education system with these social theories, designed the 1933 *Humanist Manifesto*. Signed by more than 34 community leaders and dignitaries in 1933, his manifesto was a suppression and ridicule of religions and their ability to help solve the problems of mankind. With authoritative contempt, the document denied man's spiritual nature and his need for a word from God.

The *Manifesto* called for a one-world religion, of sorts, which was not to be bound to the old standard belief system but was to be influenced by scientific and economic change. The manifesto declared that the old way was powerless to solve the problem of humans living in the Twentieth Century. It rather promoted a religion pointed in the direction of human strength—the religion of humanism.

A list of fifteen precepts was drafted. These included:

1. Religious humanists regard the universe as self-existing and not created.

2. Holding an organic view of life, humanists find that the traditional dualism of mind and body must be rejected.

3. Humanism asserts that the nature of the universe depicted by modern science makes unacceptable any supernatural or cosmic guarantees of human values.

4. Religion must formulate its hopes and plans in the light of the scientific spirit and method.

5. The distinction between the sacred and the secular can no longer be maintained.

6. We assume that humanism will take the path of social and mental hygiene and discourage sentimental and unreal hopes and wishful thinking.

In 1973 the *Humanist Manifesto II* was published, delivering an even more savage blow to the sanctity and validity of religion.

Humanists maintained that the idea of a traditional theism which promoted a connection to a prayer-hearing, and prayer-responding God by faith was outmoded and unproved—therefore invalid. Thus, the traditional moral codes connected to the traditional theism were also insufficient for modern man. Humanists considered the idea of immortal salvation, and the fear of eternal damnation as both illusory and harmful. Their idea about man was that he was a biological organism transacting in a social and cultural context with no credible evidence of life after death.

The year 1980 saw *A Secular Humanist Declaration* continue the attack, declaring that people can lead meaningful and wholesome lives without the need of religious commandment or the clergy.

Recipients of the "Humanist of the Year" award presented by the American Humanist Association include Margaret Sanger, founder of Planned Parenthood. Sanger's humanistic thoughts were observed in the publication, *Birth Control Review* as well as other publications.

She promoted the idea of the fittest of society having more children and less children from the poor and unfit. This was one of her ideas connected to birth control. Her more radical statements revealed her belief that, "The most merciful thing the large family does to one of its infant members is to kill it."

Sanger believed, not only in birth control for the fittest, but that there should be a national sterilization program to get rid of the unfit offspring in our society. Sounds similar to the Nazi sterilization programs of Adolf Hitler, does it not?

The wrong word problem did not happen overnight. Its growth has been more like the insidious nature of weeds growing in our midst over a long period of time. Suddenly, we begin to take note when the seed heads appear.

A study of over a thousand school readers in use between 1776 and 1920 illustrates how public education shifted from a religious and moral emphasis to the virtual anarchy it is today. The study found 100 percent emphasis on moral and religious content from 1776 to 1786, approximately 50 percent emphasis from 1786 to 1825, 21 percent from 1825 to 1880, and only 5 percent from 1916 to 1920. One observer has remarked that today the percentage is so small as to be immeasurable. In many instances there is a subtle or not so subtle ridicule or attack on moral and religious values.

Society was obviously spiraling downward. Many social trends were not getting better. But the humanists had a fix for us. With a humanist word becoming more prominent and the Word of God gradually becoming discredited, it was time for the humanist priests of the modern order to step in.

What followed during the 1960s was the infiltration of government funded psychologists, psychiatrists, social workers, and psychiatric programs like we have never seen before in the history of the world. One observer noted that educational psychologists increased from around 450 in the late sixties to over 16,000 in the late nineties. In 1994, child psychiatrists, psychologists, counselors and special educators in and around the U.S. public school system nearly outnumber teachers.

The *post-modern* mindset and philosophy (word) is looming like a monster over us today. Their word is that everything is *relevant*. There are no hard and fast rules—no moral absolutes. If it is good for you—it is good for me. We are free to believe or not believe without any stigma or judgment. We define *truth*—we establish our own relativistic word by which we live and you must *tolerate* it.

It is obvious from historical facts and statistics that when you put two and two together you come up with an obviously contrary word perpetuated upon our society. I call it contrary, only from my biased position that everything should spring from the foundation of God's Word as the only authorized basis for life, health, and blessing. Somewhere along the way, if it is not too late, we are going to have to wake up to the fact that we are building on a devastating word.

The Basis Of Our Beliefs

I often listen to a radio program in our city that has nothing but news and talk and no musical format. People are encouraged to call in to express their views on certain subjects. Sometimes I get so weary of listening to baseless philosophy I just turn the radio off. People will spout their view, belief, or opinion, with a fervency and zeal that smacks of authority. But where is this *word*, this opinion, this philosophy coming from? What is the basis of their belief? I maintain that the basis of one's belief means everything. By *basis* I mean the *word* of our belief.

From where does what we believe come? Does it come from our stint in the university, from grandma's homespun ideology, from the ghetto, or from where one grew up? Does it come from environment, education, or experience? Is it a combination of all of these? Why do we believe the way we do about morals, abortion, the death penalty, drug abuse, adultery? What *word* is your life based upon? Is it the word of grandpa, mother, or the professor? What we do, how we respond to situations, and what we think are based upon a *word* from some source. Everything hinges on a *word*.

Our teachers and philosophers are telling us that there are no moral absolutes and everything is relative. We are told to apply situation ethics and be politically correct. We are forced to hear that evolution is fact instead of theory and that one's opinion is what is right for them. We are taught that I'm okay and you're okay and none of us should judge another.

This flies in the face of Biblical truth. For the Bible, the Word of God, is not lenient in its proclamation of truth. It claims to contain absolute truth.

The same is applied to Jesus. He said very plainly that He was **the** way, **the** truth, and **the** life and no one could come to the Father but by Him (John 14:6). The definite articles (**the**) in the Greek text mean that He is the exclusive and only way, truth, and life.

This means that Mohammed is not an alternative way to heaven. It means that Buddha or Confucius are not alternatives. Jesus does not give the luxury of deleting Him or combining Him with alternative ways of eternal life.

Therefore, we must come to grips with what we believe to be absolutes. Absolutes are necessary if one is to determine if something is contrary. You must have an absolutely perfect circle if you can determine if a circle is not perfect. You must have an absolutely straight line to go by if you are to determine if a line is crooked. But if you have no absolutes to go by, then anything goes. If you do not have an absolute word to go by then any opinion or word will suffice. This is the precise predicament we have gotten ourselves in to today. When the absolute Word of God is removed from our society—any opinion or emotional feeling will do—anyone's word is just as good as another. When the standard is removed, you don't know what is sub-standard.

The book of Judges, in the Bible, is a terrible story of Israel's cyclical spiral downward into degradation and defeat. The last sentence in the book is a haunting refrain and a prophetic depiction of our situation today. It says:

"In those days there was no king in Israel: every man did that which was right in his own eyes."

Israel had lost more than a king. They had lost their way—their standards—their rules—their absolutes—the right word by which to live.

I once was invited to speak in a Christian university in Kiev, Ukraine, which was formerly part of the Soviet Union. While there I was able to spend time with a family who grew up there. The wife's father had been one of the top officials in the Soviet government. She, of course, grew up in a Communist Party family.

Olga gave me a tour of the city and invited me to have dinner in their home. There I was able to quiz the husband and son, as well, about life in the former Soviet Union. It was a rich experience for me as I freely shared with them how I felt about their government while I was a boy growing up during the *cold war*.

They, too, shared with me how they began to discover the truth. For all of their lives they had been living under the word of Lenin, their great leader. But, while college students, they began to notice that information about the outside world would turn up missing. Later they would become somewhat resentful to know that they had not been told all the truth. They had been living under a lie; a false word. The entire country became inflamed enough to topple over the huge statue of Lenin down in the *Center* of Kiev. Olga showed me the empty pedestal where the giant statue once magnificently loomed over the city and the people.

Adam and Eve began operating on a word from God. They, however, were persuaded to exchange that word for a word from Satan. The word they operated by made all the difference in the world. While operating by God's word they enjoyed paradise, fellowship, and fruitfulness. The word to which they transferred produced as well, but in a negative fashion. While basing their life on Satan's word they experienced thorns, sweat, abandonment, and defeat. What *word* one bases his or her life upon makes all the difference in the world. Your outlook on life, your health, your attitude, your actions, your morals, everything you are is based upon some *word*.

The Power Of Propaganda

History tells us in graphic form what can happen if we do not question the basis of the word from which we live? The characters I am going to mention are all well-known players on the stage of World War II. I think you will recognize them.

First, there was the fanatical propaganda of Adolf Hitler. He even had a full-time paid "propaganda minister." With repeated words he stirred up the German people to attack the world. A reading of his Mein Kampf will verify his remarkable understanding of repeated words. Dr. René Fauvel, a famous French psychologist, explained it by saying that Hitler had the unique ability to use the law of suggestion and its different forms of application, and that it was with uncanny skill and masterly showmanship that he mobilized every instrument of propaganda in his mighty campaign of suggestion. Hitler openly stated that the psychology of suggestion was a terrible weapon in the hands of anyone who knew how to use it.

Slogans, posters, huge signs, and massed flags appeared throughout Germany. Hitler's picture was everywhere. The chant of "One Reich, one Folk, one Leader" was heard everywhere that a group gathered. Even the German youth marched and sang, "Today we own Germany, tomorrow the entire world." Other slogans or *words* appeared throughout the motherland—"Germany has waited long enough," "Stand up, you are the aristocrats of the Third Reich," The German people were bombarded twenty-four hours a day from billboards, sides of buildings, the radio, and the press. Hitler used every means at his disposal to plant his word deeply in the conscience and subconscience of every man, woman, boy, and girl. Eventually it sank in and they began to believe that they were a superior race. Then they acted upon the word now stuck deeply in their heart and set out to prove it to the whole world. Unfortunately for them, there were other nations who also had strong national *words* on which they rested. Those opposing words eventually overcame the word on which the German war machine was built. But our point is that words can have a powerful affect—even negative words that are not true.

Mussolini, leader of Italy, used the same concept in an attempt to elevate his country. Signs and slogans such as "Believe, Obey, Fight," and "Italy must have its great place in the world," covered the walls of buildings, and waved along the roadways. Using the radio and any other means possible, Mussolini pounded his propaganda word into the minds and hearts of his people.

Stalin, the leader of Russia, used the same procedure to build Russia into a strong force. The Institute of Modern Hypnotism in November, 1946, recognized that Joseph Stalin had been using the great power of repeated words upon the Russian people in order to make them believe in their strength and power. They subsequently, named him as one of the ten persons with the "most hypnotic eyes in the world," and rated him as a "mass hypnotist."

The Japanese warlords used the power of repeated words to make fanatical fighters out of their army including suicide pilots willing to die for their country and emperor. From early childhood, the Japanese children were fed the repeated word that they were direct descendants of heaven and destined to rule the world. They prayed it, read it, heard it, and chanted it. It sank into their heart and they believed it to the point of death. Although it was used wrongly, still it worked. Words are powerful.

The subtle force of words repeated over and over again tends to overcome our sound reasoning and begins to appeal to our emotions and feelings. Finally, these words penetrate through our mind and our emotions and get imbedded upon our subconscious heart where we truly believe. This is the basic principle of all successful advertising and is a powerful tool. We must evaluate the words we are building our life upon before it is too late.

Earworms

"Earworm" is the term coined by University of Cincinnati marketing professor James Kellaris for the usually unwelcome songs that get stuck in people's heads. Since beginning his research in 2000, Kellaris has heard from people all over the world requesting help or offering solutions.

He surveyed about 500 students, faculty and staff on campus asking about the type, frequency and duration of earworms, and possible cause and cures. Among the songs respondents picked as most likely to become stuck were: "The Lion Sleeps Tonight," the Chili's restaurant "baby back ribs" jingle and "Who Let The Dogs Out?"

Most all of us have "earworm" musical lyrics stuck in our head. Whether it's the theme music of the Andy Griffith Show, a McDonald's hamburger jingle, or a song from the 70's, we all have them imbedded in our head and heart. It shows the power of words impressing themselves upon us and in us.

Hitler, Mussolini, Stalin, and the Japanese warlords used "eyeworms" and "earworms" to get their "word" imbedded in the minds and hearts of their people. The results were monumental.

Words Are Universally Available

There are three *universals* that we all can touch with in the concept we are putting forth; *words, the heart,* and *faith*. If you are to understand our concept you must come to grips with the prevalence of words. Everyone has the availability of words—to receive them and to dispense them. They come in different forms and fashions, whether it is the cave man's stick drawings, the cry of a newborn, or the intellectual verbiage of a college professor. Any kind of communication, expression, body language, video presentation, picture, etc., is a *word*. Words are prolific. We are bombarded with them from the womb to the tomb. They are universal.

There are bad words and good words. Words can help you or hurt you. What you do with words makes a difference in your life and the end result of your life.

God operates by words; the creation—the covenants—the commandments—the prophecies—the healings of Jesus—the Scriptures—the Holy Spirit's communication.

You have power in words. What you believe, think, and say has powerful affects. You have the power to build up or tear down with words. Kingdoms have risen or fallen because of words. We simply must come to grips with the power of words. The theme running through this book has to do with knowing and using the right words.

But just as you can use words, so others can use words on you. In the chapters to come I will show how and where a word gets planted to produce a harvest of weeds or an abundance of fruit. Much of the problem today is that we are not aware of the incoming missiles that plant and explode in our heart. We need to learn that we have power to accept or reject words.

I grew up watching Walt Disney movies and television productions. The theme song of the Disney television production was *When You Wish Upon A Star*. The song was from the animated movie, *Pinocchio*, and involved the miracle of a puppet turning into a real boy.

But let me assure you that miracles and wondrous things do not happen by wishing upon a star but rather by faith on a word—the right word! When you are backed up in a corner with little hope you do not want a cartoon fantasy but clear faith reality!

3

The Heart—The Place Where Words Work

There is a theme that runs through this book—*Get a word on your heart, act on this word by faith, and see a powerful result.* This idea can be applied in the secular world apart from God and the Bible or it can be applied in the world of the believer in Jesus Christ. In the Biblical mindset it would say, Get God's word on your heart, act on this word by faith, and see God's wonderful blessing materialize.

I hinted at this in the previous chapter. Now we are going to begin to analyze the components of this word dynamic concept. We are going to observe the essential and universal tools—the head, the heart, a word, and faith. For if you understand these specific elements and see how they work, you can transform your life and see wonderful accomplishments. We will deal first with our *head* and our *heart*.

The Tin Man's Search For A Heart

Three of the main characters in the story, *The Wizard of Oz*, were on a search for something. The Lion was on a journey to find courage. The Scarecrow was looking for a brain. The Tin Man was gravely in need of a heart.

I had never thought of it before, but the author of this fantasy story was identifying three elements involved in our concept; the head (brain), faith (courage), and the heart. Whether consciously, or subconsciously, the author was also identifying the element we just pointed out—*words*. Dorothy, the Lion, the Scarecrow, and the Tin Man were all on a journey down the Yellow Brick Road to find the Wizard of Oz, who, with *words*, would fulfill their desires.

Most of us realize the importance of the heart. But it is my opinion that, even though we use the heart every day, we don't know much about it—how it works—its nature—where it is located—how we can use it or misuse it—the vulnerability of it.

Your Head And Your Heart

Obviously there are parts of our body that function very differently and for specific purposes. Our lungs have one distinct function. Our liver has another purpose. Our stomach is fitted for yet another purpose and function.

Our inner spiritual-mental self has parts that function in different ways for different purposes as well. Even from the Holy Bible we are taught that there is an *outer man* and an *inner man*. The Scriptures clearly and specifically point out that there is a *body*, a *soul*, and a *spirit*. The Greek New Testament makes mention of various aspects of our inner person; our *mind* (nous), our *heart* (kardia), and the *psyche* (psuche).

The word, *heart*, is used over 160 times in the New Testament and three times that much in the Old Testament. When the New Testament speaks of the *heart* of man, it is not referring, in the vast majority of cases, to the physical cardio-vascular pump we call the *heart*. Although, the Greek word is *kardia*, from which we probably get *cardia*, as in *heart*, it is referring to something else.

Sigmund Freud, the famous Austrian psychoanalyst, brought the world's attention to the hypothesis that there was a powerful force within us, an unilluminated part of the mind—separate from the conscious mind—that is constantly at work molding our thoughts, feelings, and actions and thus, able to have outward affect. The Word of God, however, had spoken of this over two thousand years ago!

Some have called this the *soul*. Others have referred to it as the *super-ego*, the *inner power*, the *super-consciousness*, the *unconscious*, and the *subconscious*. It isn't an organ or so-called physical matter, such as we know the brain to be. And science hasn't located its tangible position in the human body. Nevertheless, it is obviously present and real. Man has known of its existence.

The ancients often thought of it as *spirit*. The physician Paracelsus called it the *will*. Some have referred to it as the *mind*, the *conscience*, the *still small voice within*, *intelligence*, and the *universal mind*.

It is my contention that whatever you call it or however you characterize it, this *heart* aspect is the most important part of our being. In the chapters to come I will seek to share with the reader why I believe this to be so. But the Scriptures, very clearly, reveal that this area is an extremely vital part of our being and an exclusive link to our Creator. If it is the entrance door into the Kingdom of God and into eternal life, as I surmise, then it becomes paramount that we investigate it to determine how it works. For too long we have been ignorant of it or have relegated it to the field of psychology instead of theology, where I think that it belongs.

Throughout this book there will be a simplification of this area called the *heart*. For our study and understanding I will seek to distinguish it as different from the *head*. When I refer to the *heart* I will be referring to the inner subconscious part of our mind. When I refer to the *head* I will be referring to the conscious part of our mind. Thus, you will perceive, right off, that I believe in a duality of mind. I lay this foundation on the basis of the clear teachings of Jesus and the New Testament writers who, also, made a distinction. We must come to grips early on that we do have dual functions of our mind or the teachings to follow will not make sense.

We definitely have dual functions of our one mind. One is subjective and one is objective. One part of our mind works while we sleep. One is voluntary. The other is involuntary. One is conscious. One is subconscious. I believe that this, all important, subconscious, subjective, and involuntary part of our being is called our *heart* in the Scriptures. Psychoanalysts can call it something else, but the Bible simplifies it as the *heart* and so will we!

If you are wondering about the *soul*, just let me assure you that we are considering it but possibly not in the way that you have always thought. The concepts we will address about the *head* and the *heart* will help clarify some of your questions. But, in order to examine this important area of our inner being we must do two important things; keep it simple and keep it Scriptural. It will not help us get to the truth if we interject psycho-analytic jargon or even concepts derived from English translations of our Bible. The concept of the *soul* with the compartments of *mind, emotions,* and *will,* may be more of a man-derived concept. I struggle to find this triune entity in the Scriptures. What you do have clearly defined in the Scripture is the concepts of the *head*, the *heart*, the *body*, and the *spirit*. Oftentimes, for instance, you will have both *psuche* (psyche) and *pneuma* (spirit) translated as *soul*. In the same way, *psuche* and *kardia* (heart) will be translated as *heart*. This confusion, I believe, is at the heart (no pun intended) of the ignorance and misunderstanding about a most important area. We must seek to keep our understanding clear and simple, without over-simplifying, and Scripturally accurate in our interpretation.

To make our distinctions it is necessary to observe the workings of our brain or our conscience mind. After all, it is within the brain that we find the mind. In the mind we find the *heart*. Some mind-science proponents will argue that the mind flows throughout our being and is not confined to the brain. But in our simple approach we will keep it confined to the brain area.

The Difference Between The Head And The Heart

Apparently, our heart, or subconscious, works twenty-four hours a day; it neither slumbers or sleeps. The head, the conscious part of our brain, goes to sleep when we go to bed at night and deactivates itself to a certain degree. Through the night our subconscious works to slow down our heart rate but to keep our physical heart pumping blood. It monitors our lungs for breathing. It oversees all the functions of our body while we are consciously asleep. We don't have to worry. But, we may wake up suddenly in a cold sweat because it also allows the playing of fantastic motion pictures called dreams. And it wakes you and makes your head *conscious* if you hear a prowler or if you need to make a trip to the restroom. We can even program our subconscious to wake us at approximately the same time every morning—without an alarm clock!

The conscious mind perceives by the five senses. The subconscious perceives independently of those outward senses. Thus, you will hear Jesus talk about people as having ears to hear but hear not and eyes to see but see not. He was speaking of this very difference. Your subjective heart perceives by intuition and spiritual perception. It is impressed by our thoughts and our words. It is a storehouse of memory. It responds to the conscious. Hypnosis or drug induced drowsiness can have effect because a person is put into a sleepy state *consciously* and communication takes place with the storehouse of memory; the *subconscious* mind.

Your subconscious heart is more like soft clay that receives and stores impressions. It does not argue or calculate logically. It just receives the words and word pictures conveyed to it. That is why people will follow and die with cult leaders. These followers allow the words and the thoughts of their leaders to sink down past their conscious and get impressed on their heart. Then they really believe to the point of blind obedience or martyrdom. Whether it is a political leader, a religious leader, a parent, or a teacher, the process is the same and the results are the same because the elements are the same.

If your heart is impressed with a word, a statement, a remark, or even a suggestion long enough it will begin to accept it as true. Once your subconscious heart accepts something as true you are in a powerful state for good or bad. You can produce evil power or move mountains. You can destroy yourself with depression or lift yourself and others with an energy beyond your normal capacity.

Because the heart is very impression oriented, it means that we have the capability of influencing it. The concepts, thoughts, and *impressions* that you permit to lay upon your heart will take root. If you have received thoughts from childhood authority figures that you are stupid—and you *believe* you are stupid—you are likely to act stupid, do stupid things, and reinforce your subconscious impressions.

The words we hear while growing up often are permitted to become entrenched in our subconscious. They become deep grooves on the pliable surface of our heart. When they harden there we become adults with a lot of childhood baggage. Thank God that we have a way of erasing and uprooting, what the Bible calls, *strongholds*.

In all probability this had something to do with God's insistence on abandonment of idols for the people of Israel in the Old Testament. An image held before you will eventually get impressed on the pliable and impressionable surface of your heart without you even realizing it.

I grew up during the era of Elvis Presley. I saw him sing on the Ed Sullivan Show. I watched my older sister's attraction to him. I observed the millions who *idolized* him. Then, while living in his home-town, I have had the opportunity of watching the crowds increase year after year around Graceland for his birthday and memorial service. It is amazing to see Elvis impersonators and look-a-likes standing around on the street corner.

The only way to understand this phenomenon is to see that this man, this *idol*, got impressed upon the subconscious minds of teenagers during the 50's and 60's. The great vehicle that helped this take place was music. His visual presence on television plus his words oiled by musical notes drove his persona deep into the subconscious. The same principle could be applied to sports heroes, and other entertainment *stars* or *idols*.

Again, this is why God forbade Israel to follow after, or be absorbed into the culture of, the heathen nations around them. The heathen nations were idol worshippers. Idols can get impressed upon the heart.

The Brain—The House For The Heart

I read somewhere that the average human brain is a complex mechanism that weighs 2-3 pounds, contains 12 billion cells which are connected to 10,000 other brain cells, totaling 120 trillion brain connections. The human brain is the most intriguing organ in all of life. Scientists tell us that the average person uses only

10 percent of his mind's capacity during an entire life-time. Most of us will die with about 10 billion brain cells unused!

Many feel that the *heart*, as it is called, is a part of the brain. They believe that it is tied neurologically to every organ of the body and activates feeling and movement. Many illnesses are emotionally induced from this area (as much as 85 percent of all modern sicknesses according to medical doctors). Some have called this the *soul*—the *inner man*—the *subconscious*.

Although we know little about the brain and the brain heart, we know they exist and that they function in a marvelous, mysterious, and distinct way. It is important for the believer in Jesus Christ to note that our heart, not only connects with our head, but also with a spiritual dimension wherein we touch with God and He with us.

The Value And Power Of Your Heart

One of the reasons that we are not inclined more toward the spiritual is because we are suffering under the old Adam. He was a man of the head—not the heart. He was crowned with fear instead of faith. He found, with a little help from the treasure thief, that outside the garden the major emphasis was on what the head and the hands could produce. The *Tree of Knowledge* related to the *head* or the logical thinker. Adam and Eve chose head knowledge over a heart relationship with God. The heart was ignored—left behind. The gates of the garden of plenty, power, presence, and possessions were shut. People are still buying in to the devil's lie that value is based on your head and your hands outside the garden in his world of chaos and defeat.

Most of us are brought up to believe that our value is related to what we can produce with our conscious head and our physical hands. When men get together and are introduced to one another, one of the first things out of their mouths is, "What do you do for a living?" Maybe we should realize that our heart can produce as well, and is the foundation for what the head and hand are capable of accomplishing.

Jesus knew the secret of cooperating with the Father in the area of His heart—His subconscious—the treasure house within. He understood the practical value of the heart. Jesus said,

"I tell you the truth, the Son can do nothing by himself; he can do only what he sees his Father doing, because whatever the Father does the Son also does" (John 5:19, NIV).

Jesus *saw* a *word* and received a word from the Father and acted upon this word with powerful results.

The Beans Are Burning!

Learn to read or see your subconscious heart. Know that it exists as a separate entity from your conscious head. Learn, as Jesus taught, to have "eyes to see and ears to hear." Develop a subconscious consciousness and you are on your way to the open door of blessing.

One Sunday morning my wife was sitting in our worship service. The ensemble was singing and she was absorbed in the wonderful music.

As she tells it, "All of a sudden it just came to me; the beans are burning and will catch the house on fire."

She jumped up, left the church, and drove straight home. Sure enough, when she opened the door of the house, smoke had filled the kitchen. The beans she had left on the stove were burned and smoking.

Now from where did this message come? Did it not come from the subconscious heart region, maybe even prompted by God? Consciously, she was absorbed in hearing, feeling, sensing the worship experience. Like a flash her subconscious set off an alarm. She saw in her mind the burning beans she had left cooking on the stove. Absolutely, the secret of success is seeing the word on your heart and responding to it. But is it still too mysterious for you? I maintain that we operate in it every single day whether we recognize it or not!

I heard a man on television the other day giving instruction on how to improve one's golf game. He said that in order to be a good golfer one had to do some proper visualizing. He said that too many would-be golfers go to sleep at night *worrying* about their game, their stance, their swing, their mistakes, and they visualize the resultant missed hole. He said that the golfer, in order to improve, must begin to see the ball going into the hole. He must stop worrying because worry was simply a form of negative vision. The golfer must see perfect form and success. He must visualize himself performing in a beautiful way and the resultant roll of the ball going in the hole.

What he was saying was that, in a perfectly normal way, we must learn to use the heart. We must plant seeds there and imagine the fruit. We must see it internally before we see it externally. When we learn to cooperate with our heart we will see good and wonderful things transpire in our life—in every area of our life. The heart is a wonderful entity.

So, let's go a little deeper.

4

The Mysterious Nature Of Your Heart

The heart is a mysterious entity. It has a certain and defined nature which allows influence, impression, and manipulation.

Scientific studies, as well as Biblical examples, have shown that the subconscious heart can receive thoughts, affirmations, and suggestions. The heart does not seem to be of a nature that judges, makes comparisons, or reasons. This appears to be the nature of our conscious mind. The heart mainly receives impressions. It is like a modern video tape that records and plays back whatever the camera of the conscious head allows to be filmed.

Obviously, God has made the conscious mind to protect the subconscious, impression-oriented, heart. The conscious mind is a logical screening device that, in its natural operation, critically analyzes information. Thus, if subconscious information is extracted from a person, that person usually has to be under hypnosis or drugs, or be in a "sleepy" state. Information has to slip past the guardian of the gate; the logical conscious. When a person is in this twilight state, answers can be retrieved that have been *repressed*, hidden on the video recording of the subconscious.

Careful—What You Say Is What You Get!

The Bible says that we are involved in a spiritual battle. We war against principalities and powers of the air (Ephesians 6:12). But there is an inward struggle as well (Romans 7). We can struggle between flesh and spirit or, according to James, the half-brother of Jesus, we can struggle with a divided mind (James 1:7,8); the struggle between the head and the heart.

So many of our problems are brought on by our innermost selves—not others or outside sources. From the time we are babies most of us are subjected to enough negative thoughts to mentally cripple us for a dozen lifetimes.

I heard an aunt say in the face of her beloved little toddling nephew, "Oh, you are so mean. You are a naughty one! Yes you are! You cute little thing."

These may sound like innocent, playful, expressions but they are part and parcel of a powerful tool. The same aunt can't believe it then when her sweet little Johnny grows up to be a juvenile delinquent.

Have you grown up hearing—"You can't"—"You won't ever amount to a thing"—"You're too old for that"—"You can't afford to do that"—"That's impossible"—"You are going to catch cold"—"You are going to end up in jail"?

These and thousands of other negative statements approach our heart throughout our life. And some negative words dressed as warnings should be received. But the important question is: have I allowed any *wrong* or negative words to become implanted on my heart? Have I allowed my heart to accept them as true?

Not only do we battle against these coming to us from outside sources, we have to be careful as to how we think and speak. We often self-impose improper negatives upon ourselves.

Jesus said, "For by your words you will be acquitted, and by your words you will be condemned" (Matthew 12:37, NIV).

There is a place for a negative word. But it must be used properly and with correct application.

Just as you can fight against impressions so you can supply constructive and helpful impressions. Most of us would benefit beyond our wildest dreams by a positive rehabilitative therapy of corrective impressions; corrective *word therapy*. You have power. You can keep feeding to your heart the impressions of, "I'm so stupid," "I can't do anything right," or you can repeat throughout the day, "I am complete in Christ," "I can do all things through Christ who strengthens me." It's up to you. What you say determines, to a great degree, what you become in life. What you imprint upon your heart has a tendency to be expressed in your world.

As a personal matter of illustration begin monitoring your statements and the statements of others. You will be surprised at the amount of baseless propaganda that is produced. Soon you will begin to notice it after you say it. Then you will recognize it while it is coming forth. Then, with practice, you will be able to recognize it in thought form. But your power for reform comes when you exchange the improper negative for the beneficial positive, never letting the improper negative seeds sprout.

The Ability To Read Word Pictures

Your heart differs from your conscious mind in that it does not argue—it just records and responds. It is very impression oriented. The conscious head tries to logically sort things out, but not the heart.

The subconscious receives and responds to words. I think it is more like word-pictures. To get that complete and clear word picture from our head to our heart, from our conscious to our subconscious, takes effort. It may take prayer and fasting. It may take repetition and persistence. That is why it is important to pray specifically. It is not that God does not hear general type prayers but that praying from the heart requires a clear word picture.

Word pictures received by the heart take root and grow. When you respond by the head (speech) to this word on your heart, you are in a position that frees God to work in your behalf. This is believing without doubt from your heart. You see it on the video of your heart as a word picture planted. You accept it as true and real before it actually appears. But it has a tendency to materialize as you have believed for this is a rule of the Kingdom of God just as surely as gravity is a law of the natural.

Garbage In—Garbage Out

In our computer driven age we have all become familiar with the term, *garbage in—garbage out*, as a formatting term indicating that how a computer is programmed will determine how it produces. If you have bugs in the programming—bugs will eventually come out.

The same concept is applied to the heart. Jesus made mention of this.

"For out of the overflow of the heart the mouth speaks. The good man brings good things out of the good stored up in him, and the evil man brings evil things out of the evil stored up in him" (Matthew 12:34-35, NIV).

Paul said the same thing in a little different way as he wrote to the church at Galatia.

"Do not be deceived: God cannot be mocked. A man reaps what he sows. The one who sows to please his sinful nature, from that nature will reap destruction; the one who sows to please the Spirit, from the Spirit will reap eternal life" (Galatians 6:7-8, NIV).

Learning The Secret Of The Heart And How It Works

Why do you think that a man who obviously learned the secret to heart power made the following statement?

"Finally, brethren, whatsoever things are true,...honest,...just,...pure,... lovely,...of good report; if there be any virtue, and if there be any praise, think on these things" (Philippians 4:8).

Why would he express the following?

"Do not conform any longer to the pattern of this world, but be transformed by the renewing of your mind. Then you will be able to test and approve what God's will is—his good, pleasing and perfect will" (Romans 12:2, NIV).

Why would he tell us to refocus?

"Set your affection on things above, not on things on the earth" (Colossians 3:2).

One of the reasons, if not *the* reason, has to do with *clarity*. Your heart receives and gives. If the signal is not clear you are not going to get clear reception. And why is this important? Because what is impressed upon the heart in clarity, harmony, and oneness is what is expressed. In other words, you are not going to have mountain-moving prayers answered if you don't have a clear, communicative heart. Things simply won't happen because they can't happen. The subconscious heart-mind is cloudy. You are foggy.

I am convinced that one of the reasons Jesus could easily perform wonders and miracles that astound us even to this day is because He kept a clear and clean heart.

In fact, He said,

"I tell you the truth, the Son can do nothing by himself; he can do only what he sees his Father doing, because whatever the Father does the Son also does" (John 5:19, NIV).

Jesus just did what He saw clearly, without doubt, inwardly, on His heart. On the other hand, the disciples struggled. Peter is a great example. In his early days, while following Jesus around, he was boastful, brash, and always operating from the head.

One day Jesus rebuked him and said,

"Get behind me, Satan! You are a stumbling block to me; you do not have in mind the things of God, but the things of men" (Matthew 16:23, NIV).

Peter was operating from the head. It appears that the devil was trying to sift his conscious and get to his heart. The culmination of Peter's head experience came when he denied the Savior. Jesus, however, reclaimed him and used the experience to awaken him to heart production instead of head production.

If you have read any of Peter's letters, it is obvious that he learned this most valuable lesson. Miracles were also recorded at his hand. Why? Because he learned the secret of the heart and how it works. There were little or no recorded miracles at the hand of Peter during the ministry of Jesus except when Jesus was present and an obvious participant (i.e., feeding of 5,000, walking on water, etc.). But after Pentecost and the coming of the Holy Spirit, Peter changed from a *head man* to a *heart man*!

Don't Be Double-Minded

James, the half-brother of Jesus, and a one-time skeptic of Jesus, later came to write in regard to prayer:

"If any of you lacks wisdom, he should ask God, who gives generously to all without finding fault, and it will be given to him. But when he asks, he must believe and not doubt, because he who doubts is like a wave of the sea, blown and tossed by the wind. That man should not think he will receive anything from the Lord; he is a **double-minded man**, unstable in all he does" (James 1:5-8, NIV, bold emphasis mine).

The Greek word that James uses here for *double-minded* is *dipsychos*, which means, two psyches, two minds, or a divided mind. The divided mind concept makes sense if one simply understands that there are two aspects to the mind; the conscious head and the sub-conscious heart. If there is disagreement between your head and your heart, faith cannot operate. God's deposited word cannot come forth from the heart so that it is confessed and acted upon.

I was counseling with a young woman once who was struggling with a decision as to whether to go to seminary and on to missions or to finish her degree in physical therapy. She argued that it would be noble to go to the mission field, but a job as a physical therapist would pay a great deal more, and she could help people as well.

It was my estimation that she had a clear case of double-mindedness. And I told her so. I said, "You have a double mind and according to James, you should not think that you will receive from the Lord. You need to settle on one or the other. If God is calling you to missions, then forget therapy. If He is calling you to be a physical therapist, then forget seminary and become a physical therapist. You, and you alone, have to get a word from God on this matter. Then you can act on it by faith in a powerful way that produces good results."

Like so many, this young lady was trying to get an answer by *logically* figuring out what was going to be best for her. Instead, she should have been seeking to get a *word* on her heart about the matter. She was foggy because she was double-minded. Her head and heart were not in reconciliation and God was stifled. She was confused. But, it is not an easy matter.

After I spoke to a group along these lines, an elderly lady came up to me and said, "God spoke to me through your message. I realize now why I sometimes cannot get my prayers answered. I am often double-minded in my praying."

In all of my years of teaching and listening to teaching, I can't ever remember hearing a sermon or lesson on this concept. It makes me wonder if laymen and preachers, alike, do not understand the conceptual difference between the conscious and the sub-conscious; the head and the heart.

If you are going to move mountains and walk on water you will do it when harmony comes between your head and your heart. If we are ever going to have our prayers answered it will happen when our head and heart are in agreement. Maybe this was what the old-timers used to call "praying through." If your head is saying to your heart that it will never happen—it is impossible—it can't happen—it probably won't! There is a wavering message being sent to the heart. You are being double-minded and God is stifled.

Many things operate by means of sound waves, rhythms, cycles, and rates of motion. Man has made great communicative advancements when he has been able to build devices that would reach into the air and retrieve sound waves, separate them, and process them through an apparatus that would transfer them to our ears. We take radio and television capabilities for granted today. Our great, great grandfathers would have called them miracles. But, even though the sound waves are there and perfect, we cannot receive or convey the message if our receiver or broadcaster is low power or faulty.

I have a little cheap transistor radio that I try to use sometimes to hear the news. It is scratchy, full of static, and stations tend to overlap giving me mixed messages. I have to try to get the little dial just right in order to hear. It is not the message signal. It is not faulty sound waves. It is the receiver. For I soon get fed up with it and go across the room to my high powered stereo receiver, flip a switch, smoothly dial the knob, and it is as if the people are in my living room reading me the news in a crystal clear fashion. It wasn't the sound waves (words), it was the receiver (heart).

If you learn this difference, God will be freed and activated to work in your life and experiences. If you see this difference and apply the principle, mountains will move for you. Things you thought impossible will come to pass. It is a universal truth principle. It is one of those *whosoever* laws that Jesus gave. But if you are *double-minded*; if you are cloudy, and foggy; if there is conflict; if there is not harmony; if you can't see what the heart is saying, there will be doubt that short circuits faith.

The Issue Of Integrity

The English dictionary says that *integrity* refers to soundness, a firm adherence to a code or standard of values, the state of being unimpaired, the quality or condition of being undivided. Words that relate are words like *integer*—a whole number, *integral*—essential for completeness, *integrate*—to make into a whole by bringing all parts together.

Integrity is an important concept regarding the heart. If the heart is divided it does not have integrity. If we allow God to work in our life it will be when we are focused and undivided toward Him. One reason we do not have our prayers answered in the positive is because we do not have integrity of heart. Our heart is divided. We are double-minded.

King David lost the integrity of his heart when he sinned with Bathsheba. Thus, he cries for the thing he lost—a whole heart toward God. Listen to him.

"Behold, thou desirest truth in the inward parts: and in the hidden part thou shalt make me to know wisdom.... Create in me a clean heart, O God; and renew a right spirit within me" (Psalm 51:6,10).

On the other hand, when David was just a lad, with an undivided heart, he slew a lion and a bear. His heart had integrity and God was able to work for supernatural strength. It was the same when he slew Goliath. It was not just his physical prowess at slinging a stone. God directed the stone because David's undivided heart allowed Him to work.

The same is applied to Daniel facing the lion's den and the three Hebrew men who faced the fiery furnace. I am convinced that God was able to work on their behalf because they had *integrity* of heart. Their heart was whole and undivided before God.

Jesus, likewise, was always able to work mighty miracles and wonders because He maintained integrity of heart. His heart was whole and undivided before the Father. He repeatedly said that He *always* did those things that were pleasing to His Father.

If we are going to serve God in power, we are going to do it in the integrity of our heart. A half-hearted service for God will not last or produce much fruit. The same could be applied to salvation. We cannot halfway believe on Jesus! This becomes frightening and alarming when we realize that so many so-called believers are living such a divided, half-hearted, lifestyle. Power comes from an undivided heart of integrity.

5

The Tin Man's Search

Someone coined the phrase, "knowledge is power." But what a lot of people don't understand is that power not only can come from the *head* but from the *heart*; the subconscious part of our mind. Many people miss the treasure and bypass the gold mine because they seek to operate solely from the conscious; the head. Even though they use the subconscious heart every day, they are not made to be conscious of the subconscious! Head knowledge without heart understanding produces sophisticated morons. To lack heart understanding produces fools and foolish decisions. The Bible book of *Proverbs* has a lot to say about this.

The Bible says that salvation in Jesus Christ comes because a person *hears* the gospel, *believes* in his heart and *confesses* with his mouth that Jesus Christ has been raised from the dead and is his Lord (Romans 10:9,10). Salvation comes *through* or by means of the head (confession, hearing, knowing,) not *from* the head. Head knowledge about Jesus will not save. The devils believe but are not saved (James 2:19). Atheists can know about Jesus from studying the Bible but not be saved. Theologians and Bible professors can know Biblical and historical facts and agree mentally that Jesus was the Son of God but not be saved. Salvation is a heart matter. It comes *from* the heart. We must believe *from* the heart.

Proverbs 4:23 says, "Keep thy heart with all diligence; for out of it are the issues of life."

Jesus said:

"But the things that come out of the mouth come from the heart, and these make a man 'unclean.' For out of the heart come evil thoughts, murder, adultery, sexual immorality, theft, false testimony, slander" (Matthew 15:18-19, NIV).

Jesus also said that from the heart comes the power to move mountains and do marvelous things. In Matthew's gospel there is an incident where the disciples were caught out in a boat in a storm. Between three and six in the morning Jesus came walking to the weary and frightened disciples on the water. They expressed fear. Jesus comforted them. Peter then asked if he could come to Him on the water. Jesus gave him a word—"Come." Peter bounded out of the boat to walk to Jesus on the water and was doing the impossible until his head got in the way. He walked on water by means of heart (subconscious) action. Then he saw the boisterous wind and waves. When his head (conscious) realized his location and condition, fear entered in, settled down into his heart, replaced faith, and Peter sank. The Lord Jesus reached down, rebuked him for having such little faith, saved him from the waves and carried him safely into the boat (See Matthew 14:23-33).

A thoughtful observation of this passage will reveal the four elements we are observing in this book; the *head*—the *heart*—a *word*—*faith*. The theme we are driving at is clearly seen here in this story. Get God's word on your heart—act on this word by faith—walk on water!

Am I saying here that we, too, should try to walk on water or that it is a viable possibility? I will address this in a later section, but for now, just begin to realize that the heart is a real entity within us and has value that we should observe.

Enlightenment And The Treasure You May Not Know About

From where do inventions and ideas come? What is that *flash* of inspiration that artists, architects, inventors, and thinkers seem to possess? Where is it located?

The heart is a wonderful creation of God. It is not only a connection point to Him but it is a source place for inspiration. It is where everything comes together. Your logical conscious receives information, sorts it, weighs it, calculates it, figures with it, and passes the digested information on to the subconscious. There it is filed. There it incubates. There it is assimilated. There the embryo is formed. If allowed to be born it will come forth as *fruit*; as illumination—invention—revelation—a new idea—enlightenment.

The so called *Dark Ages* of medieval history (476-1450 A.D.) were dark not because they had no candles but because the freedom for *enlightenment* was stifled. The sourcebook for true inner enlightenment, the Bible, was kept from the people. The Bible is material for the *heart*; the subconscious. All that the people of the Dark Ages possessed was pre-digested consciousness given to them by the clergy.

The *Reformation* broke down the wall that had been built for conscious robotics and men began to *see* and think, and be enlightened. Their hearts burned with a new brightness. Inventions came forth. Progress was made. Barbarism of the conscious was by-passed by enlightenment from a fertile subconscious heart.

I know a brilliant Christian architect. He has won several prestigious awards. He has designed wonderful and complicated structures.

He told me that when he was just beginning his life work, he would often, and daily, go into a quiet place and pray. He would get on his knees and say, "God I need help. You and I are the only two who really knows my capabilities and inadequacies. These people are expecting a great design. I must have your help."

He would gather information. He would apply learned and technical expertise. Then he said, "I would wait for that *flash of inspiration*. Then it would come; the concept—the vision of the design—the mental picture that was right."

This successful architect, like musicians, artists, writers, and inventors of the past, is relying not only on acquired learning in his conscious, but also upon the fertile treasure chest of his subconscious heart. And his heart produces. It gives forth the treasure. It produces the fruit. The fruit of the heart is important, if not more so, than the fruit of the head. Head fruit, or expressed knowledge, tends toward pride and haughtiness that short-circuits the power of God. As the Scripture says, "Knowledge puffs up" (1 Corinthians 8:1, NIV).

My son took a college course on Mozart, the musician-composer. He loves to listen to this musical artist and is intrigued with his genius for composition. He told me how Mozart would compose an entire piece (and some were long!) in his head with all the different instruments, notes, and musical flow. And where did it originate? Certainly his conscious mind worked but the heart was involved as well. The heart is a wonderful instrument. It is a treasure house.

Interconnected To The Divine?

It is most likely that that our subconscious heart is the closest to God of any aspect of our being. And why would I think that? We are saved from our sins by heart belief, not head knowledge. When we are saved, we say that we have "invited Jesus into our heart." We say that the Holy Spirit *speaks* to our heart, convicts our heart, or burdens our heart. Jesus said that we were to believe in and from our heart. How is it then, that we do not see the interconnectedness of God and our heart?

One description of God's dimension is characterized by the *internal* Kingdom of God concept that we find in the Scriptures. There were several aspects of the meaning of *kingdom*; "Kingdom of God," or "Kingdom of heaven." One was outward and visible. One was inward and invisible. One was present and one was future.

W.E. Vine, writing in his classic, *Expository Dictionary Of New Testament Words* declares:

"Thus, speaking generally, references to the Kingdom fall into two classes, the first, in which it is viewed as present and involving suffering for those who enter it, 2 Thess. 1:5; the second, in which it is viewed as future and is associated with reward, Matt. 25:34; Phil. 2:9-11; 2 Tim. 4:1,18.

The fundamental principle of the Kingdom is declared in the words of the Lord spoken in the midst of a company of Pharisees, 'the Kingdom of God is in the midst of you,' Luke 17:21, marg., that is, where the King is, there is the Kingdom. Thus at the present time and so far as this earth is concerned, where the King is and where His rule is acknowledged, is, first, in the heart of the individual believer, Acts 4:19; Eph. 3:17; 1 Pet. 3:15; and then in the churches of God, 1 Cor. 12:3, 5, 11; 14:37; cp. Col. 1:27, where for 'in' read 'among'" [W.E. Vine, *An expository Dictionary of New Testatment Words* (Old Tappan, New Jersey: Fleming H. Revell Co., 1966), p. 294].

Jesus told the Jewish religious leaders that "the Kingdom of God is within you" (Luke 17:21). Several study Bibles translate this as "in the midst of you" and make a commentary on it in the footnotes. But the Greek (*entos*) indicates the concept of "within" or "inside." It is used only twice in the New Testament; here and by Jesus when he was admonishing the Pharisees to clean, not only the *outside* of the cup (their bodies) but the *inside* of the cup (their inner mind and heart).

A. T. Robertson, the well-known and respected Greek scholar of the twentieth century, not only speaks from his own authority, but from the authority of other scholars when he writes regarding Jesus' statement in Luke 17:21:

"*Within you* (*entos humon*). This is the obvious, and, as I think, the necessary meaning of *entos*. The examples cited of the use of *entos* in Xenophon and Plato where *entos* means 'among' do not bear that out when investigated. Field (*Ot. Norv*) 'contends that there is no clear instance of *entos* in the sense of among' (Bruce), and rightly so. What Jesus says to the Pharisees is that they, as others, are to look for the kingdom of God within themselves, not in outward displays and supernatural manifestations. It is not a localized display 'Here' or 'There.' It is in this sense that in Luke 11:20 Jesus spoke of the kingdom of God as 'come upon you,' (*ephthasen eph' humàs*) speaking to Pharisees. The only other instance of entos in the N.T. (Matt. 23:26) necessarily means 'within ('the inside of the cup'). There is, beside, the use of *entos* meaning 'within' in the Oxyrhynchus Papyrus saying of Jesus of the Third Century (Deissmann, *Light from the Ancient East*, p. 426) which is interesting: 'The kingdom of heaven is within you' (*entos humon* as here in Luke 17:21)" [A.T. Robertson, *Word Pictures in the New Testament, Vol. 2, Luke*, (Nashville, Tennessee, Broadman Press, 1930) p. 229].

As the scholars point out, the Kingdom can be in the *heart* of the believer. If we understand the meaning to be *within* rather than *in the midst*, we will come to a greater understanding of the Kingdom concept. And if this was the meaning of Jesus, it means that this area is within the unbelievers as well. This has thrown some interpreters of the Bible into such a quandary that they translate Jesus to say that it is in the midst, rather than in the mind! Properly understanding the concept of the heart and the sphere in which God operates, we will realize that the Kingdom of God is within even the ungodly. If God is omnipresent, He is everywhere—in every person—in every cell—in every fiber of every thing. And where He is you will find His Kingdom. But, just as a person can live in a country under a king, does not mean that the person will acknowledge or obey the king. The ungodly do not submit to the Kingdom of God, recognize it, or operate in it. It was *inside* the ungodly religious leaders—in their heart—their subconscious—but they kept its doors shut. If you don't understand the concept of the *heart* you will, of necessity, have to translate it as being *in the midst of*, or *around in the vicinity*.

Jesus further amplifies on this when he spoke to the disciples about the people who did not understand his teachings. He said:

"Though seeing, they do not see; though hearing, they do not hear or understand. In them is fulfilled the prophecy of Isaiah: 'You will be ever hearing but never understanding; you will be ever seeing but never perceiving. For this people's heart has become calloused; they hardly hear with their ears, and they have closed their eyes. Otherwise they might see with their eyes, hear with their ears, understand with their hearts and turn, and I would heal them'" (Matthew 13:13-15, NIV).

Our Inner Invisible Realm

As I have studied the life and works of Jesus, I have discovered that miracles, most often, and without question, resulted from an inward activity. These inward actions which resulted in outward miraculous occurrences were themselves, an invisible inner-working combination of elements. Jesus did not deny these elements and, in fact, pointed them out to us.

This realm is invisible but very real. It is within each of us and operates by certain rules and actions that many do not use in the right way for the best of purposes. Though each person possesses this realm, it does not necessarily follow that they are spiritually minded or even God oriented. Even the ungodly religious leaders of Jesus' day had this inward area but did not operate in it correctly. Sometimes we are blind to it. Sometimes we harden it so that the essential seed of success does not get planted. But sometimes we allow enough light to get in, a seed no bigger than a mustard seed, to get planted and we discover the gold mine. For it produces. Dreams come true. Desires are fulfilled. Prayers are answered. Things happen. There is a direct reason—a cause and effect, if you please.

Jesus told worried Peter to go catch a fish and find enough money in its mouth to pay both their taxes. He told the fishermen who had toiled all night on which side to cast their nets for a haul so large the boat couldn't contain them all. Where did He get this knowledge? Was it peculiar to Him because He was the Son of God? Or does He show us what could be as He operates from this mysterious inner realm?

Do not neglect, reject, or be afraid of this concept. After all, it is the realm where God operates. It is also a realm that we operate in every day of our life. It is hardly possible to live without using this area. Do we not operate in this realm for salvation and service? Do we not operate in this realm when we pray or intercede for someone? When we meet at church to pray for the sick or for missionaries seven thousand miles away, are we not operating in this realm?

Could it be that by virtue of our heart, like a spiritual telephone modem, or cell phone, our computer brain is linked to a greater source? Is it by means of a heart network called the *Kingdom of God* that we are linked to a divine power and source that goes beyond our normal capabilities?

Possibly, this is the explanation of why common men in the Bible could interpret dreams (Daniel, Joseph), prophesy of future events (Isaiah, Ezekiel), and perform miracles (Elijah, Peter, Paul).

In the Old Testament the prophets saw visions, interpreted the dreams of kings, and had the future revealed to them. Where did this occur? Was it not mostly communicated to their heart? The Apostles Paul, John, Peter, and others in the New Testament had divine enlightenment, communication, revelations, and visions of the future. Where did it occur? It occurred mostly in the regions of their subconscious heart. Before, God would communicate with people by the use of angels, burning bushes, whirlwinds, prophets or even a talking donkey. Today, and since the day of Pentecost, God speaks to us primarily through the revelation of His written Word and by the Holy Spirit in our heart.

The gospel proclaims that Christ came to bridge the gap—to reconnect man to God—to be the mediator between God and man. Jesus said, "No man can come to the Father but by me." Jesus claimed to be the only one who could bridge the God-man dimension. He proclaimed salvation or eternal life as a reconnecting to God's dimension. Those who do not get reconnected are called "lost." *Lost* never refers to deficient knowledge on God's part. *Lost*, in the Bible, means *separation*. Being *lost* means to be disconnected from God's eternal dimension.

Though God has revealed himself by many means to mankind, it appears that His preferred method of connecting to man is through the subconscious heart. God could speak to us through angels, burning bushes, donkeys, or rocks but He uses those only in a secondary, Old Testament, or last resort sense. He has spoken to us through prophets, His divine Word, and our own intellect. But, from my observation of the Scripture, it is clear that God prefers to deposit His word on our heart and have us respond, accordingly, by faith.

6

Faith—The Activator Of Words

The cowardly lion, in the fantasy story, *The Wizard of Oz*, was on a journey down the Yellow Brick Road in search of *courage*. Another word that could have been used instead of courage would be *faith*. Faith and courage are very similar.

The Bible describes faith as "...being sure of what we hope for and certain of what we do not see" (Hebrews 11:1, NIV). Bible faith is tied closely to action and resolve on the basis of something. That something is the word, the promises, the covenants of God. Although it is hard to define, it is easy to observe. Throughout the Bible, from Genesis to Revelation, we have people acting by faith.

Faith is one of the key ingredients in our success soup. The others are: *a word from God* and the *heart*. **Get God's word on your heart—Act on this word by faith—God will be free to show you great and marvelous things**.

You Don't Need Much

The strange thing about faith is that you don't need much of it. It only takes a small amount of faith. The big element is the word. The important instrument is the heart. It only takes a speck of faith.

Jesus rebuked His disciples on more than one occasion concerning their microscopic faith or lack of it all together.

"Then the disciples came to Jesus in private and asked, 'Why couldn't we drive it out?'

He replied, 'Because you have so little faith. I tell you the truth, if you have faith as small as a mustard seed, you can say to this mountain, 'Move from here to there' and it will move. Nothing will be impossible for you'" (Matthew 17:19-21, NIV).

Jesus said the same thing in another context.

"If you have faith as small as a mustard seed, you can say to this mulberry tree, 'Be uprooted and planted in the sea,' and it will obey you" (Luke 17:6, NIV).

It has been my understanding that a mustard seed is about the size of a pepper flake or a tiny grain of salt. The point that Jesus is making is that it doesn't take much faith.

This flies in the face of many preachers of the gospel today. I hear them all the time preaching that we need abundant faith—more faith—strong faith. One television evangelist's program is entitled, *Ever Increasing Faith*. What many do not understand is that the issue is not much faith but a clear word on a clean and whole heart!

Jesus paralleled the mustard seed faith concept to the "leaven of the Pharisees." He told His disciples to "beware of the leaven of the Pharisees." They knew how leaven worked in making bread rise. They knew that it only took a pinch to affect the whole loaf. The leaven Jesus was referring to was their unbelief, ungodliness, and untruth. Their teaching was poisoning the Jewish nation.

Blasting Caps And Dynamite

I remember as a boy getting to go with my father to set off dynamite. It was a fun and interesting thing to do. Since he worked for a company that allowed him to use dynamite, he could take on weekend projects of blasting rocks and holes for people in the surrounding countryside.

I would watch him prepare the dynamite stick by stuffing a little object into one end called a *blasting cap*. It was an ignition device with electrical wires running back to a small battery. He would prepare the charge, stuff the stick of explosive into a crevice in the rock, and make his way to cover. I would watch as he yelled, "Fire in the hole!" Then he would touch the electric wires to the positive and negative posts of the battery. The tiny charge in the current would ignite the blasting cap which, in turn, would set off the dynamite. I would cover my ears and head as a sudden blast shook the earth. Dust and smoke billowed and rocks rained down all around. I was always anxious to jump up and see the results of the blast.

The powerful explosion was the result of a charge igniting the little blasting cap. The blasting cap, like faith, was very small but oh, the power that it ignited.

Now follow this. The dynamite was like the word. It was the power charge. The rock in which it was placed was like the heart that receives a word. The tiny blasting cap was like a tiny amount of faith. The action of touching the wires to the battery post was like our activation of faith. This, of course, is an imperfect analogy. The word we receive in our heart does not explode and destroy us. But energy is released in that God causes things to happen as a result of the word in the heart, acted upon by faith. We then see the result.

Faith—A Universal Element

A word is a universal element. There are all kinds of words from all kinds of sources and can be used by all people. Words are universal. The heart is universal within the human frame. Everyone has a head and a heart. Faith is also a universal element. Anyone can use faith. The good, the bad, and the ugly can use faith. Jesus used faith and so did Adolf Hitler. Faith is universal and can be applied for good or ill.

One author writes:

"When we talk about faith—and belief—we have to refer to the greatest book ever written, and the greatest Teacher of the ages on the subject. He summed it up when He said: 'Go thy way; and as thou hast believed, so be it done unto thee.'

...Dr. Ernest Holmes, who devoted his life to teaching this great truth, explained it another way. 'Here is a power which every person has, but which few people use consciously. One individual does not possess this power above another, or to a greater degree. Everyone has it, since everyone lives and has consciousness. The question then is not: Do we have the power? It is merely: Are we using it correctly?'" [Dennis Waitley, *Seeds of Greatness* (Old Tappan, New Jersey: Fleming H. Revell Company, 1983), p. 148].

Everything about our life is based on a word or words. Knowing what word or words to base one's faith actions upon is of utmost importance. It is like the blasting cap and the stick of dynamite. You can act by faith on the wrong word or words and blow yourself up and do a lot of damage to others. The heart is universal. Words are universal. The ability of anyone to use faith is a universal ability.

Good Intentions—Disastrous Results

Many, many people throughout history have based faith actions on the wrong word. And as we have seen, a bad word can get planted on the heart as well as a good word—if not easier.

The opening up of the new world was delayed because people believed the *expert's* word who proclaimed the earth to be flat! This sounds preposterous to us now. But mankind has been stifled by ignorance about the true word on a subject.

People have been slaughtered because of the promotion of a wrong word too. Millions of Jews were exterminated because followers of a German mad-man believed his word of Aryan superiority. German people, and especially the leadership of Nazi Germany, believed the word of Nazi psychiatrist Ernst Rudin perpetuating the 1933 Nazi sterilization law. This law led to the sterilization of 375,000 "unfit" Germans and set the stage for the Holocaust.

In another era, hundreds of men, women, and children followed religious cult leader, Jim Jones, like the Pied Piper, to Guyana and committed suicide because they acted by faith on his word. The news footage of the bloated bodies of men, women, and little children that lay dead in the hot sun spoke volumes concerning the power of words.

Every day young people base their hair styles, clothing purchases, and activities on words they receive from pop music, movies, and star's endorsements or television commercial words and images. We are even living in a day when *subliminal* messages, or slightly hidden words, influence people to make purchases.

I listened to a documentary recently on television regarding the effect of verbal abuse on the brain. Brain scans have revealed that the physical brain is severely affected by verbal abuse. Studies showed that adults who were verbally abused as children had dramatic differences within the structure of the brain, specifically in the area that divides the two halves of the brain. This difference that lasted on in to adult-hood affected neuro-transmission and resulted in reactive behavior. Words make a difference!

Seemingly innocent words, if not the best or proper words for our life, can have devastating results. There must be a screening process. There must be something by which we gauge the right word so that we can act by faith.

Everything Hinges On The Right Word

Just because one makes choices in life does not mean that success will follow. Making the right choices or faith choices based on the right word is the key to success.

Sometimes this gets a little confusing when two *good* words from reliable sources are coming at you. So who do you believe? This can happen with political election decisions, conflicting decisions between parents, or the differences in religious dogma.

In the Old Testament there were two prophets, supposedly representing God; Hananiah and Jeremiah. Hananiah was prophesying a more pleasing prophecy regarding their victory over Babylon. Jeremiah was prophesying a warning regarding a harsh Babylonian captivity. The people chose the word of Hananiah. But they were wrong—dead wrong! Hananiah also received God's personal word of judgment and died that very year.

God felt so strongly about a right and true word going forth that His prescription for a false prophet was stoning to death! The right word was absolutely essential for it affected those who based their faith and life upon it.

Know God's Word And You Know His Will

A young woman who was desperately seeking God's help in her own life asked the question in one of our seminars, "How do you know when you are acting upon God's word on your heart?"

Others, who want to be in line with God's word, have asked it another way: "How do you know God's will?"

Oftentimes I have heard people conclude their prayer with, "if it be thy will." Certainly these people are sincere. They are seeking to be humble. They do not, in any way, want to violate or disregard God's will. But the truth is that they are praying from ignorance or habit as much as from humility.

You will struggle to find this type praying in the New Testament. In the Garden of Gethsemane Jesus prayed, "Not my will, but thine be done." But His prayer was from knowledge of the Father's will, not ignorance of it. In the, so called, *Model Prayer*, Jesus said that we should pray for God's will to be done on earth as it is in heaven. But there was no "if" involved.

It sounds humble to pray this way but it is the wrong way to pray. Can you imagine Jesus standing at the tomb of Lazarus saying, "Lazarus come forth if it be God's will." Or, "Man stretch forth your hand, if it be God's will."

One prominent characteristic mentioned time and again was that Jesus spoke with "authority," not like the religious teachers.

Again, the principle is: get a word on your heart and act on it by faith. Jesus could respond with authority because He always acted from the Father's word on His heart. That is why miracles happened. That is why miracles will still happen.

Knowing The Word And Acting By Faith Is Not Easy

If this experience was easy, everybody would be doing it and it would be so common as to not even be considered as something unusual. The road to the right word is straight and narrow and often requires effort and energy. Sometimes it requires patience and persistence. It is not for the lazy and insensitive person.

In Old Testament times, the prophet Elijah prayed for rain seven separate times. The first time or two nothing seemed to be happening. Then a little cloud appeared. Then it rained in abundance. Daniel prayed for twenty-one days. Jeremiah prayed for ten days. Jesus gave illustrations concerning asking, seeking, and knocking. He told parables about persistent individuals.

The proper word that comes to our heart has to come through many obstacles before it gets planted. Listen to the conversation that an angel had with Daniel as he prayed for many days.

"Then he continued, 'Do not be afraid Daniel. Since the first day that you set your mind to gain understanding and to humble yourself before your God, your words were heard, and I have come in response to them. But the prince of the Persian kingdom resisted me twenty-one days. Then Michael, one of the chief princes, came to help me, because I was detained there with the king of Persia" (Daniel 10:12-13, NIV).

Alignment Is The Key

God's good is the best good. God's word is the best word. Lining up by faith with God's word on our heart is the key to true success and blessing.

The other day I took my car in to have my tires rotated. The attendant came back and said that he wouldn't advise rotating them because they were so worn. I argued that they did not look that worn to me. Then he pulled the wheel off and showed me the inside portion of the tires. The rubber was worn down until the metal strands within the tire were protruding. I stood amazed. He said it was because the front end was out of line. He also told me that I was lucky I had not had a blowout and wrecked. I agreed to a front end alignment and new tires.

Many people, living in our high stress world, have blowouts and often wreck because their life is out of balance, out of alignment, and out of control. Some will "turn over a new leaf" every New Year only to see it reversed before Valentine Day. Some will make commitments to exercise and eat properly only to revert to former unhealthy eating patterns before a month is over. We struggle to stay lined up with what is right, good, and healthy for us.

The struggle is actually a spiritual one that involves our mind, our heart, words, and priority choices. Jesus addressed this in His sermon on the mount when he said:

"But seek first his kingdom and his righteousness, and all these things will be given to you as well" (Matthew 6:33, NIV).

Jesus was saying that food, clothing, houses, and other *things* would be given to them by the Father when they did a very simple thing. This thing that Jesus mentioned is so often missed by those who read this Scripture. For most, it means a commitment to live right. But it is much more than that.

Notice that this is a contrasting verse: "but." The contrast is in regard to worry over having things. Notice that it is a personal verse: "(you) seek." Notice that there is a priority: "seek first." Notice that there are two items mentioned as priority goals: "His kingdom and His righteousness."

So what is His kingdom and His righteousness? This is where people miss the interpretation. And proper interpretation here is crucial to receiving from the Father.

First, remember that Jesus told the Pharisees that the kingdom was within them. Then understand that this kingdom within is locatable within the heart for it is in the heart that God relates to mankind. I think that we would be safe to say that this area of the kingdom within us *is* the heart. So, we need to seek within the kingdom of the heart.

Once we begin to look inward with spiritual eyes and *search our heart* we are to look for something else; His righteousness. What is His righteousness? His righteousness may be more than His word but it certainly includes His word. The Bible tells us that His word abides for ever and is a light unto our path. The Bible tells us that His word is sharp and powerful with the capability of dividing "soul and spirit" (Hebrews 4:12). Certainly, His righteousness has everything to do with His word, if not indistinguishable from it.

So here is how it makes perfect sense to me. If the kingdom refers to the heart and righteousness refers to His word, it means that we are to line up with His word on our heart. This fits perfectly with our model: **Get God's word on your heart—Act on this word by faith—God will be free to bless**.

Do you see it? If so, you are ahead of where I was just a short time back. For over thirty years I have been looking at this Scripture verse without this clarity. When I saw it, it not only made sense but I wanted to jump and shout for it relates perfectly to our theme.

This verse makes perfect sense in light of the response Jesus made to the unbelieving Pharisees in his day. Remember what He said? "…the kingdom of God is within you" (Luke 17:21).

The Pharisees could search for it and find the inward kingdom but the righteousness or word that was there in their kingdom heart was their own word; their own righteousness. This is why Jesus would tell one of the religious leaders,

Nicodemus, that he must be "born again." He must learn to look inward from the spiritual perspective—from the heart—from God's word on his heart.

All of this is about *alignment*. It is about lining up our life, our head, and our word with His word on our heart. If we can ever learn this and learn to act on the proper word by faith, all these other things will be given to us as well. Jesus said so!

7

Every Farmer's Struggle

Jesus gave us a wonderful parable, or story with a spiritual meaning, when He spoke of the man who went forth to sow seed. It is often called *the parable of the sower*. It is probably more accurate to call it the parable of the *soils* or the parable of the *seed*. The parable is given in Matthew, chapter thirteen.

Jesus describes a farmer who went forth to scatter seed on the ground. Some seed fell on the path, never took root, and the birds ate it up. Some seed fell on rocky soil where it tried to take root but couldn't, and withered away. Some fell among thorns that choked out the growth. Other seed fell on good ground where it took root, grew, and produced varying degrees of abundance.

One unique thing about this parable is that Jesus explains to the disciples what is meant. The birds represent the evil one who comes and snatches away God's word as it tries to get planted on the heart. The rocky soil represents trouble or persecution that causes the seed to wither away. The thorny soil represents the worries of life and the deceitfulness of wealth that choke out the plant causing unfruitfulness. The good soil, of course, represents a heart that receives God's word, acts on it by faith, and a wonderful harvest is produced.

The seed represents the word. It is interesting that *seed* in this passage comes from the Greek word *sperma*. Our word *sperm* or *spermatozoa* comes from this word. God's word is like sperm that impregnates our heart. The condition of our heart will determine the result of the seed; whether it is received at all; whether it gets planted and stays planted; whether it is nurtured for production or not.

Paul addresses our responsibility for a positive outcome, in a coordinated relationship with God, when he prays for the believers at Corinth.

"Now he who supplies seed to the sower and bread for food will also supply and increase your store of seed and will enlarge the harvest of your righteousness. You will be made rich in every way so that you can be generous on every occasion..." (2 Corinthians 9:10-11, NIV).

Enemies Of The Seed

As the parable points out, there are outside enemies that influence us to reject or neglect the seed. We have the capability of rejecting the seed altogether, receiving it but allowing it to get choked out, or downright aborting it.

The *evil one*, evil spirits, or demons, are very real today and work through the world system to distract us or to steal the word from us. They also can whisper their own seed words in our ear. Yes, they can give forth words as well.

Trouble or persecution can so distract us that words do not get planted. Some of the top causes of stress in our life are (1) the death of a family member or spouse, (2) divorce or marital troubles, (3) sickness or major health issues, (4) getting fired, laid off, or job transfer, (5) relocation of the home, (6) financial woes, etc. Any of these can so distract us that we don't even think about the right word getting planted. When these issues arise, we need to make time to get alone with God in prayer.

Worries of this life and the deceitfulness of wealth can cause any of us to neglect the word and miss being fruitful. Priorities are very important. Some begin with noble pursuits but get redirected along the way. Temporal *things* can so distract us that a heart word becomes unfruitful. Sometimes we have to make some hard choices and steel our resolve at the beginning in order not to be distracted. Remember, there is a reason for getting alone in the closet of prayer. There is a reason for fasting. There is a reason for focus.

One of the things the Bible predicts will be the case when the end time comes is that people will be caught up in everyday things so much that they will not be ready for the return of Jesus.

"As it was in the days of Noah, so it will be at the coming of the Son of Man. For in the days before the flood, people were eating and drinking, marrying and giving in marriage, up to the day Noah entered the ark; and they knew nothing about what would happen until the flood came and took them all away. That is how it will be at the coming of the Son of Man" (Matthew 24:37-39, NIV).

If there ever was a distracted society it is the one we are living in now.

Inward Hindrances

In studying the healings of Jesus, I discovered an interesting truth, or another *common denominator*. That is, faith seemed to be a constant and necessary factor in the individual being healed, but the application differed. His requirement for the heart was consistent; a word on the heart acted on by faith. His application to the head and body varied.

The Scripture validates the variations. Jesus spoke to some. He touched others. He put his fingers in a deaf man's ears. He spat on the ground, made mud, and applied it to blind eyes. Sometimes he healed from a distance as in the case of the centurion whose servant was sick. One woman simply touched his garment and power came out of Him to heal her. It is marvelous and amazing the varieties of methods found in the ministry of Jesus. Varieties are also attributed to the healing accounts of Peter and Paul.

But why do the methods and applications differ? I think that it has to do with the *head* or our logical mental brain. The head, brain, mind, or whatever you want to call it, is a marvelous computer. It assimilates information and stores information. Our mind is a reservoir of our past experiences, thoughts, and imaginations. It has been influenced by our environment and stands in the results of that influence that we have received through the years. Thus, we all come from slightly different backgrounds needing different applications for our mindset.

If God could only deal with our heart without the hindering influences of fear and knowledge He could work so much better. But we throw up all kinds of mental barriers. What we see Jesus doing in the pages of Scripture is simply getting past the conscious to the subconscious—past the head to the heart. Since people thought differently, so His methods differed. Possibly, the *tree of knowledge*, spoken of in the Garden of Eden account, refers to this aspect. Maybe, before the fall, faith in the heart was unhindered.

We are operating with constant hindering influences. If we could ever get to the place where these hindrances were alleviated, it is my conviction that God could, more readily, get His word to us for implanting upon our heart.

Not only is it hard for us to receive a word, it is also difficult to keep a word on our heart.

A Delicate Matter

Often, Jesus would heal someone only to instruct them *not* to tell anyone. There are two possible reasons for this. One is that it was not time to reveal Himself as the Messiah. But if that was the total issue, why did he start healing? I believe there is another reason. Maybe He knew that the skepticism of others would take away what had been gained. Skepticism, or the unbelief of others, can affect a seed word staying planted or growing in our heart. Unbelief, like a virus that floats through the air, has a way of lodging in our head and heart, depriving the word of food and oxygen, so that the word weakens and moves back up to the logical mind where its power dies. This is also a reason we should be careful in broadcasting our dreams and goals. Someone is liable to send an anti-faith, anti-word, virus our direction.

If you have a dream or a desire it is sometimes best not to share it. The negative thinkers and skeptics abound, ready to spray the water of unbelief and doubt upon your fire of heart faith. Let it be a thing of your heart—between you and God. Give testimony to it after the results are validated. You have trouble enough believing in a thing. You don't need help with doubt.

Therefore, Jesus said, "See that you tell no one."

Knowing the word is not easy. Keeping a word is difficult. This, possibly, is why we do not see more people operating in this way and why there is a need to promote this idea. The old adage is true: "If it was easy, everybody would be doing it!"

We need all the help and support we can get to get a word on our heart, act on it by faith, and see a wonderful result.

Help For Knowing, Getting, And Keeping The Right Seed Word

Like children, we want things simple, easy, and colorful. The reason we have difficulty presenting a little three-step *formula* here is because we are, in fact, dealing with the subconscious heart and the supernatural unseen world. The conscious sensory head wants it otherwise. But let me give you some helps for developing the ability to see and hear the word on your heart.

<u>1. Transform Your Mind</u>

The first thing that Jesus began to proclaim in His public ministry was *repentance*. This word is made up of two Greek words which came to mean "to change one's mind." Repentance means to change your thinking with a view to changed actions. Obviously, this was important to Jesus.

Likewise, the Apostle Paul spoke of this in his letter to the Romans.

"Do not conform any longer to the pattern of this world, but be transformed by the renewing of your mind. Then you will be able to test and approve what God's will is—his good, pleasing and perfect will" (Romans 12:2, NIV).

Again, changing one's mind or renewing one's mind is not necessarily quick or easy. It may take time. Attitudes do not change over-night. You have been affected by time and experiences. Childhood baggage may still be in place. Some transformation may appear to be instantaneous. For the most part we are talking about a process that takes time.

2. Take Baby Steps To Build Confidence

Confidence is related to faith and experience. Confidence comes from repeated experiences that produce the expected result.

If you will begin to act upon what little light, knowledge, and experience you can muster you will gain confidence. Faith builds faith. Hearing builds greater ability to hear. Seeing builds greater ability to see. Act on what you see, hear, and know now. You will be given more. If you don't—you won't! You will eventually come to the place, that even though you cannot explain it, you know that you know that you know!

To come to the place where you can say, "I have absolutely no doubt," is to have confidence. Often, this confidence is a result of progressively building our heart soil and consistently using faith.

When I first started a garden on our new property I discovered that the soil was mostly hard clay. After years of adding compost and cultivation it became loose and rich. The first year I didn't have much confidence that it would produce. Through the years my garden's soil had a transformation. I came to have confidence that it would produce. A transformation of your mind and the cultivation of your heart's soil will allow confidence to develop as seed words are progressively acted on by faith.

3. Operate From Bible Truth

Jesus said that His disciples would know the truth and this truth, acted on by faith, would set them free.

"To the Jews who had believed him, Jesus said, 'If you hold to my teaching, you are really my disciples. Then you will know the truth, and the truth will set you free'" (John 8:31-32, NIV).

The Psalmist wrote, "I have hidden your word in my heart that I might not sin against you" (Psalm 119:11, NIV).

The best document for truth and for written words from God is the book of Holy Scriptures we call the Bible. This author considers it not only to contain the word of God, but to be the word of God. It is alive. It is living. It is unlike any other body of words. You can apply it and it will produce.

If one is serious about knowing God's will and word for his or her heart, then the Bible must be considered. The reason is obvious—God will not contradict Himself. In fact, the Scriptures will bear witness for or against the word we get for our heart. The key is acting upon what the Bible means, not on what it says. Languages and translations differ. My seminary professors, who taught Greek and Hebrew, were always telling us that in any translation from the original into any modern language, you will always gain or lose something in the translation. Even though the Scriptures are timeless, we must come to understand that the Bible means what it said in the original manuscripts, in the original language, and in the original context of the society and circumstances of the day. Many people misinterpret the Scriptures and come up with all manner of weird decisions based upon what they believe the Word of God is saying.

The word you receive on your heart needs to ring true with Scripture truth if you want to know or live up to God's will. His Word will not disagree with His will. His Word, oftentimes, will bear witness with our word. When it does not we stop and see why.

I have seen people make important decisions based upon tradition, emotion, race, and exaggeration rather than upon truth. You will bypass the genuine Word if this continues to be your response. You must get to the truth.

4. Rely Upon The Holy Spirit

The Bible says that the Holy Spirit or Spirit of God bears witness with our spirit. The Holy Spirit bears witness of Jesus. The Holy Spirit communes with God the Father and with Jesus as a part of the Holy Trinity.

It makes sense to me that the Holy Spirit who indwells believers would also serve to convict us, correct, and confirm. And so He does.

Sometimes we don't have or can't get a clear word from ancient Scriptures about a modern-day problem. This is where the Holy Spirit becomes vitally important. The Holy Spirit becomes the law, the governing inner traffic light, the roadmap, the flag waver. Learn to rely on the Spirit of God. He has been promised by Jesus to every believer to be the intercessor and comforter. He will help you to know the true word, either by conviction or comfort. He will bear witness to the true word within the will of God.

Mind science practitioners who miss or explain away this important element, show that their philosophy lacks a vital relationship with God. We are not just dealing with an unexplainable *ether* or *universal mind*. We who believe in Jesus Christ are connected to God in a personal, spiritual, and real relationship by means of the Holy Spirit.

You must learn to listen to the Spirit of God as He impresses your heart. You don't just commune with a *higher being*, a *force*, or your *inner self*. You must learn to commune with God by the Holy Spirit.

5. Maintain A Clear Heart

Jesus said, "Blessed are the pure in heart: for they shall see God" (Matthew 5:8).

Jesus also said that one of the requirements for moving mountains by faith was *forgiveness* (Mark 11:25,26).

Both of these aspects refer to the importance of keeping a clean and clear heart. Reception of a word, holding a word, and asking by faith on a word are all tied to this important concept.

Fast, pray, forgive, tithe, confess sin, love your enemy, do good to those who persecute you—do whatever you need to do to keep a clear heart. This is absolutely essential if you would have "eyes to see and ears to hear." Part of the reason we have trouble getting a word on our heart is because of sins and transgressions against God, unforgiveness toward others, or even disappointment toward ourselves. The more this is corrected the easier it will be to operate with a word on our heart.

6. Maintain A Devotional Lifestyle

Maintaining quality time alone with God is absolutely essential to developing your ability to hear God's word. Force yourself, if need be, into a consistent pattern of time alone with God. Have a set time when you read from the Bible. Learn to pray by praying. Walk with God. Commune with Him often, throughout the day, in the early morning, and during the night. Like athletes conditioning their physical bodies for performance, so there is a certain conditioning that must take place over time with consistency in our heart. The ability to get a word from God is, oftentimes, a developmental process.

7. Be About God's Business

This may sound strange, but it is my conviction that God, much more often, prefers to give forth His word to those who are about His business. In other words, we cannot live just any old way and expect that God is going to eagerly let us in on His will and word. God does not often share His glory or His word with those going in ways contrary to His purpose. If you are stepping out by faith into the darkness, trusting in the Lord, you are most likely to enjoy His favor, His blessings, and His word. The Scripture says that faith pleases God. It just makes sense to me that He would be more likely to share His word with someone walking in His way by faith.

We, who believe on the Lord Jesus Christ, are reborn as instant saints, from God's perspective, based on the finished work of Christ. But from our perspective, we are in need of growth, maturity, understanding, enlightenment, and purging. The key to our forward progress is captured in the concept of *getting a word from God on our heart, acting on it by faith, and seeing a wonderful result.*

When To Walk On Water

There is a particular religion in America that practices handling poisonous snakes as a part of their worship experience. Their primary reference is the passage in Mark, chapter sixteen, that says that believers will take up serpents and not be harmed. I have not actually seen this experience, except on television documentaries, but I am told that many actually hold copperheads, moccasins, and rattlesnakes without being bitten or poisoned. Others handle them, are bitten, and die.

I will not try this for two reasons. First, I don't interpret the Bible as saying this is necessary. I don't believe we are obligated to this behavior. Secondly, I don't do it because the picture I have engraved upon my subconscious heart and conscious head and in every fiber of my being since childhood is that of an aggressive, fang manifesting, poison dripping reptile bent on biting me with all its power. With this *in mind* I wouldn't dare pick up a poisonous snake. The word engraved on my heart would surely allow the bite to occur. If I ever did pick up a snake for this purpose, I would have to pray and fast until I got another *word* engraved and the old one erased.

The same holds true of walking on water. I have never walked on water except as ice. My heart has a picture burned upon it of the law of gravity and of sinking. To walk on liquid water, I would have to get another word picture burned upon my heart—not only of my capability, but of my actual performance of it without any doubt. There would have to be a word from God to do it and there couldn't be a conflict between my head and my heart or I would surely sink like Peter sank (Matthew 14:22-33). I do not have that *word* on my heart. Therefore, I better not even try it. All things are possible to him who believes but getting to the "believes" is often a real stretch.

Some, however, will not even consider things that extend beyond their own understanding and experience. This is a common response as there has always been a disparaging conflict between fact and fiction, head and heart, conscious reasoning and subconscious faith, myth and reality. Sometimes, the struggle is due to our lack of knowledge or experience. Sometimes, it is a result of fear and foolishness. But the tragedy comes when we refuse to consider the possibility, choosing rather to stay in our own little conscious comfort zone.

Many things in the realm of physics were once thought impossible. Sir Isaac Newton, the founding father of engineering, and a devoted Christian, believed that, according to prophetic Scripture, men in the last days would travel at a high rate of speed across the earth.

When he came to the prophecy in Daniel 12:4, where it talks about men running to and fro throughout the earth and knowledge increasing, he said:

"I honestly think that some day as we come to the close of time and when Christ comes back, we will see knowledge expand at a tremendous rate. I think we will see men travel at rapid rates of speed. I think that we will see people travel at the rate of thirty, forty, even fifty miles an hour."

Voltaire, the contemporary atheist of Newton's day, said:

"See what a fool Christianity makes of an otherwise brilliant man such as Sir Isaac Newton. Does he not know that if a man traveled at forty miles an hour he would suffocate and his heart would stop?"

Is it any more absurd of Voltaire to expound such a negative unbelief than it is for us to say that other laws of nature or physics, as we know them, cannot be set aside on certain occasions and under certain conditions? Can we not, at least, investigate the possibility of operation in the realm of uncommon experience? Let us be careful not to unnecessarily lock ourselves into such negative impossibility thinking to the point that truth from the supernatural realm cannot be investigated.

So let us consider for a moment, that certain physical laws, as we *know* them, can be placed in suspension. Let us suppose that strange occurrences, like the Bible miracles, actually happened at the hand of Jesus and His apostles. How are these uncommon acts accomplished? Is it demon power, God power, or mind power? If it is possible, what makes it so? Are there certain rules inherent in this action that should be adhered to by the believer? I hold that there are responsibilities incumbent upon the Christian believer that deal with this area.

I, personally, do not have the water-walking word or the snake-handling word. Therefore, you are not going to see me tempt God in these activities. Jesus refused the devil's temptation to turn stones to bread and levitate off the pinnacle of the temple. Jesus operated on the basis of a higher relational law; respect and submission to the Father's word on His heart. This should be our guideline as well. Responding to a word on our heart from God by faith is the ideal. Responding to any other word may be foolishness.

This is where the imposition of improper word impressions can become dangerous or damaging when used in isolation from the truth of Scripture or the impressions of the Holy Spirit. Rather, we who are believers in Jesus, volitionally choose to submit to God's word on our heart. The religionist who handles snakes or walks on hot coals may have used the universal law of faith but the word may be his own. It may not really be from God. We need to get a genuine word from God before we act.

You can impress many things upon your subconscious heart and achieve wonderful, if not miraculous, results. But our position takes into account Jesus as the *Living Word* which has come to us from the Father and the *written Word*, or the Bible, as our authority for the faith-life.

We volitionally choose God's Word. We believe that it is the proper seed to plant upon our subconscious heart for eternal results. Therefore, we choose to submit to God's Word. Our responsibility is not to try to manipulate laws of physics or nature in an irresponsible and indiscriminate way. Rather, our choices revolve around God's word on our heart. This is how we know *if* and *when* to walk on water. And *if* and *when* are important considerations.

8

The Internal Operation Of Word Dynamics

I knew some mechanics once who were always building engines for their cars. One day I stood over the two brothers in their shop and watched, in amazement, as they put together an automobile engine. There were so many parts, nuts, bolts, wires, wrenches, sockets, and screwdrivers! It looked like a big steel jigsaw puzzle to me but they seemed to know what they were doing. I went back in a few days and they had it installed in an old car of theirs.

One of the brothers turned to me with a greasy wrench in his hand and a smile spreading across a grease-smeared face and said, "You want to see if she'll crank?"

Deep down inside I wondered if it would take off like the space shuttle, blow up like a bomb, or be dead as a hammer. "Sure," I said.

The younger brother got in the driver's seat, inserted the key in the ignition, and turned it.

The engine hesitated for a split second then started right up. It sat there and purred like a kitten. The sense of accomplishment was obvious on the brother's faces.

I sat there and tried to imagine all those pistons firing, the crankshaft turning, the carburetor pumping gas in just the right amounts, the distributor turning in sequence with the crankshaft and pistons, the water being pumped around the engine block to keep it cool, and all the tiny parts of the transmission ready to engage. It was amazing to me that all those parts could come together to distribute energy in a way to provide transportation horsepower for man's use.

Everything about that engine was a closed system of sorts. That is, everything was contained within its system to produce the desired results. All of the internal components and the combustion that took place within the cylinder walls were contained in a closed system that was mostly hidden from human eye. The internal combustion engine is uniquely tied to specific cycles and procedures. If the timing is off and the sequence of piston firing does not take place in specific and determined order, the engine will not run properly. The result will not be the desired effect of horsepower.

The concept of *word dynamics* works much the same way. The operation of getting a word on our heart and acting upon it by faith is an internal matter within a closed system requiring certain timing and procedures. In a way it is simple. In another way it is quite complex and requires everything to function with precise order if we would achieve the desired energy and result.

Farming is probably the oldest profession and activity of mankind. It has been around for a long time. Most everyone knows about soil cultivation, seed planting, germination, growth, and fruit bearing. It seems simple. In a way it is. In another way it, too, is quite complex. Yes, anyone can understand dropping a seed in the ground, letting it grow, and watching it bear fruit. But what happens underground, in the earth, hidden away in the nucleus of the seed? That spark of life that brings about germination is still a mystery to many. And what about the genetic structure deep within that seed that causes it to grow to be an apple tree or a corn plant? What about the genetic structure that protects it against disease and pests? And what if it gets too much moisture or not enough? What about the growth cycle—the degree of heat or cold—the normal seasons of the region. Men of science go to school and take involved courses to study the complexity of seeds and how they grow.

Again, the concepts we are about in this book are much like the simplicity or complexity of agriculture. Words are like seeds that get planted in and on our heart. In that hidden and closed system there are certain activities going on that require attention, proper procedures, timing sequence, and proper environment. Yes, it is simple to plant a seed in the ground and allow it to grow. It is simple to get a word on our heart and see a result. Yet it is complex and mysterious.

There is another illustration from the Bible that could very well be the pinnacle of all illustrations regarding the subject matter of word dynamics. It has to do with the impregnation of Mary and the birth of Jesus.

But if you are one that does not believe in the virgin birth of the Lord Jesus Christ then what I am about to say won't make any sense to you. On the other hand, if you take the story of Mary being impregnated by the Holy Spirit as true, the following will make perfect sense and enlighten you to this whole theme.

In Luke's gospel, you have the story of the angel coming to Mary with the news that she would be the bearer of the long-awaited Messiah. Observe carefully:

"The angel went to her and said, 'Greetings, you who are highly favored! The Lord is with you.'

Mary was greatly troubled at his words and wondered what kind of greeting this might be. But the angel said to her, 'Do not be afraid, Mary, you have found favor with God. You will be with child and give birth to a son, and you are to give him the name Jesus.

…'How will this be,' Mary asked the angel, 'since I am a virgin?'

The angel answered, 'The Holy Spirit will come upon you, and the power of the Most High will overshadow you.'

…'I am the Lord's servant,' Mary answered. 'May it be to me as you have said.'

Then the angel left her" (Luke 1:28-38, NIV).

Understanding God's Abundant Seed Pool

In the sexual process of creating new life, the male participant, out of an abundant sperm pool, sends sperm toward the female egg. One sperm swims and swims, and out of all the other thousands, makes its way to the egg. There it penetrates and attaches itself to the egg forming the beginning stages of what we call life. The embryo develops and nine months later the mother gives birth to a child.

God (the male counterpart to us) has a seed pool Himself. It is rather a *word* pool. He sends forth words—many words toward our heart (the egg). We can receive this word (sperm, seed) or we can reject it. We can even abort it later!

The angel that came to Mary with the word about Jesus' conception and birth was serving as the vehicle by which God was sending seed; sperm; word to her heart. In the longer version of the Bible story you will notice that the angel had to send several words toward Mary before she would believe. He told her plainly. He used the reinforcement story of the miraculous pregnancy of old Elizabeth. He encouraged her.

The Scripture says she was "greatly troubled" and "wondered" (NIV) or "cast in her mind" (KJV) what the angel was saying. This word means to *toss back and forth*. She was vacillating between her head and her heart; between fear and faith. But then she responded.

Her response reveals her faith. It was only then that the messenger was free to leave. He could not leave until she had believed. Why?

God was sending Mary a word seed. The angel was delivering this word seed. Mary was to receive it but had the privilege of rejecting it. When she believed, she received, and only then, was Jesus conceived.

God has a seed pool with many, many words. He sends them our way. But like the fragile sperm, not all of them get to our heart. Some die, for whatever reason, along the way. The conditions must be right for pregnancy to take place. The conditions must be right to receive a word in our heart.

The same illustration is made by Jesus in the parable of the soils. Many seeds were scattered. Only those that found receptive soil where the conditions were right germinated and produced.

Oftentimes we lay blame or resignation on the sovereignty of God for wonderful things not happening when, in fact, it is the condition of our heart soil. There are many factors involved in fruit production. We cannot always lay the lack of productivity on God's sovereignty.

Many Riches Are Never Mined

God has a vast amount of words; seeds; sperm in his pool. Could it be that you have riches and wonders waiting to happen? When we get to heaven I would not be surprised if the Lord opened a door and showed us millions of words that we could have touched with and received but did not because of ignorance or unbelief.

It is a fairly sure thing that if the male does not send sperm toward the female egg no baby (miracle) is going to be birthed. If the female is not in the right cycle for reception, no baby is going to be formed.

If you do not expect, watch for, make the conditions right, participate with God, and carry the baby to term you will not see a live birth either.

It appears from Scripture that we have the ability to neglect words, reject words, or abort words that are incubating blessings. We would be absolutely astounded if we only knew how many people were on the verge of birthing a wonderful blessing but they gave up—they aborted through unbelief.

Sweating Great Drops Of Blood

On the night before His arrest, Jesus was praying fervently. He was asking the Father to remove the cup of suffering He was being asked to drink. No human or God-man wants to face the horrors of crucifixion.

So He prays, "Father, if you are willing, take this cup from me; yet not my will, but yours be done" (Luke 22:42, NIV).

Now, please understand, He is not praying from ignorance. He knows and sees the word. And, it is my opinion that He knows about the *word pool*. He is seeking for another word; another new seed. But there is no other word that He can draw upon except the word *crucifixion*.

He is in such turmoil that He sweats great drops of blood. Then, when He finds no other word in the Father's word pool, He quietly resigns; "yet not my will, but yours be done."

This, to me, is where the sovereignty of God is displayed. It was not God's will, and there was no word to be given for Jesus, to bypass death.

Likewise, the Apostle Paul could not get another word about the "thorn in his side," although he sought the Lord many times (1 Corinthians 12:8,9).

Maybe it is not God's will and word to heal or give wonderful results in every case. But my point is that we need to stop focusing on the one out of a hundred that does not apply and start being impregnated by the ninety-nine! You could be losing out on blessings every day of your life because you mistakenly think that the sovereignty of God limits you.

Aren't We Leaving God Out?

Most people who conclude a prayer with, "if it be thy will," are praying from ignorance even though their motives and intent are pure. They have no idea what the word is or if there is a word. So they respectfully bow to the *sovereignty of God*.

This method of praying shirks one's responsibility to see and know the word that God wants to give on the situation. Know the word and you will know the will. Thus, you will never be guilty of over-stepping the bounds of respect for God's sovereignty. Maybe it is that knowing the word becomes work and takes time!

Again our premise and foundational truth is: Get a word from God's vast word pool on your heart—act on this word by faith—God will be free to act in your behalf to provide a wonderful blessing!

Stop worrying about *His will* and concentrate on knowing and getting *His word*. Stop being depressed about the positive occurrences that did not happen and believe—receive—conceive—and birth the ones that will happen. Leave the problems of predestination, God's sovereignty, and man's free will with the theologians. Go for the practical aspect of God. Go for positive God occurrences and don't stop until you see some doors open in wonderful fashion.

God loves us. He wants to *marry* us. The fellowship of New Testament believers is called His *bride*. In this marriage relationship God desires to create (produce babies) in conjunction with us. Will you allow it? Will you cooperate?

There are riches to be mined in your heart—wonderful riches of eternal value. Will you begin with God today? You can experience a positive God occurrence, the fruit of good success, or the positive manifestation of God's ability sometime in your life. But these will **not** be forced upon you. You have a definite part. Begin now to exercise your God-given right to birth a joint creation—a miracle baby—a blessing from God.

"'Test me in this,' says the Lord Almighty, 'and see if I will not throw open the floodgates of heaven and pour out so much blessing that you will not have room enough for it'" (Malachi 3:10, NIV).

Unlocking The Door Of Your Heart

Our hearts are fragile and somewhat peculiar. We talk about a person having a "broken heart." But we can also have a wicked heart, a good heart, a doubting heart, a believing heart, an impressionable heart, or a calloused heart. Our heart can be open to receive or closed in rejection.

God has made the heart to be receptive and sensitive. It is the micro-chip receptor of God's word. It was designed to be free and uncluttered—able to commune with God at a second's notice.

But, since the Garden of Eden episode, man has struggled to hear God, see God, commune with God. The reason is simple—there is so much clutter, sin, and so many calluses upon the heart that we are insensitive.

Like the old prospector's mineshaft we try to mine gold when there is so much dust we can't even breathe. When we do go down the shaft, the old timbers of doubt and fear creak and move ready for a cave-in. Most people just never go down. It's too dark and dusty.

What we propose to do here is to unlock the door to the mineshaft, expose the dust and debris, and show how it is to be removed so that the gold can be extracted. There are several things that cause us difficulty in hearing the right word and receiving the right word upon our heart. Two of these problem areas are mentioned in Mark's gospel by the Lord Jesus.

In Mark 11:23-26, when Jesus told the disciples that they could move mountains, he pointed out a couple of potential problems. One was *doubt* and the other was *unforgiveness*. Doubt keeps the seed from being planted. Unforgiveness keeps a seed that may be planted, dormant.

The heart is a sensitive object. It will allow planting and sprouting, but it will not function in these activities when there is cloudiness, confusion, or disharmony. It operates best from a clear signal. Like the internal combustion gasoline engine and the planted seed, so there must be a proper sequence of elements functioning in a prescribed manner within a proper environment.

Jesus told His disciples to get into their closet when they prayed (Matthew 6:5-8). He said that the Father "who sees in secret," would reward them openly. Apparently, what goes on in the quiet secret place is heart communication. Real prayer involves getting some place where it is still and quiet so that we can hear and receive the word that God wants to place upon our heart. The heart is a sensitive instrument.

I knew a photographer once who developed his own film. He was very particular about the recipe for the developing solution and whether or not it was fresh. He was also very particular about the length of time for development and the room light during the process. He had good reason.

If the chemical solution, film, and room lighting are not right the negative or the finished photo will not turn out right. It is a sensitive process.

Your heart is sensitive in the same way. It is much like the darkroom where film is developed. If things aren't right and conducive to development you will not get a good image. The word you are seeking from God will not develop out clearly so that you can act upon it by faith and confidence. Many people do not act by faith because they can't seem to get a clear word on which to act. Jesus repeatedly told His disciples that it was not an issue of much faith. Just a little faith would do. The real issue was a clear word on the heart.

If we cannot get a clear word developed on our heart, we cannot have confidence. If we don't have confidence, we will doubt. And if we doubt, faith is stifled and the mountain will not move. "Doubting not" is a real issue.

Learning To Operate In An Ordered Universe

God is orderly. He has designed things to function in orderly fashion. His whole creation functions in timing and order from the smallest atom and molecule to the spin of the largest planet. If anything seems to be in disarray, it is only because we don't see the whole picture. He is a God of order.

"For God is not a God of disorder but of peace" (1 Corinthians 14:33).

This holds true in relation to our physical bodies, our minds, and our hearts. If we allow our physical bodies to get out of "balance" we will get overweight, unhealthy, and sick. If we allow our minds to get out of balance we will make bad decisions and foolish mistakes, encounter depression, anxiety, or other forms of mental illness. If our heart is out of balance, like poor photo development solution, we will not hear God or be able to respond to His word that He wants to give to us.

The Importance Of Harmony

One of the things that I have fought to sustain in the churches that I have pastored has been a harmonious fellowship. It takes some doing but it can be accomplished and is so very important. Church harmony doesn't mean that everyone sees eye to eye mentally, politically, socially, or even theologically. But it does mean that there is oneness and harmony of Spirit. A quarreling, fussing, self-centered, back-biting church fellowship is out of harmony with God. God is not the author of confusion or disorder. As such, I would think that He would hesitate to give forth much of His will and word to a congregation in such disarray.

Much phenomena of nature depends upon ordered motion. It is another example of the concept of harmony or agreement. Certain rates of motion give us sound, temperature, expansion, solid, liquid, or gas. Every motion is a movement of *something, in some direction, at some rate of speed*. For instance, it is the rate of motion of matter that determines the audibility and then pitch of sound. It is the rate of the motion of the bullet that determines the force of its blow. The harmonious motion of our very life produces health, success, and blessing.

God is the creator, organizer, and sustainer of proper *life* vibrations of harmonious motion. Maybe this is why Paul wrote of Jesus: "And he is before all things and by him all things consist" (Colossians 1:17).

Possibly, this is why the Scripture says, "A cheerful heart is good medicine, but a crushed spirit dries up the bones" (Proverbs 17:22, NIV). When our hearts are merry we move in synchronization with God, others, and especially our self. When we are out of synchronization, we are out of harmony. Our life is disordered. When we live a positive, thankful life, we harmonize. Singing, praising, and giving thanks to God are important tools for putting one in harmony with God and with one's self.

Recent medical and scientific studies have shown that people who live in ordered family units and attend church tend to be healthier and live longer with fewer diseases and sickness. Maybe it is because there is a certain degree of harmony in their lifestyle.

Many people respond with wonder and amazement at *coincidences*. Was it just a coincidence? The word means that something occurred at the same time (coincided). The dictionary goes on to say, "taking up the same position in space at the same time. Being in exact agreement...."

What we consider a coincidence may oftentimes be the result of harmony between our word and God's word regarding a given matter. The *wonderful result* we want to see from prayer is the fruit of coincidence; the coinciding of our word and God's word on our heart in harmony and agreement.

The Importance Of Agreement

I took some film to be developed. It was an experimental batch. I was trying out a new flash attachment to see if it was working properly in conjunction with my old camera. The sad look on the developer's face told me something was wrong with my pictures. Sure enough, on some the image was barely visible—on some there was only half an image—on others it was very dark—some had too much light. This was an intentional experiment and it taught me something; the flash was not synchronized with the camera. The flash, the light which exposes the subject to the film, was not in harmony or agreement with the camera's shutter.

Jesus said: "That if two of you shall agree on earth as touching any thing that they shall ask, it shall be done for them of my Father which is in heaven" (Matthew 18:19).

If you have ever read the Bible book of Acts, you will note that many wonders were performed and observed by the first Christians. It is likely that one of the reasons for the prolific number of supernatural occurrences in the early church was because of oneness—harmony—agreement. "They had all things in common" (Acts 4:31-37). Their flashes and shutters were synchronized! Conversely, maybe one reason wonderful results are so scarce in churches today is because of the lack of oneness. There must be agreement in the heart. If there is disagreement, God has difficulty planting his word. We then have difficulty receiving it and seeing it. We have already mentioned the concept of being *double-minded* and how it negates God's work in our lives (James 1:5-8).

Matthew 5, 6, 7 constitutes the *Sermon on the Mount*. I must admit that the sections where Jesus told the followers to "turn the other cheek," and "go the second mile," have always been a little uncomfortable for me. I must say that I really did not understand the *reason* until I put the context into the template of our theme regarding getting a word on our heart.

Oftentimes, I look for common denominators within a context to discern the main truth of the passage. If there was one word you could put over the entire section on "turning the other cheek," it would have to be *agreement*. Agree with God. Agree with self. Agree with your adversary. Get in agreement with your enemy (not agreement with sin or lies or wrong, but with the individual) so that your prayers will not be hindered and wonderful *word results* can happen. The secret of being blessed is tied to agreement, and has much to do with harmony.

9

Your Heart—The Golden "Mercy Seat"

The heart is like the mercy seat or top lid of the golden *Ark of the Covenant* of the Old Testament. According to the Scriptural account, it was the place where God touched with man in the physical domain. But, He would not touch down unless atonement had been made. The blood had to cover. Forgiveness and appeasement had to be in place. Think of the word *atonement* as meaning *at-one-ment*. God demanded harmony, oneness, and agreement.

The same applies to God's word on our heart. There is a loosing or a freedom that must take place in and on the heart. You will not get a clear word imprint from which you can respond by faith if your heart is cluttered with resentment, bitterness, or unforgiveness. You must let it go; forgive. Stop holding grudges. Get in agreement. You may think you can win with bitterness. You may win in court, or whip the bully on the playground, but you may lose divine capability and connection.

Obviously, there are many good, Bible-believing, church-going, Christians who are not having their prayers answered or the desires of their heart met because of this one concept. The *mercy seat* is cluttered and God will not touch down with His word.

This is precisely the law Jesus is displaying in His insistence on turning the other cheek. It is what Paul is driving at in 1 Corinthians 6:7-9 when he suggests that it is best to suffer wrong. You will not understand why Jesus taught us to "turn the other cheek" unless you understand the principle of a clear heart.

God never intended for us to become martyred floor mats for the ungodly. His higher motive was to keep us from clouding our heart with bitterness and unforgiveness. Just as the most perfect of internal combustion engines will not run on bad fuel, so we cannot function on the poison of bitterness and unforgiveness.

God will not touch down and share the mercy seat of our heart with unforgiveness. He reserves it all for Himself. Once it is clean, He sends his word. We are able to see it. The chemicals are right for development of the picture. The flash and the camera are in synchronization. We see it develop on our heart before we see it materialize. We hear it from our heart before we hear it with our outward ears.

Recording On The Right Track

Unforgiveness has disagreement going in two directions—toward an individual and toward God. The heart is cluttered and confused. The mind keeps feeding it reminders. It keeps recalling and playing back the video of the wrong. The conscious even helps it formulate vain imaginations—"Why if I get my hands on that culprit, I'll choke the life out of him for what he did to me." And your mind records this imaginative video.

Like a VHS video tape there are tracks. There is a video track and an audio track. If you have an old video camera like mine, the video tape can be recorded over on either the video or audio. But you cannot have two different audio tracts or two different video tracts on a regular VHS tape recorded on my old camera. You can only record over them.

So how do I come to the place of a clear heart for answered prayers? You must record over that which is playing on your heart. You do this by consciously feeding your heart replacement words of love and statements of forgiveness. To begin to "say" to that mountain of unforgiveness is the first step in seeing it removed. Say, "I forgive so and so. I let them go."

Say, "I will to extend love toward my wrongdoer." An extension of outward good-will performs marvelously to replace bitterness with clear heart confidence. That is why Jesus said: "Do good to them that despitefully use you," and "pray for your enemies."

Again, Jesus is not trying to get us to be compliant floor mats for the evil persons but to have a clear heart for answered prayers and kingdom living.

These affirmations and thanksgivings are reprogramming tools. You reaffirm Scriptural truth to your heart. You give thanks in all things.

The design is to get our heart in a clear and receptive state. Fasting, forgiving, turning the other cheek, loving, praying for enemies, doing good to abusers, giving thanks in all things are simply means to gain freedom on the surface receptor of the heart.

The Healing Power Of Forgiveness

Some years ago a conflict arose in our church. One of the men involved, who happened to be a wealthy and influential man, stormed out, left our fellowship, and joined another church. Although I was never bitter or unloving toward the man I never contacted him after that incident. The years passed and his health began to fail. For months he was in and out of the intensive care unit. The doctors had given him up to die on several occasions.

One day, while I was visiting one of our church members in the same hospital, a word came to my heart about this man. It was an unusually clear impression that I should go by and see him. So, I mustered some courage, dispelled fear, and got off the elevator at the Intensive Care floor. I didn't know what to expect or how I would find him.

There was a long hallway leading directly into his room. Being a minister I can walk right in to the ICU anytime I desire. So I walked down the long hall looking directly into the room. The closer I came I realized that the man staring back at me was the man I was coming to see. I hadn't seen him in years but I recognized him and he recognized me.

He was hooked up to all kinds of wires and monitors. A plastic oxygen mask covered his mouth. He was so weak he couldn't talk. I just had to read his eyes and lips.

At that point I was really relying on a *word* for which to speak. I was uncertain as to how he felt physically. So I watched the heart monitor to make sure my presence didn't send him into cardiac arrest.

Yet, I must admit, that there was the strangest warmth there that moment. His eyes reached out to me with a longing as if grasping after something. I greeted him and then knelt on the floor beside him as I grasped his hand in mine.

I searched my heart for some *word*. What seemed to come forth was a brief message of love and forgiveness.

I called him by name and said, "I just want you to know there is absolutely no hard feelings toward you (He had always used the term "hard feelings" and I knew he would relate). You are loved."

Tears came to the old fellow's eyes. He tried to speak but could not. His lips moved. He clinched my hand. I asked if I could pray for him. He nodded affirmatively. I had a confident word on my heart to pray for his healing. And so I prayed.

As I knelt beside him and offered a prayer, I had the strangest sensation. I had never felt before or since what I was feeling in that moment. The best way that I can describe it is by picturing an invisible blanket of warmth and love descending over us both. It was a strange sensation.

I left his room that day not knowing if he would live or die. I expected that he would probably die there in that very room. I simply did not have that revelation. He was very close to death's door. But I felt confident and was glad for reconciliation. I think that a forgiveness, a *letting go*, took place there that day. I think that something was set free there that had been bound for a decade or more.

I went about my business for the next few weeks not really thinking much about the incident. Then one day, in passing, an old church member who kept up with former members said, "Did you hear about _____? A few weeks ago, after the doctors had given him up to die, he suddenly recovered, gained strength, and is home doing very well!"

I rejoiced! I couldn't help but believe that my obedience to God's word helped free a man from the bondage of unforgiveness. Harmony and agreement allowed a healing word to be received. I checked my calendar and discovered that the day of his turn-around and unexpected recovery coincided perfectly with my visit and prayer.

We must remember that we have certain powers for "binding" and "loosing." The word we get on our heart is not always for us. Often, it is for others.

A day or so later the man wrote me the following letter that I cherish. Other than our hospital visit it was the first correspondence I had received from him in nearly ten years.

"Thank you brother Jerry for visiting me while I was so very sick. I remember you being there. I appreciate your prayers. Prayer brought me through. The doctors gave me up many times during the 4 1/2 months in the hospital. After cardiac arrest twice and three kinds of pneumonia at the same time, and another fatal disease, I'm still here. God is good.

Thanks again,
Sincerely, _____."

Forgiveness allows healing. Would this man have died if this occurrence not transpired? His turnaround was not due to any change in medication. It was not due to any surgery. The only change was a heart change—a forgiveness.

You say, "Well, it was just coincidence." But remember that the *coinciding* of necessary elements is not always happenstance. It could very well have been the ordered alignment of necessary *words*.

Forgiveness is vital. Jesus said it was a necessary part of the formula for moving mountains.

Forgiveness—The Key To Success

Forgiveness needs to take place in three directions; toward others, in our relationship with God, and toward ourselves. There must be a "letting go"—a freedom in each of these areas. We are to forgive the offenses of others toward us. We are to believe and receive forgiveness from God for our offenses toward Him. We are to forgive our selves for the mistakes and blunders of the past.

One of the great passages of Scripture I have relied upon through the years in regard to forgiveness is a passage in 1 John.

"If we say that we have no sin, we deceive ourselves, and the truth is not in us. If we confess our sins, He is faithful and just to forgive us our sins and to cleanse us from all unrighteousness" (1 John 1:8,9, NKJV).

This is a powerful word to us. We can confess, "agree," with God about our sin and He forgives. He lets it go. How wonderful. God, it appears, is desirous to forgive. He waits for us to respond so He can forgive. Jesus taught forgiveness and went about eager to forgive. God is in the forgiveness business!

One of the great illustrations in this regard involves the story of Joseph in the Old Testament. Joseph was his father's favorite. He was even given a special coat of many colors. But his brothers were jealous. One day when Joseph went out to the fields to meet his brothers, he was taken by them and thrown in a well. His coat was taken, dipped in the blood of an animal to look as if he had been killed by a wild animal, and returned to his father and mother. Joseph was then sold by his brothers to Ishmaelite traders on their way to Egypt. The traders, in turn, sold him to the captain of Pharaoh's guard.

Joseph's faithfulness and demeanor won him the respect of Potiphar, the captain who had purchased him. Potiphar set him up in charge of his entire household. Things went well until Potphar's wife tried to seduce Joseph to sleep with her while her husband was away. The wife grabbed him. Joseph ran away leaving his coat behind in the hands of the lustful wife. When Potiphar returned she concocted a false story of Joseph trying to take advantage of her. Potiphar had Joseph thrown in prison.

His leadership abilities again rose to the surface and he was made a ruler in the confines of the prison. While there, two of the Pharaoh's servants were imprisoned. Joseph interpreted their dreams which were relayed to Pharaoh. They came true just as Joseph had predicted. One was slain and Pharaoh's cupbearer was released. But the cupbearer did not return the favor of remembering Joseph as they had agreed would be the case. Joseph was forgotten again for two years.

Then Pharaoh had a dream. The search was on for someone who could interpret the dream. Finally, the cupbearer remembered the interpretive ability of Joseph. He was called to come before Pharaoh to interpret the dream. Joseph interpreted the dream as an upcoming seven year period of prosperity in the grain fields followed by seven years of famine. He suggested to Pharaoh that leaders be put in charge to manage the storehouses in view of the famine to come. Pharaoh was so impressed that he put Joseph in charge of all of Egypt. The only higher position was that of Pharaoh, himself.

The years of prosperity came followed by the years of famine. Joseph's dream interpretation had come true. It not only affected the local region but extended all the way up to the territory of Joseph's family. Joseph's brothers appeared one day seeking to buy grain for their famished families. Joseph kept his identity secret and complied with their request. Eventually, he revealed himself to their dismay. They expected to be killed. Instead Joseph forgave them and cared for them. When the father died, the brothers came and cast themselves before Joseph and pleaded for their lives thinking that it was only because of their father that Joseph had spared them thus far.

"When Joseph's brothers saw that their father was dead, they said, 'Perhaps Joseph will hate us, and may actually repay us for all the evil which we did to him.' So they sent messengers to Joseph, saying, 'Before your father died he commanded, saying, "Thus you shall say to Joseph: 'I beg you, please forgive the trespass of your brothers and their sin; for they did evil to you. Now, please, forgive the trespass of the servants of the God of your father.'" And Joseph wept when they spoke to him. Then his brothers also went and fell down before his face, and they said, 'Behold, we are your servants.' Joseph said to them, 'Do not be afraid, for am I in the place of God? But as for you, you meant evil against me; but God meant it for good, in order to bring it about as it is this day, to save many people alive. Now therefore, do not be afraid; I will provide for you and your little ones.' And he comforted them and spoke kindly to them" (Genesis 50:15-21, NKJV).

This is one of the most remarkable stories in the Bible. It reveals several important truths that are pertinent to the theme of this book. First, it shows the importance of forgiveness. All along the way you see Joseph as a forgiving person, not holding grudges, or seeking revenge, even in the face of injustice and unfairness. One will also notice that Joseph operated from his heart. His success depended upon his ability to see and interpret dreams from his heart. If he had harbored a cluttered heart of bitterness and unforgiveness, it is likely that he would not have been able to read the message God sent his way that he gave forth from his heart. He was promoted and became successful and blessed because he operated from a clear and clean heart. He did not allow unforgiveness and bitterness to rob him of a great blessing. In other words, the secret of his success was in his ability to hear and see God's word upon his heart.

Unblocking The Life Flow

One reason we are told not to sin is because sin puts guilt upon our heart that leads to unforgiveness toward ourselves. Whether against someone else or ourselves, unforgiveness blocks a clear reception. In the field of mental health it is being constantly assessed that resentment, condemnation of others, remorse, and hostility are behind a host of maladies ranging from arthritis to cardiac disease. One doctor has listed 51 diseases that result from these emotions.

Jesus gives a conditional statement in Mark 11:25-26 pronounced in the text by the little word "if." *If* you forgive, the Father will forgive you. *If* you do not forgive, the Father will not forgive you. Apparently life is to flow from our heart. Doubt caused by fear, vain imaginations, lust, and unforgiveness, blocks the flow. Only God can forgive sin. Sin blocks the life flow in whatever form it takes. If you don't get God's forgiveness the divine cycle of life is blocked. It is in this life-word in your heart that we find the power for supernatural living. Most people do not have supernatural power, even answered prayer, because they continue with the life flow blocked. They pray and pray but see little, if any, results. One evangelist told our congregation once that many of them had probably not had a single prayer answered in forty years because of sin in their heart!

Jesus told the disciples that some miracles would not happen in their life except through prayer and fasting. Why prayer and fasting? Because there was a short in the divine circuit.

If one electrical leg of a house current is all you hold, you will know little difference. But pick up the other leg allowing the flow to continue and your body will instantly acknowledge the effect. There must be a complete and clear circuit in our heart area too.

The "if" in Mark 11:25, 26 ("if you do not forgive") is a very big word. It may, in fact, be bigger than faith, because faith cannot respond on heart soil covered in unforgiveness.

But when you forgive and God forgives, the heart is made ready to be impressed with your desire. Confidence is built. Faith has something with which to work. The vision is not impaired. You see it before you see it. You abide in His word. His word abides in you. You ask what you will and it is done unto you to the joy and glory of the Father!

Help For A Clear Heart

Again, the Apostle Paul gives us some aids to heart clarity in Philippians 4:8:

"Finally, brethren, whatsoever things are true,...honest,...just,...pure,...lovely,...good report; if there be any virtue, and if there be any praise, ***think on these things***."

Some practical therapy might include work on our thought life, on the words that come forth from our mouth, and on the actions that we do.

Notice Paul's added advice in Philippians 4:9:

"Those things, which ye have both learned, and received, and heard, and seen in me, DO: and the God of peace shall be with you" (capitalization mine for emphasis).

The NIV translates it: "Whatever you have learned or received or heard from me, or seen in me—put it into practice. And the God of peace will be with you."

Anything that helps us to have a clear heart is important; forgiveness—meditation on God or His Word—purity—fasting. A clear heart is essential. You must strive to get into agreement and harmony if you hope to get a word from God on your heart.

10

Prayer And The Power Of Word Dynamics

People talk about prayer all the time. Many assure others, "We'll be praying for you"—"Our prayers are with you." But do we really understand, both the simplicity and complexity, of prayer? Do we pray properly? Do we pray for the right things? Do we seek for a word on our heart from which to pray? Does our praying show forth fruit and results? Has there ever been anything in our life that could be directly attributed to our praying? I believe that we all, in general, are poor prayers. And when we do attempt to pray we don't pray properly or powerfully. Yet, prayer is, if understood properly, one of the most powerful activities in the universe.

E. M. Bounds once wrote,

"Prayer is as illimitable as God's own blessed Son. There is nothing on earth or in heaven, for time or eternity, that God's Son did not secure for us. By prayer God gives us the vast and matchless inheritance which is ours by virtue of his Son. God charges us to 'come boldly to the throne of grace.' God is glorified and Christ is honored by large asking."

God spoke through the prophet Jeremiah and challenged us,

"Call unto Me, and I will answer you, and show you great and mighty things, which you do not know" (Jeremiah 33:3, NKJV).

The disciples of Jesus observed that He was a man of real prayer. They saw a difference between Him and most of the other religious leaders of their day. Thus, they were always imploring Him, "Lord teach us to pray."

Prayer is most important. It is vital for the true believer. It is, therefore, incumbent upon us that we see how prayer really works and how Word Dynamics fits into its structure and end result.

The Common Denominators Of Prayer And Faith

Some time back I did a study on the aspects of prayer, faith, and the heart from the mouth of Jesus. I took His teaching about alms, prayer, and fasting from Matthew 6. Then I combined the accounts of the healing of the lunatic son in Matthew 17 and Mark 9. I combined the two similar accounts of the withering of the fig tree and moving mountains in Matthew 21 and Mark 11. I included the brief statement of Jesus in Luke 17:5-6 regarding the uprooting of the sycamine or mulberry tree. I put these six accounts into a grid. My purpose was to discover the emphasis or common denominators. I have learned much from this technique in the past and it proved fruitful here.

What I discovered is pertinent and important to our theme in this work. Observe the following:

1. <u>The problem of unbelief</u>. Jesus rebuked the disciples and even the lunatic son's father for having little or no faith. It is not that we don't believe in general terms. It is that we are not applying specific faith to the specific situation.

2. <u>The problem of focus and definition</u>. Jesus told them to speak to "this" mountain. He identified and rebuked the demon in the lunatic son. Jesus said, "say to this mulberry tree." Is it better to pray, "Lord, bless all the missionaries on foreign soil," or "Lord, give strength, energy, and protection to missionary John Doe today as he works on the water well project there in Africa, in Chief Kammami's village. Let them find water within the next forty-eight hours"?

A lot of our ineffective praying is like a man standing on the ground with a loaded double-barrel shotgun. He has it loaded with tiny bird-shot. He aims it at the sky and pulls both triggers hoping that a pellet will strike a bird flying overhead. Some praying is like this; firing prayers heavenward, hoping something will stick. This is not good praying. We need to be specific and focused. There is a reason for this.

3. <u>The necessity of faith</u>. In each of these accounts there was *faith*. But never was there a requirement for much of it. Jesus used the term "mustard seed" to describe the amount of faith that was necessary. A mustard seed was about the size of a pepper flake or a grain of salt. Faith is like the blasting cap in the stick of dynamite, I mentioned earlier. The dynamite (word) is what is important. Faith is the igniter of the word.

4. <u>The heart receptor</u>. Jesus said, "and does not doubt in his heart." The heart was essential in each of the accounts. Jesus focused on the heart—not the head—not emotions—not positive thinking. He taught that the issue was a word on the heart.

5. <u>The human expression</u>. Jesus said, "say to this mountain," "speak to this tree." For some reason, God expects the participation of the human believer. It is like this for salvation.

"That *if you confess with your mouth*, 'Jesus is Lord,' and believe in your heart that God raised him from the dead, you will be saved. For it is with your heart that you believe and are justified, and *it is with your mouth that you confess and are saved*" (Romans 10:9,10, NIV, italics mine for emphasis).

The saying is agreeing. Confessing the word in your heart is like the man touching the positive and negative posts of the battery to ignite the blasting cap (faith), that ignites the dynamite (word).

6. <u>Authority</u>. One of the characteristics of the teaching of Jesus was, "this man speaks with authority." His authoritative method in teaching was in contrast to the religious leaders of His day. There was a *confidence factor* in each one of these accounts. Confidence, or acting in authority, comes from observing a clear word on your heart. If you have a clear word on your heart, you can act by just a little faith and see wonderful results. A clear word gives you confidence to act in authority. The issue then is one of obedience or courage to act.

7. <u>Cooperation in grace</u>. In each of the accounts there was an intimation of the Father's involvement or granting the request. It is not necessary that the Father be involved. But this is His desire. It is to be a goal of the believer. We must understand that an unbeliever, a mind scientist, or a voodoo witch can use faith, a word, and the heart for powerful results. The magicians of Pharaoh's court performed magic apart from Jehoveh. Simon, the magician performed mighty deeds and was rebuked by the disciples when he tried to add the power of God to his repertoire of tricks. The point is that evil spirits or the devil can work wonders. Our goal is to receive from the Father by His love and grace.

What Happens When Mountains Refuse To Move?

We know from our personal experience that mountains can be stubborn to move sometimes. So what are we to do or think if they don't move? I have observed five responses or reasons in this regard:

1. <u>This kind comes not out but by prayer and fasting</u>. This concept is mentioned in Matthew's account of the disciples being unable to help the lunatic boy. It is recorded in Mark's account but is not in the best manuscripts. Obviously, what is talked about is a diligence, determination, and focus.

2. <u>The need for forgiveness</u>. In the account of moving mountains, from Mark's gospel (11:25-26), you have the necessity of forgiveness. I addressed this

previously. It could be that bitterness and unforgiveness have clouded the heart so that it is difficult for faith and a word to operate.

3. <u>Misalignment</u>. It could be that there is a conflict between His word and our word. We simply must discern the word of the Lord in order to line up properly for powerful results.

4. <u>Faith not being applied in the specific situation</u>. We may believe something in general, but for specific situations, we must apply specific faith.

5. <u>Timing</u>. Although *timing* is not addressed in these accounts particularly, we know that God's timing and our timing could be misaligned. Every mighty work does not have to happen instantaneously. The Bible says to pray for the peace of Israel. I pray for the peace of Israel. I believe that peace is going to come. But I do not believe that it will be because of envoys from the United States or any other country making it happen. There will be war and conflict between Israel and other nations until the Prince of Peace returns and creates lasting peace. I pray. I believe. I have confidence. But it is not immediate.

Why We Should Pray For Mountains To Move

People do not pray for mountains to move for several reasons. For some it is as simple as ignorance or unbelief. Others are discouraged because their experience or track record in this area is dismal at best. Some do not pray for mighty things because it takes work and effort. Others may not approach it because fear has replaced faith or sin has produced an unreceptive heart.

Let me tell you why we should pray for mountains to move.

1. <u>It forces us to use faith</u>. The Bible tells us that without faith it is impossible to please God.

2. <u>It reinforces our faith</u>. It makes our faith stronger and gives us courage to be obedient.

3. <u>It gives confidence toward the future</u>. Confidence gives us energy for operating in authority.

4. <u>It forces us to have a working relationship with God</u>. God is after this anyway.

5. <u>It allows God to bless</u>. God, not only desires to bless us, but to bless through us.

6. <u>It provides a testimony to the power of God</u>. God is honored and others receive a witness.

7. <u>It blesses God</u>. God is honored by those who cooperate with Him by faith.

Everybody Prays—So What

As in many of the more *unseen*, mystical, or supernatural things there can be ignorance and misapplication. Blindly, we skip over Scripture passages that we don't understand or have fear about. Sometimes tradition will out-weigh truth. But, however you want to say it, there are many misconceptions regarding prayer; what it is; how it works.

Obviously, Catholics pray, Protestants pray, Buddhists pray, Moslems pray, New Agers pray, and Satanists pray, but they are different in several ways. Could it be that we are dealing again with a universal truth? Yes, to one extent, we are dealing with a universal truth available to all. Anyone can pray. And any prayer can have results. But, the object and method becomes of utmost importance.

I pray to God, the Father, through the Holy Spirit's intercession, in the name of Jesus. Sometimes I address Jesus alone in my praying. The mind scientist may pray to the ethereal universal consciousness that surrounds the earth and resides in every cell of every living thing. Roman Catholics may pray to or through Mother Mary. The Moslems will pray to Allah. The Satanists will make Satan their object. The idol worshippers will bow down and pray to an image. The object makes a great difference in your praying.

Again, The *Word* Is The Key

Praying words alone is no guarantee of praying properly. Repetition, Jesus said, was not the key to proper praying. Praying in some kind of trance is not necessarily the proper way. Praying on your knees with folded hands is not the only way. What, then, is proper and real prayer?

Let me first try to simplify the concept of prayer; real prayer. Real, genuine, God honoring, result-oriented praying is: (1) getting a word from the true and living God on your heart, (2) and responding to this word by faith.

One reason to go into your closet and pray (as Jesus taught) was to be able, in quietness and meditation, to see God's deposited word on your heart. Your response in adoration, praise, thanksgiving, confession, intercession, or petition is the connecting link we call *prayer*.

The Old Testament prophets of Baal prayed all day, cut themselves with swords and spears, and went into ecstatic religious frenzy trying to perform a miracle of calling fire down from heaven. Elijah, God's prophet, simply spoke a few words and the altar was completely destroyed by God's fire. This was a test to determine the true God but it also revealed true prayer.

As I have mentioned before, I don't pray for people or situations just any old way or offer a standard recitation from a prayer book. When I go into my quiet time of prayer I begin with praise and thanksgiving. This is the way to enter His courts and stand in His presence. I then watch for a word from Him or I bring one of my own. Sometimes this requires that I confess sin. Sometimes some one is brought to my attention for which I intercede. Then, oftentimes, I ask or petition for something.

If someone asks me to pray for a loved one lying in the intensive care unit of the hospital, or for marital trouble, or for financial woes, I seek for that word on my heart. Sometimes I pace back and forth in my study or sit up at night at home seeking for a word on my heart. I want to do this so that I can pray accurately. I do not always pray for someone's healing. It is amazing how many times I have received no clear word to pray for recovery and the person in a critical condition dies within a day or two. I really try to honor God's word from which I pray. Other times I have gone in confidence, prayed for healing when the situation seemed hopeless, and watched the sick individuals recover.

Obviously, when someone implores you to pray on behalf of their sick or injured loved one, they usually have only one way they want you to pray—that God would restore and heal. But, I maintain that we ought to be seeking God's word on the situation so that we will know *how* to pray, and so that we will have *confidence* to pray in faith.

A man shared a testimony about this very thing in our church one day. He said that the little country church where his sickly mother was a member, prayed faithfully for her. She was on their weekly prayer list. They prayed fervently for her healing.

The son testified that his saintly old mother, in her late nineties, lying in a miserable hospital bed asked him to relay a message to the little church. Her request was that they stop praying for her healing. Yes, she told them that she was ready to die and wanted to go on to heaven. "Son," she said, "tell them to stop praying for me to be healed!"

The son relayed the request to the church. Though a little surprised, they stopped praying for healing. The old lady died not long after that. Whether her death was due to the church ceasing to pray for her or it happened just in the course of God's time and providence is something we will never know for sure.

But here's the point. The well-meaning little church was not praying from a word from God. They had not thought to seek for a word from God. Out of "duty" they were faithfully calling out their word. How often, in our corporate or small group prayer meeting, we list a series of prayer requests. Then we dutifully go down the list praying for this or that as listed in the request with no regard or consideration for God's desire. We are not obligated to pray for every request as the person may desire. We need to get a word from God on *how* to pray for the individual. If we neglect to get a word from God on how to pray for something, we are no better than the hypocritical religious leaders of Jesus' day or the prophets of Baal in Elijah's day.

We should be finding out what God's word is and be obedient to respond accordingly. This is real prayer in a true spiritual relationship—not mere religion. Again, it is about Him—not us!

Making Deals With God

In trying to get a sure *yes* answer from God, some people will make a deal with Him. "God, if you do this, then I will do such and such." This can be very dangerous. I have discovered that God deals with man through *covenants*. There are several of them throughout history in God's dealings with mankind. The Scripture also shows us covenants or vows that man has made with God. One will discover that God takes these very seriously. In fact, there is a warning in Scripture about making vows and not keeping them.

"Guard your steps when you go to the house of God. Go near to listen rather than to offer the sacrifice of fools, who do not know that they do wrong. Do not be quick with your mouth, do not be hasty in your heart to utter anything before God. God is in heaven and you are on earth, so let your words be few. As a dream comes when there are many cares, so the speech of a fool when there are many words. When you make a vow to God, do not delay in fulfilling it. He has no pleasure in fools; fulfill your vow. It is better not to vow than to make a vow and not fulfill it. Do not let your mouth lead you into sin" (Ecclesiastes 5:1-6, NIV).

Why does God take these so seriously? A covenant is a promise, a contract, a solemn vow—a *word*. Words are important to God. One of His Ten Commandments is about bearing false witness. One of the final judgments has to do with this:

"But the cowardly, the unbelieving, the vile, the murderers, the sexually immoral, those who practice magic arts, the idolaters and **all liars**—their place will be in the fiery lake of burning sulfur. This is the second death" (Revelation 21:8, NIV).

Words are critical. God deals with us by means of words. We, too, operate toward God with words. When God gives you His word it is a true word. You can count on it. He expects the same from us. There is no deviation in this concept. Thus, He takes vows very seriously. Be careful!

Putting Out A Fleece

In the Old Testament there is a story about a man of God, named Gideon, who wanted to know God's will and word on an important decision he was contemplating. He decided to put a fleece of wool out on the ground and asked God to use the dew that fell on the ground as a sign of what he was supposed to do. If the dew fell all around but not on the fleece, it was a miraculous sign.

In the Old Testament there was also a *will telling* device called the "urim and thummim" used by the High Priest to determine God's direction and word on a matter. We don't know much about these devices except that the words meant, *light* and *perfection*, and that they were exclusively for the priests. They were also part of the multi-jeweled breastplate worn by the High Priest. God instructed that it be included as a part of the High Priest's garb and used to discern the will of Jehoveh. Some scholars believe that God made the jeweled breastplate, with the multi-colored stones, to glow. The stones with a particular Hebrew letter would glow spelling out God's desire. Possibly, the urim and thummim were *yes* and *no* stones. Much of this is speculation but we do know that this device was given by God and was to be used to discern His will.

By the New Testament time there was a dice-like unit called *lot* or *lots*. These units were used for hundreds of years before the time of Christ, going back to the institution of the priesthood and the sacrificial system for Israel.

It was not solely a Jewish custom. At the crucifixion of Jesus we find the Roman soldiers "casting lots" for His garment.

Lots were cast in the beginning of the early church as they sought a replacement for Judas in the Apostle's band. In the book of Acts we find the leaders casting lots to determine between two candidates; Justus, and Matthias.

"So they proposed two men: Joseph called Barsabbas (also know as Justus) and Matthias. Then they prayed, 'Lord, you know everyone's heart. Show us which of these two you have chosen to take over this apostolic ministry, which Judas left to go where he belongs.' Then they cast lots, and the lot fell to Matthias; so he was added to the eleven apostles" (Acts 1:23-26, NIV).

The concept of casting lots to determine God's word and will fades out. Why? It probably had to do with the coming of the Holy Spirit on the day of Pentecost. We have no record of Jesus relying on the urim or thummim or the casting of lots. He relied on the Holy Spirit that was present inside of Him. Likewise, the apostles and disciples began to rely upon the indwelling Holy Spirit. The casting of lots to determine the apostleship in Acts 1:23-26 is immediately followed by the coming of the Holy Spirit on the day of Pentecost in the very next verses of chapter two. After the coming of the Holy Spirit there is no mention of *casting lots* in the remainder of the New Testament.

I mention these outward methods for two reasons. First, we should be extremely careful about using any kind of fleece, sign, or will telling device, if we use them at all. Secondly, God's preference for communicating His will and word to us is by means of His word on our heart, prompted and interpreted by the Holy Spirit. Otherwise, we, like the carnal beings of all time, will seek after an easy, outward way of future telling and fortune telling. The next thing you know, we will be gazing into crystal balls or rolling dice in an attempt to discern our future.

Real Prayer Keeps It Simple

Prayer—real prayer—is not complicated. But it is a sensitive matter. Thus, Jesus will instruct us to get into a closet and shut the door. There, in quiet, we can listen without distraction for God's word. God does not want to have to compete for attention. Once we are quiet, we can get His word upon our heart and activate that word by faith. He is then free to reward us and reward us openly.

The problem of unanswered prayer or lack of results in prayer is not on God's side. The problem is on our side. The individual must get his heart *right*. The individual must see and receive God's word upon the heart. The individual must activate this word by faith and have the courage to express it. Then God can provide a wonderful result.

Real prayer—powerful prayer—is simple. Get God's word on your heart. Act by faith on this word. See a wonderful and powerful result.

11

The Power Of Positive Word Dynamics

Positive Word Dynamics refers to the use of words in a positive and constructive way for success and blessing. Positive word dynamics can change your world by changing your vocabulary. Change your words and you will change your heart. Change your heart and you will change your actions. Change your actions and your will change your world. Everything about our life is based on a word. Words are vitally important. Words are the result of heart belief. Heart belief stimulates faith action. Faith action is energy and power. Words are not only important but words are powerful.

The struggle we encounter when we start examining this theme and approach is that we realize we tend to operate in *negative word dynamics*. It is like the person that determines to start a new and healthy diet only to realize how much they were addicted to junk food. It is like the person who decides to quit caffeine only to go through headache withdrawals. It is like the alcoholic who professes that he doesn't really have a problem. We may not realize just how much we are involved with junk words, caffeinated hypertension due to negative thinking, and word pollution that keeps us in denial.

Some of the most important things we can ever do in our life is to recognize the power and importance of words, realize the difference in positive and negative word dynamics, and realign our lives with positive word dynamics. In this chapter we are going to try to expose the growing proliferation of junk words and show how to overcome them with positive word dynamics for success and blessing. A word of warning—there could be withdrawals!

The Growing Blight Of Foul Words

A recent article revealed what we were already suspecting—profanity is increasing in use in our society.

"The use of foul language on television shows in the past five years has increased dramatically on nearly every network and in nearly every time slot—including the so-called 'Family Hour' from 8 to 9 p.m. ET—according to a study by the Parents Television Council.

The report, released Sept. 15, examined all prime-time entertainment series on the major broadcast television networks from the first two weeks of the 1998, 2000, and 2002 November sweeps periods, analyzing a total of 400 program hours.

Foul language, including curses or intensives, offensive epithets, scatological language, sexually suggestive or indecent language, and censored language, increased by 94.8 percent during the Family Hour between 1998 and 2002. During the 9 p.m. ET time slot, such language increased by 109.1 percent, though the smallest increase (38.7 percent) occurred during the last hour of prime time—the hour when young children are least likely to be watching.

'It's easy to be dismissive of foul language on TV, but it does have an impact,' the Parents Television Council said in a news release" (*Baptist and Reflector*, Baptist Press, October 8, 2003, p. 8).

Recently, Bono, the lead singer of a famous Irish rock group called *U2* went before a national and international audience to receive a Golden Globe award. The following is taken from a news report:

"The singer-songwriter was so enthused about U2's Globe win that he must've forgotten he was on TV.... 'Ah, this is really f—king brilliant (crowd cheers),' Bono said."

Bono's vulgar adjective prompted a ruling by the Federal Communications Commission who ruled that it could be used anytime as long as it was used as an adjective and not referring to sexual conduct. What this means is that the door has swung a little wider for "anything goes" on TV, Radio, movies or any public venue.

For the last decade or more, movies have pushed the envelope of decency in regard to language. Long gone are the days when the world is shocked because Rhett Butler turns to Scarlet and says, "I don't give a damn." The shock waves of that one statement on the big screen movie, *Gone With The Wind*, pales in comparison to the flood of filthy language we are inundated with today.

I was driving up the street one day in our neighborhood. I stopped at the stoplight. Another car pulled up in the lane next to me. The man had a young boy in the car with him that was around five years old. What caught my attention was the rap music he had blaring from his car speakers. The music, if you can call it that, could be heard all around the intersection. It literally vibrated the windows in my own car. I do not own a rap music album of any kind. I don't think that I have ever listened to a complete song. I don't like that style of music at all. But I was forced to listen to this. I couldn't understand all the words but I understood enough that I discerned that the story line was about a woman getting raped and a policeman getting brutally killed. The vulgarity and profanity was unlike any I had heard in a brief span of one or two minutes. I couldn't help but feel sympathy for the child that was being taught these concepts that were literally being pounded into his mind and engraved upon his heart. Unconsciously, the boy was receiving all of these powerful negative and destructive words into his subconscious heart.

The shock factor in movies and music is a powerful selling tool. The philosophy behind the shocking words has to do with capturing attention and impressing an image or attitude. This is exactly what we have been saying—words are powerful entities. The problem is that words don't just grab our attention, they affect our lives, dull our sensitivities, awaken certain images, press us down or lift us up. Words are powerful.

One of the growing complaints that we hear from teachers in city schools is the growing use of profanity and vulgarity coming out of the mouths of young people. I watched a local news report on one of our stations in the Memphis, Tennessee area regarding this problem. But it was not just with the children. The report gave an audio recording of one of the children's mothers calling in about their child. One could hardly piece the conversation together because of all the deleting beeps on the tape trying to cover up indecent language coming from—the mother!

One of the prominent arguments that we hear in this regard has to do with "free speech" and how we all have a right to say anything we want. But the other side of the coin is a creeping unconscious corruption. We have become so desensitized that we hardly think anything about the vile and negative words that come into our conscious and our subconscious.

Hung By The Tongue

James, the half brother of Jesus, said,

"But above all, my brethren, do not swear, either by heaven or by earth or with any other oath. But let your 'Yes,' be 'Yes,' and your 'No,' 'No,' lest you fall into judgment" (James 5:12, NKJV).

Like unconscious robots, we often grow up parroting what we hear around us without any consideration for how those words are affecting us or how they are getting implanted in our subconscious. Then, seemingly innocent "by-words" come forth from our tongue because they have been planted in our heart.

Most of us have heard all kinds of word derivatives, abbreviations, slang, and profanity without giving it much consideration. We may even be in a habit of saying words that have no value or have a negative impact upon ourselves or others. Do we consider the meaning of such seemingly innocent words such as *gosh, golly, darn, dern, jeez, gosh darn,* and *freakin*? What are the meanings behind these expressions—where did they come from? Moral, church-going people would never think of using God's name in vain or even cursing with profanity. Yet I have heard them use these words.

Webster's dictionary says that *gosh* and *golly* mean, "an alteration of God—used to express mild surprise or delight." It says that *darn* is an "alteration of damn" (Webster's New College Dictionary, 1995). But how many folks who use *gosh, golly, darn,* or *gosh darn* realize that they are using derivatives and veiled forms of *God, damn,* and *God damn*?

I used to carry our children and some neighbor children to school every morning on a twenty minute drive. Often I would overhear them say a word they had heard someone say at school—usually a questionable word. I would ask them if they knew the origination or real meaning of that word. They would sometimes take a stab at the meaning. Other times they would remain closed-mouthed indicating that they surmised it was a naughty word. If I knew the meaning or origination in Greek, Hebrew, or Latin, I would tell them. Sometimes it required that we look the word up in a dictionary.

One day I overheard them referring to someone as a *dork*. I said, "Do you guys know what that word means? Do you know the origination of that word? Do you know what you are calling that person?"

I really didn't know what it meant either, but it made them think about what they were calling another person. Other times they were surprised to discover what words meant. I think it helped condition them to be more conscious of their words.

People just don't think. I overheard a church member going out the door of our church one day. He thought it was cute to respond, "Jeez Louise!" I confronted him by asking if he knew what *Jeez* meant. He looked surprised. I said, "I think it refers to *Jesus*." Here was a man who would never use God's name in vain but was unconsciously using a derivative of Jesus in a vain slang expression.

The ancient Hebrews so reverenced the name of God (Yahveh) that when they were reading Scriptures they would not read the name Yahveh or Jehoveh (our transliteration of Yahveh) but would say "Adonay" (Lord). To take the name of Yahveh in vain carried the penalty of stoning to death. Words and names are important to God—especially His personal names. In the New Testament to "name the name of Christ" was to belong to Him. To "hold fast His name" was to be true to Him. Believers prayed "in the name of Jesus." New converts to Christ were baptized "in the name of the Father, the Son, and the Holy Spirit." The third commandment says that we are not to take the name of God in vain.

"'Vain' is the adjective of 'vanity,' and it is virtually synonymous with empty, hollow, or idle. 'Vain' implies either absolute or relative absence of value; 'empty' and 'hollow' suggest a deceiving lack of real substance, soundness or genuineness; and 'idle' suggest being incapable of worthwhile use or effect.

This reveals an even darker side of the third commandment. When we misrepresent His name, we are guilty of malfeasance, misfeasance, or nonfeasance as His ambassador. 'Being a witness' is more than giving out tracts or responding with theological clichés" (Chuck Missler, website article; *What's In a Name*, www.khouse.org).

Not only do we contribute unconscious speech but we spew forth unnecessary, and oftentimes, uncontrolled speech. Listen again to the half-brother of Jesus as he warns us about our tongue.

"So then, my beloved brethren, let every man be swift to hear, slow to speak, slow to wrath; for the wrath of man does not produce the righteousness of God. Therefore lay aside all filthiness and overflow of wickedness, and receive with meekness the implanted word, which is able to save your souls" (James 1:19-21, NKJV).

James uses more than one analogy to emphasize the importance and power of the tongue.

"My brethren, let not many of you become teachers, knowing that we shall receive a stricter judgment. For we all stumble in many things. If anyone does not stumble in word, he is a perfect man, able also to bridle the whole body. Indeed, we put bits in horses' mouths that they may obey us, and we turn their whole body. Look also at ships: although they are so large and are driven by fierce winds, they are turned by a very small rudder wherever the pilot desires. Even so the tongue is a little member and boasts great things. See how great a forest a little fire kindles! And the tongue is a fire, a world of iniquity. The tongue is so set among our members that it defiles the whole body, and sets on fire the course of nature; and it is set on fire by hell. For every kind of beast and bird, of reptile and creature of the sea, is tamed and has been tamed by mankind. But no man can tame the tongue. It is an unruly evil, full of deadly poison. With it we bless our God and Father, and with it we curse men, who have been made in the similitude of God. Out of the same mouth proceed blessing and cursing. My brethren, these things ought not to be so" (James 3:1-10, NKJV).

The Apostle Paul warns the believers at Ephesus about their contributing foolish talk and course jokes in their conversations.

"But fornication and all uncleanness or covetousness, let it not even be named among you, as is fitting for saints; neither filthiness, nor foolish talking, nor coarse jesting, which are not fitting, but rather giving of thanks" (Ephesians 5:3,4, NKJV).

We can do a lot of damage with our tongue. How many lives have been ruined by the gossip of others? How many kingdoms have been toppled by whispers in the inner chambers? How many people have been discouraged to quit or to commit suicide because of criticism and demeaning words? How many churches have split in bitterness because of harsh unloving words? How many marriages have divided because of words? Words have great power.

We need to be conscious of our words and our speech. We need to guard against unnecessary verbiage. We need to constantly work on controlling our tongue.

One of the great sins of Christian believers is unspoken words of witness. We fail to speak a good word for God. We fail to witness to others. We fail, even when we have opportunities, to minister to others with our words, to pray proper words, to witness the Gospel to others with our words, to encourage with words, to forgive, and to bless with words. We need to learn to control our tongue in regard to using wrong words and not using right words. We have power in words for good or evil.

The Spoken Word—God's Power Tool

I like power tools—most guys do. They sure make projects go a lot faster, easier, and with more accuracy for the most part. Those who use an electric power saw usually don't want to go back to the old fashioned hand saw.

The spoken word is like a power tool. And like power equipment of most any type, we can get hurt by them, hurt others, or get a lot accomplished. The use of words should be a skill we develop for accomplishing great good. Instead we often make a mess. Just because a guy has a shop full of power tools does not mean that he can make a prize-winning cabinet. One must learn how to use the tools with safety and precision. Plans have to be followed from the raw cuts to the assembly and to the fine finish. We should all seek to be word craftsmen with the goal of superior craftsmanship, creating quality works.

I am well aware of the importance of words. I have spoken to audiences nearly every week for over thirty years—over 5,000 different audiences. Sometimes I feel like I communicated and built a worthy message with a fine finish. Most of the time I feel like I crafted a Little Rascal's clubhouse out of apple crates.

On Sunday mornings a few of us gather a little early before the services start at church and pray. We join for a group prayer and then we break off to be alone in prayer. Hardly a Sunday goes by but what I don't get alone, kneel in prayer, and pray the prayer of David in Psalm 19:14:

"Let the words of my mouth and the meditation of my heart be acceptable in your sight, O LORD, my strength and my redeemer."

I know how vulnerable I am. I know how deceptive my own heart can be. I want God to guard my heart lest I speak from the pulpit or even to someone walking down the hallway with harmful or unnecessary words. A slip of the tongue has done great damage. But I also want to use the power of my tongue to bless and build up. So I pray for God's help.

What was God's primary power tool for crafting the earth, the universe, and all the multitude of creatures? What was the primary power tool of Jesus? What did He use to heal the sick, cast out demons, and raise the dead? You guessed it—His spoken word.

The spoken word is God's great gift to us all. How we use it is up to us. It is a power tool. The problem is like the guy who has a shop full of power tools but doesn't have electricity to the shop. Or the guy who never uses his tools. Or the guy who uses dull tools. Or the guy who never learns how to use them. Or the guy who uses them to create harmful and hurtful objects.

The Scriptures are clear in this respect.

"So Jesus answered and said to them, 'Assuredly, I say to you, if you have faith and do not doubt, you will not only do what was done to the fig tree, but also if you say to this mountain, "Be removed and be cast into the sea," it will be done.'" (Matthew 21:21, NKJV).

"For by your words you will be justified, and by your words you will be condemned." (Matthew 12:37, NKJV).

"That if you confess with your mouth the Lord Jesus and believe in your heart that God has raised Him from the dead, you will be saved. For with the heart one believes unto righteousness, and with the mouth confession is made unto salvation" (Romans 10:9,10, KJV).

Each of these verses tell us plainly that we have a power tool: "if you say to this mountain...it will be done," "for by your words," "if you confess with your mouth." This power tool is so powerful that it can move mountains and justify us before the court of God.

12

The Practical Use of Positive Word Dynamics

Positive word dynamics can change your life and affect others around you. Changing your words, however, is not always easy. Much of what we are today is a result of a lifetime of words being implanted into our head and heart, either voluntarily or involuntarily. We all need to do an objective inventory of the words we use and the word we live by. This is basically what a psychiatrist would do with a patient—try to get at the word the person is living by and seek to change or redirect that word. It is not complicated. If we can honestly take inventory we can set about a process for change. And if we can change our words and the word we live by, we can change our world. If we can change our words and the word we live by we can rebuild a better life for ourselves.

Words Set The Tone

In 1973 I married a wonderful young lady. She is still my wife today. I wanted to do something special for her wedding gift. I decided to order her the inner workings of a grandfather clock and build her a clock. I ordered the parts and went to work on the case. I had taken wood shop in high school and crafted a few projects with limited tools. But, I felt that I could borrow the power tools I did not have and complete the project. I worked and worked on drawing the plans. I selected the maple veneer plywood. I had a man cut the glass for the doors. I applied every ounce of knowledge and expertise to this project to make it the best I had ever attempted. Sharon seemed pleased with the gift.

The clock stood in our house and ran perfectly for many years. One day our preschool daughter accidentally pulled it over. The corner of the clock case hit the floor at just the right angle and shattered into thousands of pieces. I was glad our daughter was not hurt but I knew the clock was history. There would be no way to put it back together again.

As I gathered up the pieces I kept noticing how weak I had crafted the joints. I noticed how I had not used the proper screws and glue. I noticed how I had cut a corner here and there that allowed a weakness in the structure. I was older and more experienced in woodworking now and couldn't believe how I had created such a shoddy piece of "heirloom" furniture. I gathered up the wood pieces and threw them in the trash.

Sharon seemed really disappointed in the destruction of the clock so I decided to build her another one. Only this time, it would be built right. If she thought that much of it, then my pride was on the line!

I spent hours working up the drawings. I collected the native hardwoods from our hometown—no veneers this time. I had already collected most of the power tools and had them in my shop. What I did not have, I purchased. I determined that I would take however long it took, would not cut any corners, and not install a piece until it was exactly right. I believed that I had gained a greater degree of expertise in woodworking and what I did not know, I would learn. I would seek to make every piece perfect and not cut a single corner. I had established a "word" and was determined to live by it.

It took me months to finish the project. The clock case stood over six and a half feet tall made out of solid native oak, sanded and finished to feel like silk. The old clock works were installed and I had an old glass craftsman hand bevel the glass for the doors. I even hand carved the rams horn finial out of solid oak and mounted it upon the hood. It was the pinnacle of my years of woodworking experience.

People come into our house now and look at the clock. Many are amazed that I could create such a beautiful piece of furniture. I must admit that it looks stately. I also know that it was built properly and expertly, giving me a great sense of accomplishment and satisfaction. You could push this clock over and the glass would break but not the wood case. It was strong. But what was the difference in the two clocks? Believe it or not, the difference had to do with the word on which they were built.

The first clock was built on the word of inexperience, inferior materials, improper tools, and an attitude of "I've never built a clock case before. I sure hope I can do this." The second clock was built on a stronger word that was fixed at the beginning—"I can do this and I can do a much better job than that first clock. This time I am going to do each stage exactly right. I will not cut corners or use any inferior materials. I don't care how long it takes—this clock will be built strong and beautiful." Do you see the difference? The word at the beginning set the tone.

Oftentimes a company fails or succeeds by how they set the tone for their production at the very beginning. The corporate charter and by-laws are to be in place to provide the word or the guidelines for the operation of the company. A marriage continues strong and productive by how it sets the tone with the vows at the beginning of the union. Goals are words that are set at the beginning to set the tone for our journey. Set no goal or have shoddy goals and the end result will be a telling sign. Sometimes we don't realize what word we set at the beginning until our work topples over and bursts into a million pieces. Then we realize how we built upon a faulty word.

Oftentimes, my associates and I have had to do marriage counseling with people who have come to us as a last resort. We have often compared these folks with the analogy of someone jumping out of an airplane without a parachute. Somehow, they want us to fix it or install a parachute before they splatter on the ground. Sometimes it is too late.

An Objective Inventory for Positive Correction

Once we do an objective inventory (and hopefully it will not be the result of a crash) we can begin to develop a new word on which to build. And establishing a word goal at the beginning is very important. There will be *words* we operate by but there will also be *the word* at the beginning that we build upon.

Before we can help others we often need to help ourselves. That is, we need to take an objective inventory of how we feel about ourselves as evidenced in the words we say about ourselves and the thoughts we think about ourselves. Most of us can look in the mirror or reflect upon our past and easily find things we don't like. The thing that we must not do is to build a negative self-image. Regardless of how you look in comparison to others or how you feel about yourself begin to cast aside those words and thoughts and build new ones. Even if you cannot find a single thing you like about yourself, begin to visualize something good about yourself and begin to thank God for things you like now or for things you expect to see in yourself in the future. This is not an introspective self-centered concept as much as it is recognizing the attributes God has given you and believing Him for the changes that are coming. It is recognizing God's image in you, God's good in you, and God's potential for you. In a way, it is not self-centered but God-centered. Certainly, you are not going to be helped, God is not going to be glorified, and others will not benefit if you are moping around with negative word dynamics ruling your life.

Like many teenagers, I too, had a difficult time coming through the adolescent years. I was sickly, anemic, weak, pimply faced, and shy. I had low self-esteem and little confidence in my self or my abilities. I wanted to hide under a rock. It was not until my personal clock crashed and burst to pieces—a crisis point in my life—that I began to rebuild myself. It took years but it worked and my life has been better for it and I have been able to help others. Once you get yourself running on a new word you can help others with a word.

What we are about here is not a complicated formula. We just must realize a few things, get educated about word dynamics, and make a commitment or decision to get on with it. We may even have to force feed ourselves and force expressions out of our mouth that seem contrary to the situation and contrary to how we feel, how we look, and how things are at the present time. Much of what we do is out of habits formed over many years, emotions, peer pressure, fear, or physical/mental feelings. Yet these will have to take a back seat. Begin to think with positive word dynamics, speak positive word dynamics, and act on positive word dynamics regardless of how you feel or what you have always done. Only you can decide to break the mold.

I heard of a young woman who broke her leg but did not get it set properly and it grew back improperly. She finally went in for surgery. They had to put her to sleep and actually re-break her leg in order to reset it so that it would heal and grow back properly. Re-breaking word patterns that we have allowed to form in our life will take effort and will probably be a painful experience. To begin to tell someone that you love them when you are emotionally opposed to them is difficult. To forgive someone when you really want to retaliate with anger is painful. To begin to think and speak positive words when you really feel negative is difficult. You must do what God did at creation—speak as though it is when it has yet to materialize. You cannot wait until it materializes and then speak to it. You are the initiator. You must act by faith rather than sight, feeling, or emotions. So force feed yourself. Examine your negative word dynamics and formulate your strategy and plan to reestablish positive word dynamics in your life. As the Nike commercial says, "Just do it!"

Our Power To Use Positive Word dynamics To Bless Others

As I just mentioned, when you get your act together, you can begin to use positive word dynamics toward others. And again, it is not complicated. Just a few choice positive word dynamics directed at others can do wonders.

I learned something along these lines during my high school days. I am not sure where I picked it up but it was a neat little trick for becoming well-liked and more popular. It had to do with expressing respect. It was as simple as speaking to everyone—the popular kids—the geeks—the jocks—and the outcasts. Say "Hi" to everyone. Leave no one out. Make the lowliest feel like you notice them and you care. Just the simple "Hi" can do wonders if it is backed by a genuine attitude.

A second respect impact that anyone can do with a little effort is to say "Hi Joe," "Hi Sue." Most people like to hear their own name mentioned.

A third level is to greet someone with a "Hi Joe" and a sincere question regarding something important in their life. If you can't think of any or you don't really mean, "How are you?" you might just say "Hi Joe. Good to see you today." And I know it is not cool any more to address people as "Sir" or "Ma'am" in a lot of circles but it is a form of respect and done in a genuine rather than in a patronizing way is a great positive word dynamic.

A fourth level of ministering to people is by genuine compliment. Flattery has a bad connotation because it often smacks of a negative or self-serving ulterior motive. But genuine compliments are power words. Encouraging words, when honest and appropriate, are powerful ministry words as well.

My wife's grandfather was a respected businessman, a state senator, a Christian man, and a true gentleman. We all learned many things from him. He taught us to greet people with a smile and a handshake. He was conscious of others and made them feel important. He stood when someone came into the room and greeted them with respect. He remembered people and made them feel important. I have seen him respond in this way to children and adults, to hillbilly farmers and to chief political leaders, to the poor and to the wealthy. He always gave forth a good word whenever he could regarding any individual. I can never remember him speaking harshly toward anyone. He blessed with his words and his actions. Somewhere along the way he learned the power of personality, positive word dynamics, and ways to bless people. As a result, he was successful, blessed, and a blessing to many. He was elected again and again to the state senate because people respected him and believed in him. People lined up at his place of business to ask advice. He was a powerful man and important man because he understood the power of positive word dynamics.

The true Christian believer has many power words or expressions in his or her arsenal to use toward others. Let me give you three; the power to love, the power to bless, and the power to forgive.

Jesus put it this way, "But I say to you, love your enemies, bless those who curse you, do good to those who hate you, and pray for those who spitefully use you and persecute you" (Matthew 5:44, NKJV).

Again, Jesus said, "But I say to you who hear: love your enemies, do good to those who hate you…. But love your enemies, do good, and lend, hoping for nothing in return; and your reward will be great, and you will be sons of the Most High" (Luke 6:27, 35, NKJV).

Paul reiterated what Jesus said, "Bless them which persecute you: bless, and curse not" (Romans 12:14, NKJV).

We have the power to express words of love instead of hate. Genuine words of love are powerful instruments for change and affect.

During my seminary days, my wife and I took in a troubled teen to live with us. He had many problems which would often manifest themselves. One day he went off on one of his tantrums. When I tried to control him he became further enraged and engaged me out in the front of our apartment. I was just trying to hold him. We both tripped and fell to the ground. They next thing I knew he was on top of me with a large rock in his hand raised and getting ready to crush my skull. All I could think of was, "It's okay, James. We still love you. It's okay. We still love you."

His hands began to quiver and tears welled up in his eyes. He slowly lowered the rock and removed himself from atop me. The positive word dynamic of love won the day and I was thankful.

We also have the power to bless. It is not just a catch phrase either. We can actually speak blessing upon someone else or curse upon someone else. Our ability to bless and curse is real and powerful. Jesus and Paul understood this power. It is the reason they both said to bless and curse not. We have a positive word dynamic working when we gain enough confidence to speak blessing upon someone. Learn to bless with your words of compliment, encouragement, and love expressions. You will be surprised at the positive response.

For years I have given away ink pens to friends, family, and leaders in our church at Christmas time. On the side of the pen I have the pen company laser engrave the phrase, "May God Bless You." It is a prayer that I pray for each of those to which I give a pen. I believe that the phrase comprises a *word* to the individual and is worth a whole lot more than the pen itself. We have power to bless people and we should practice giving forth that important word.

Thirdly, we have the power to forgive. "I forgive you" is a positive word dynamic statement and carries great weight with God. Remember that in Mark, chapter eleven, Jesus said that we could move mountains if we truly believed, spoke to the situation, doubted not, and forgave. We can hold ourselves and others hostage with unforgiveness or we can release power with forgiveness. Forgiveness means *letting it go* and is most honored by God. Forgive whether you feel like it or not and see the power that is released. Forgiveness is a positive word dynamic.

Positive Word Dynamics Toward God

There are also positive word dynamics that we can initiate toward God. These are mostly words of privileged relationship for true believers. But they are important and powerful primarily because they connect us to God in a better way. And the better we are connected in relationship to God, the closer we are to the power source. For instance, Scripture says,

"Let us come before his presence with thanksgiving, and make a joyful noise unto him with psalms" (Psalms 95:2).

"Enter into his gates with thanksgiving, and into his courts with praise: be thankful unto him, and bless his name" (Psalms 100:4).

We have the ability to issue positive words toward God in prayer. We draw close to him by thanksgiving and praise. We can also bless His name with our speech. This can be a part of a quiet time alone with God in our closet or in corporate worship. It appears that God likes these expressions. If so, it means that they are powerful word dynamics.

1 Peter 2:9 says,

"But you are a chosen generation, a royal priesthood, a holy nation, His own special people, that you may proclaim the praises of Him who called you out of darkness into His marvelous light" (NKJV).

Not only does the Scripture say to give forth praise but to give thanks in all things as a definite part of God's will.

"In every thing give thanks: for this is the will of God in Christ Jesus concerning you" (1 Thessalonians 5:18, NKJV).

If there ever were powerful relationship-building tools that could be used toward God, they would have to include praise and thanksgiving. These positive word dynamics get us into his courts and before his throne like nothing else.

Another powerful word tool that the believer has in his arsenal is intercessory prayer. In fact, we can build a case and argue our point before the Lord. C. H. Spurgeon used to say that proper arguments in prayer were like forceful rappers on the door of heaven.

It is also interesting to listen to Job as he speaks of coming before the Lord.

"Oh that I knew where I might find him! that I might come even to his seat! I would order my cause before him, and fill my mouth with arguments. I would know the words which he would answer me, and understand what he would say unto me. (Job 23:3-5).

Spurgeon, in a sermon on prayer, quoted from Job and proclaims that we, as believers, have the privilege and right to come before the Lord to argue our case. As His children, we have the privilege of pleading for and even winning a judgment!

"And if we know that He hears us, whatever we ask, we know that we have the petitions that we have asked of Him" (1 John 5:15, NKJV).

Yes, the believer has more power in prayer than he might imagine. Few employ positive word dynamics toward God in prayer. Yet God says,

"Call to Me, and I will answer you, and show you great and mighty things, which you do not know" (Jeremiah 33:3, NKJV).

Positive word dynamics are to be used toward ourselves, others, and even God. What power we would have for daily living and ministry if we were aware of these truths, understood the power of these truths, and employed these truths. The use of positive word dynamics is an important and practical concept.

13

Learning To Use Positive Word Dynamics

One of the most haunting statements from the mouth of Jesus was,
"For by your words you will be acquitted, and by your words you will be condemned" (Matthew 12:37, NIV).

The larger context is even worse,
"For out of the overflow of the heart the mouth speaks. The good man brings good things out of the good stored up in him, and the evil man brings evil things out the evil stored up in him. But I tell you that men will have to give account on the day of judgment for every careless word they have spoken" (Matthew 12:34-36, NIV).

Chilling, isn't it? "Every careless word" covers a huge territory for those of us who live a lifetime communicating with our mouth. Not only do we have power to receive words and act on words, we have a responsibility on the expression of words. Not only are we supposed to receive good words but we are to give them forth. How we have failed!

In view of this pending judgment we should consider using the right words—positive word dynamics. This, however, is not a natural process. It must be learned. We must learn how to uproot the ingrained, negative, defeating words that have become a habitual part of our life and replace them with positive words for success and blessing. We must *learn* to do this.

Learn To Reject Negative Words

Back in college when I first felt called into the ministry, and before I really knew how to deal with words, I was confronted with a normally devastating negative word. My college speech teacher, who happened to be an avowed atheist, told me that I would never make it as a preacher or public speaker! In fact, I still have her note that she wrote me detailing why I would not make it. I have kept the note in my files all these years. But why didn't her words persuade me as she had implied?

I didn't know much about a lot of things but I was convinced of God's *call* upon my life. He had engraved His word upon my heart. He had drawn me out to go forth and proclaim His truth. This I knew. No one could persuade me differently. I was responding to this word upon my heart by faith, not by how I felt intellectually, emotionally, or by what anyone else thought.

Yet, I found myself mentally agreeing with the teacher. She said that I was monotone, disorganized, could not communicate verbally, was too nervous standing before people, and that I would NEVER make it! I mentally agreed with her to an extent. I was introverted, backwards, shy, and verbally weak. I was a pathetic communicator and a frightened public speaker.

Obviously her words didn't sway me completely as I have been speaking before audiences for over thirty years. But why? What allowed me to reject her word? Why didn't it discourage me or cause me to quit? As I look back on the situation, I realize that I had firmly received into my heart a stronger word from God. I had received it by faith, no matter what, even though I could not understand it by reason. Her words went to my head. I related to them sympathetically, logically, consciously, and historically. In many ways, she was right on target. But, her words were based upon what is or has been and not upon what can be. Her words were based upon head knowledge, not heart knowledge. Her words were motivated by outward perception, not inward reception. I was, however, firmly convinced, beyond logic, beyond sight, and beyond sense of a greater word upon my heart. Thus, it didn't bother me because I never let it get past my head. It never replaced the word on my heart. The word on my heart was greater. This is not to say that I didn't learn from her caustic criticism. I am still learning and watchful of things related to her criticisms. I always try to improve. But, assuredly, the best way to combat folks that want to mess with your head is to have a more solid word firmly implanted in your heart.

What is really difficult to deal with is the impressionable young child that is bombarded by parents, teachers, or authority figures with negative, and often devastating words. For an adult authority figure to tell a child that he is stupid, ugly, lazy, worthless, and so on, can be a damaging word to that child in an unfair situation. The child usually has no recourse other than to just take it as it comes. He is usually not strong enough, mature enough, or knowledgeable enough to retaliate. He does not know how to reject the negative word and may even come to believe it if it gets engraved on his heart. We need to learn to reject negative words.

Learn To Reject Untrue Words

Some years ago I was teaching a pastor's class. At the time, we were dealing with cults, "isms," and various religions. I knew that we had some in the class that had come out of these areas and probably did not know the whole truth. There was an obvious awakening as I presented the historical and theological truths.

One day, one of the ladies burst out in tears. "Do you mean that I have been living with this lie for all of my life?" she asked.

I told her that there was usually truth embedded in every religion but that we better make sure we knew the important truth if our eternity depended upon it. I told her that she would have to come to her own understanding regarding that which was true and that which was false. It was difficult for her to reject that which she had grown up believing in order to embrace the truth. She went away that day and pondered the truth. It wasn't long until she came back and made a profession of her faith and allowed me to baptize her. In fact, her whole family came around to the truth and became faithful members.

It is difficult to reject what we have always believed when we realize it is not the truth. It is not natural to do so. But when it comes to essential Christian doctrine and issues of eternal importance, we better come to grips with it and reject that untrue word.

Jesus told His disciples to "beware of the leaven of the Pharisees." What He meant was that it was not the ninety-nine percent that was bad, but the one percent that would corrupt them. Heresy is such not because it is half bad but because it has just a tiny bit of corruption. The truth is that the tiny bit makes the whole batch sour. You wouldn't want to eat an egg if it was only half rotten or one third rotten. We wouldn't want to eat a pie if it only had just a little cow manure mixed in with it. The small amount corrupts the whole.

Many religions contain wonderful truth. Many households contain large amounts of moral fiber. Many educational institutions contain a large amount of truth. Most every political platform has a large number of planks that are true. But the small amount of untruth can spoil the whole. We must learn to sort out the truth in areas where our life is affected, both now, and for eternity.

Real wisdom is being able to sort out the truth and courageous enough to live by it. The truth I try to live by is found in the Bible and in the person of Jesus Christ. Jesus was always about the business of the truth.

"Then Jesus said to those Jews who believed Him, 'If you abide in My word, you are My disciples indeed. 'And you shall know the truth, and the truth shall make you free'" (John 8:31,32, NKJV).

When we know the truth we will be confident. Confidence in the truth will enable us to operate in authority—the authority to reject the untruth that tries to be put upon us. Maturity in this confidence will enable us to come to the place where we can reject a negative or untrue word that someone tries to put upon us without rejecting the person.

One of the things most of us dislike is for another person to "put words in our mouth" or try to label us a certain way, or misquote us, or tell us that we are a certain way when, in fact, we are not. This usually grates on us or makes us angry.

In anger a child may respond to a parent with, "You just don't love me. You hate me. You never let me do what the other kids are doing. You are always putting me down. Everyone else gets to go, why can't I?"

Every one of these statements could be true or false. Most of the time they are false and are simply defensive words to try to win the case. A cautionary flag ought to go up anytime we hear an argument with words like, *never, always,* and *everybody*. But let us suppose that the parent is a loving and responsible parent and the child is just blowing off in anger. Some parents might want to absorb these words, accept them as true, agree with them, feel like a bad parent, and "give in" so the child will "love" them. A wise parent will first examine the statements. The obvious will come forth—"I do love them. I don't hate them. I do allow them to do some things the other kids are doing. I don't always put them down. I often try to encourage them. And, everyone else does not get to go."

The parent doesn't have to receive these statements as true. The loving parent can refute each and every statement and say something to the effect of, "I understand how you must feel but what you say is not true and I do not accept those statements as true. I reject them. They are not true statements. You can say them but I don't have to receive them."

You may accidentally get over into another person's lane while driving down the street. The other person may yell at you out the window and call you a moron or an idiot that doesn't know how to drive. You then have the choice of accepting his words as true or rejecting them as false. You can go off into depression and decide to never drive an automobile again, or you can reject those negative and untrue words. You may even want to say to yourself, "No, I am not a moron or an idiot. I just wasn't watching what I was doing. I do need to be more observant while driving but I reject those negative words. I choose not to accept them as true."

When sports teams gather on their little battlefield to do battle there is often what is referred to as "trash talk"—words designed to inhibit, offend, or demoralize the opposing team. Sometimes it can come from the fans in the stands. It is not new. Goliath taunted the Israelites in the valley of Elah for forty days with trash talk, defying the God of Israel. It was only when David showed up that the words were turned around. David spoke the truth from confidence. You know the end result. But many of us today will listen to the negatives that come against us and fold up our tents and go home in defeat. We must learn to recognize and reject negative words.

The Bible predicts that in the last days "men's hearts will fail them because of fear." How much we need a sure word of promise imbedded and engraved in our hearts. How we need the truth! How we need to stand up and reject the negative and untrue word that comes against us. Words are powerful but we have the ability and authority to reject them and deflect them if need be.

Learn To Use The Tools!

I have learned through the years of working with wood and shop tools that there is usually a tool for every need. Tools are designed to do specific things. A hammer cannot do what a sharp chisel can do and vice versa. If they are used improperly a devastating result can ensue.

I was out in the shop one day working on a project. I got in a hurry and decided to just use a flathead screwdriver instead of a sharp chisel. The end result was that I damaged the screwdriver by pounding on it with the hammer and the piece I was working on looked like…a screwdriver had been hammered into it instead of a sharp chisel! We have to use tools in an appropriate way or we will have a mess.

There are two "psycho tools" that we have at our disposal in dealing with positive word dynamics that are very important. Let me explain.

There is a concept or definition in Psychiatry or Psychology circles with which I hesitate to be associated. It is the concept of *suggestion* or *autosuggestion*. To me it smacks of metaphysical or mental manipulation by secular mind scientists.

The dictionary describes *suggestion* as "The sequential thought process by which one idea or concept leads to another. The psychological process by which an idea is induced in or adopted without argument, command, or coercion."

Autosuggestion is described as, "The process by which a person promotes self-acceptance of an opinion, belief, or plan of action: self-hypnosis."

I understand the concept of suggestion and autosuggestion. I see the parallels in regard to the concepts I am trying to get across in the theme before us. But, allow me to coin a concept that does not smack of the mind science jargon. How about *implantation* and *autoimplantation*!

The concept of *implantation* will describe the work of impregnating our heart with a word, say from the Scriptures or from the Holy Spirit's impressions. *Autoimplantation* will refer to the self-imposed implantations, hopefully orchestrated by the Holy Spirit, and based on the Word of God as well.

I am convinced that by the proper use of Biblical, spiritual, autoimplantation we can overcome great obstacles and do wonderful things. Habits can be broken and changed. Life can take on new meaning.

While locked away in prison, the Apostle Paul said, "I can do everything through him who gives me strength" (Philippians 4:13, NIV), and "I have received full payment and even more; I am amply supplied..." (Philippians 4:18, NIV).

Then he told the Philippians, "And my God will meet all your needs according to his glorious riches in Christ Jesus" (Philippians 4:19, NIV).

These statements are what mind scientists call *suggestions* and what we are calling *implantations*. Those statements directed toward himself as in Philippians 4:13 and 18 would be called *autosuggestions* or self-directed suggestions—*autoimplantations*. The statement directed toward the Philippian church in verse 19 would be simply a *suggestion* or *implantation*.

There is power in suggestion and autosuggestion—implantation and autoimplantation. They can be tools for good or evil. Parents can use them for good or ill toward their children. Cult leaders can use them to brainwash their followers. You can use them on others. You can apply them to yourself.

Autoimplantation can be used to banish fear or worry. Or, unwittingly, we can use it to bring such negatives into our life that we can experience sickness, poverty, and death.

What we are today, and even what we have and what we do, are a result of permitted impressions of the heart that are being expressed. We cannot avoid head and heart implantations.

Manipulating The Heart With A Starter Word

Most automobiles have an electrical starter motor. It is about the size of a loaf of bread and operates from your battery. When you turn the key to your car the starter turns a gear, which, in turn, connects to a larger gear that turns your engine's crankshaft. This begins a sequential movement of pistons and a firing of sparkplugs which causes the engine to run.

One day my starter went out. Let me assure you that your engine is not going to start without that little device. So, I went to the parts store and bought a new one but it was the wrong one. My engine was still dead. I returned and bought another one, had it installed, and was off down the road again. The right starter is very important.

The teaching of Jesus indicates that the spoken word, in connection with the word on the heart, without doubt, produces powerful results (Mark 11: 23, 24). We also know that the Apostle Paul believed this as well, especially in regard to the miracle of salvation.

"But what does it say? 'The word is near you; it is in your mouth and in your heart,' that is, the word of faith we are proclaiming: That if you confess with your mouth, 'Jesus is Lord,' and believe in your heart that God raised him from the dead, you will be saved. For it is with your heart that you believe and are justified, and it is with your mouth that you confess and are saved" (Romans 10:8-10, NIV).

The word of the mouth is the starter motor. The right words, like the right starter motor, are important.

You can lift yourself up or bury yourself with words. These words can come from many sources; preachers, philosophers, the Bible, God, Satan, parents, rock music, news media, or from your own mouth. When we allow words to enter into our life we give them opportunity to impregnate our heart.

Words, like human sperm, or vegetable seeds, can implant on the heart. Not all get planted, germinate, take root, or produce. But some do.

You can receive negative words or positive words. God's design is for us to receive positive, life-giving words—His words. He promises that His words produce life.

But what about self-imposed manipulation? Do we have legitimate grounds to mess with our heart? Can we legitimately autoimplant words on our heart? My study indicates that we can and should.

Once a person gets a word from God, he or she can act upon that word from the heart. It is also my contention that we can, with discretion, and discernment, take a *word*, not specifically or immediately tied to the Scriptures and apply it to our heart.

Yes, it is possible to manipulate our heart. We did it all the while we were growing up. We did it during classes at school. We impressed words on our heart while listening to music, reading books, and watching television. We do it every day of our life. The formation of the habits in our life today are the result of words we allowed to impregnate our heart. In a good or bad way we can manipulate the heart with a powerful change agent—words. It is not *if it happens*, it is *how much* and *of what kind!* Hopefully, we will realize our power and begin to manipulate our heart with the Scriptures and by the impressions of the Holy Spirit.

Can We Start With Our Word?

I discovered that Jesus refrained from putting parameters on the subject of asking for things in prayer or autoimplanting words. This is puzzling but obvious. Jesus said, "whatsoever you shall ask in prayer, believing…" and "whosoever." So, to the question of legitimate autoimplantation—yes! Yes, we can impose words upon our heart. Jesus allowed it. He did not hesitate. In fact, He seemed to encourage it. Yet, I must admit that I am not sure if we push our own word toward our heart in hopes that it will line up with God's word or if God is the originator of the desire before we even think of it.

The work of autoimplantation is an important work. You can transform your life and bring things to fruition by the use of autoimplantation. In a way, you are doing something similar to what God did at creation when you speak as though it is while yet it is not and then see it come to pass. But, again, the key for the believer is to autoimplant from God's word. This is different than a wide-open, indiscriminate, "name it and claim it" philosophy or theology.

I feel compelled to point something out here, again. That is, it is interesting to see how conservative Bible believers will tend to isolate this aspect most solely to the act of salvation and not to other areas of life. It seems to be acceptable in two areas; when Jesus performed a miracle, and when a person experiences the new birth. Everything else seems taboo. This, however, is not the restriction of Jesus or the New Testament writers.

Autoimplantation—Conveying Word Pictures

The manipulation of the heart has been a technique picked up on by psychoanalysts of all sorts. Mind science practitioners, hypnotists, preachers and faith healers have all employed the universal principles given by Jesus. As a result, many have fled away in fear as if dangerously approached by snake oil salesmen. But, I think it behooves us, as seekers after truth, to examine this aspect, either for refutation or acceptance.

The questions we want to ask are legitimate. Can we, who believe in Jesus Christ and adhere to Biblical principles, follow this approach and maintain integrity? Did Jesus use it? Are we permitted to employ it?

As I have surveyed the Bible, I must conclude that it is there and that Jesus and the disciples used it. It is even in the Old Testament. But you will not find it defined as a science. You will find it used as a tool. You will find numerous examples of it. You will find outlines to guide you. You will find it summarized; "Have faith in God."

It does not seem to be primary. It is secondary. It is not the most important aspect of our lives. It is a means to an end. Thus, the Bible does not give a scientific outline. But it is there. The closest thing to a formula was Jesus' teachings to the disciples about the withered fig tree and moving mountains.

Wonderful and mysterious results have been documented all over the world because the heart was allowed to be impressed with a suggestion or implantation. But what about autoimplantation or self implantation.

Historically, psychologists, mesmerists, and so-called faith healers have proven that their suggestions to a patient, once received, can produce certain behavioral responses. But again, this is heterosuggestion; suggestion from another.

One does not observe Jesus using autoimplantation; self imposed words. Why? The reason is simple. He didn't need it! He did only that which He saw the Father do (John 5:19). He was not "double-minded" (James 1:8). He always possessed a clean and clear heart. He did not have the same sin-saturated heart hindrances as we possess.

Autoimplantation is valuable to us because we harbor a cluttered heart. We struggle with being double-minded. We don't give a clear impression to our heart. We doubt. We struggle with faith. We harbor unforgiveness. Our prayers don't work.

Self implantation or autoimplantation refers to the process of clearly imprinting the word of a desired result upon your heart. Again, this can be done by an unbeliever or secular minded person as well as by a true follower of Christ. Our goal, as believers, is to line our desire up with the desire of God; our word with the word of God.

Getting A Specific Word

Most of life can be lived on the obvious and literal words of God as contained in the pages of Scripture. But sometimes there arises specific instances in our modern world where we need a word from God on a particular matter that doesn't seem to be readily discernable from the ancient texts of Scripture.

If we are seeking to abide in the obvious Word, God will most likely be inclined to reveal the not so obvious word. But abiding in the obvious Word takes time and energy. It takes discipleship and growth. If we are willing to cooperate, God can and will reveal the specific and not so obvious word.

The Scriptures give us a case in point. The Apostle Paul was on board a ship in a storm at sea. There were no Scriptures that outlined what to do in that specific situation. But because he was abiding in the *general* word, the Holy Spirit was able to implant upon his heart a *specific* word. Therefore, he was able to tell the captain what to do and what would happen. It happened just as he prophesied and lives were spared.

The Scripture says that we don't always know how to pray for a specific word. But the Spirit of God intercedes for us with groanings and words that communicate to God which would not be understood by us in our conscious mind (Romans 8:26-27). God, it seems, has a tendency to help those serious about His word—receiving it or expressing it.

Words Can Make A Difference

Jesus said that, "by our words we shall be justified and by our words we shall be condemned."

It is said that He could, in one place, do no mighty work because of the people's unbelief.

"He could not do any miracles there, except lay his hands on a few sick people and heal them. And he was amazed at their lack of faith" (Mark 6:5,6, NIV).

How was the unbelief of the people manifested? Was it not by their talk; their words?

Maybe it is that nothing much has come from our lives because we have manifested negativism or unbelief by the words we have spoken, even about ourselves, and our circumstances. Or maybe we can look back and see that a resolve was made at some point to accept a challenge. The challenge was engaged and victory ensued. We trace the success back to the *word* we began to live after.

God doesn't even assume that we will be prepared to give ourselves a proper word. So he gives us a model to follow—a model prayer—a success formula. Read Psalms, chapter one, and you will see it. Read God's instruction to the military general in Joshua, chapter one, and you will see it. Hear what Jesus has to say in John, chapter fifteen, and you will discover it. It is all about responding to His word on our heart.

14

Repairing The Damage Of Negative Word Dynamics

The damage done by negative word dynamics is real. I have seen the results in my own life and in the lives of others. Maybe there are some adults who grew up with little or no negative word dynamics in their home, school, or community but I would think the number would be few. In fact, statistics and normal observation tell us that our children are being bombarded with negative and harmful words that crop out in adulthood.

I interviewed two psychologists, both with a Ph.D, specializing in testing children with learning difficulties and applying curriculum for their learning needs. They both told me that the problem of learning difficulties and brain function processing problems has increased and would probably get worse. The cause of the problem, it seems, is multifaceted; parents conceiving children with illicit drug histories, improper nutrition, chemical imbalance, watching television and video games at early growth stages, and a lack of discipline and educational guidance in the home.

Sometimes our brains just function differently. One of our own children was diagnosed with a peculiar processing problem. Another one of our relatives was diagnosed with a processing problem. My wife tutors children, who, when tested properly, are diagnosed with differences in learning and processing. It doesn't mean that they are mentally incompetent or have a low IQ. In fact, many of them have been able to squeeze through the public education system only because they worked harder than most others. Some students can read and comprehend with one reading of a passage. Those with processing problems or eyesight problems may have to read the same material slower and up to a half dozen times to be able to process the information.

I know now that there were intelligent children in my grade school who had learning problems. I remember one boy named Kent, who would try to read in the reading circle every day when we were in the second and third grade, but would break down and start crying. The other boys saw him as a sissy and told him so. The teacher would even speak to him harshly. Kent grew up and was able to overcome the negative word dynamics thrown at him to become a successful adult, but it was not easy. I am sure that he still carries mental baggage and scars from those days in grade school.

Sometimes the brain responds in definitive ways that clinicians have termed *Attention Deficit Disorder* (ADD) and *Attention Deficit Hyperactivity Disorder* (ADHD). I know very little about these disorders but believe that too often chemical medications are applied to them for a quick fix without regard for the cause of the problem, the cure of the problem, or other alternatives for helping alleviate the problem. Chemicals are also insufficient when the child experiences the results of negative word dynamics in his life. I would venture to say that with every ADD or ADHD diagnosis, there is an accompanying negative word dynamic problem.

What I am saying is that most all of us have had, are having, or will have negative word dynamic baggage. It could be from a poor environment or home life. It could be the result of a chemical imbalance or processing problem. It could be because we don't fit in or look the way society says we should look. Most of us, regardless of what causes it, have to face negative word dynamics that come against us sometime in our life. The increased number of plastic surgeries, facelifts, breast implants, and television "makeovers," tell us that society is fighting against the negative word dynamics either from others or when they look in the mirror.

Repairing Damaged Heads And Hearts

An allegorical story is told of a meeting of the devils of hell. It was a strategy session and the issue was how to defeat Christians in their daily living. Many suggestions were given including, casting of suspicion on the Bible and on Jesus, persecution, and infiltrating the ranks of believers. At last, a young demon came up with an idea of systematically planting bits of bad and negative news here and there until discouragement set in. The idea pleased all the devils. They would go forth to discourage and then defeat the beleaguered Christians.

Some call it discouragement. Some call it depression. Some call it having a bad case of the "blues." Some call it burnout. Some say it is brought on by physical changes, chemical imbalances, mental illness, poor eating habits, circumstances of life and even demons. But whatever you call it or wherever it comes from, it is often a problem in our path somewhere along our journey. This problem is a serious one as it strikes at the nerve center of our being—our heart.

"Each of us is a potential target for burnout. Increasingly we find symptoms showing up in ministers, lawyers, physicians, housewives, psychologists, social workers, police officers, parents, computer professionals, nurses, industrial workers, secretaries, counselors, corporate executives, managers, missionaries, teachers, and students. Half the parents in America—according to professor Joseph Procaccini, as well as one of five ministers today—according to an Alban Institute survey—suffer burnout" [Frank Minirth: The Minirth—Meier Clinic, *How To Beat Burnout* (Chicago, IL:Moody Press, 1986), p.17].

We have been under a certain assumption that your subconscious heart is healthy, strong, and in perfect working order. This may not be the case. Just as your body can be damaged or in ill health, so your heart can get damaged, weakened, and in ill health. Without infringing upon the psychiatrists and "shrinks" of our day, let me give the believer in Jesus Christ, a trouble-shooting guide that I have found helpful and rewarding for repairing a damaged heart.

You will notice that I have confined my repair list to "believers in Jesus Christ." There is an obvious reason for this. The Bible is very clear that a person apart from God has a heart that is closed off, in darkness, blind, and unable to hear. Listen to what Paul wrote to the Ephesian believers:

"So I tell you this, and insist on it in the Lord, that you must no longer live as the Gentiles do, in the **futility of their thinking**. They are darkened in their understanding and separated from the life of God because of the ignorance that is in them due to the **hardening of their hearts**" (Ephesians 4:17-18, NIV, bold emphasis mine).

What I am about to say is for believers only. It is for those who have been regenerated; born again by the Spirit of God; blood bought; and made new by Jesus Christ. It is for those who see with inner eyes and hear with inner ears. It is for those whose hearts have been indwelt and touched by God.

Like so many men, I too, experienced somewhat of a "middle-age crisis." Along about the age of thirty-eight I started having feelings about myself that I had not had before. Physically, I could not do what I did at eighteen or even twenty-eight. I would play basketball with the guys only to discover that my body would not coordinate with my mind. In my mind I would be down the court on a fast break only to realize that my body was about ten steps behind. My body was changing before my very eyes. Gray hair was sprouting on my head. My muscle tone was diminishing. I found that it was easy to gain weight and hard to get it off. I had aches and pains that I knew nothing about at eighteen. Add to this the stresses in our modern day of being a responsible father of a large family, a responsible husband, a responsible leader of a group of people, and feelings of discouragement and even depression can set in.

Although I have never actually had "clinical" depression, still I can sympathize, to some degree, with those who suffer with feelings of depression, worthlessness, and despair. Most all of us have touched with this to some degree. Often, it ties directly to negative word dynamics in our life whether real or imagined.

The great preacher, C. H. Spurgeon, of England, said that he had boughts of depression he would not wish upon any human being. He wrote:

"I remember when, like a broken, bruised, and worthless thing, I seemed set aside from Christian service, and from my work for God, which I loved. It seemed to me as though I should never return again to preach the Word; I marveled at how the work of my hands under God would fare, and my spirit was overwhelmed within me. I made diligent search after comfort, but found none; my soul took counsel within herself, and so increased her woes, but no light came."

Hudson Taylor, the great pioneer missionary to China wrote of his trial of sorrow and depression:

"Just at this crisis my dear wife had an attack of cholera from which she rallied with difficulty; and a little one was born and lived only a fortnight....The very evening after the funeral of the baby my precious wife had an attack of syncope, from which she did not fully recover, and early the next morning she too was taken.

An illness of some weeks followed, and how lonesome were the weary hours when confined to my bed; how I missed my dear wife and the little pattering footsteps of the children far away in England now! Perhaps twenty times in the day, as I felt the heart-thirst coming back again, I cried to the Lord...."

Elijah, possibly the greatest and most powerful Old Testament prophet, experienced depression so severe that he fled to the wilderness and sat in a cave. The remarkable thing about his story is that his depression and burnout came immediately after the great miracle of fire consuming the sacrifice in his challenge to the prophets of Baal on Mount Carmel. The fire of God came down and burned up the altar, but a fire of another sort burned up the prophet.

The prophet wasn't alone. He was one of three great men in the Old Testament that prayed to die. The other two were Moses and Jonah. It can happen to the most spiritual of men.

Likewise, the believer in Jesus Christ is not immune to depression, discouragement, and burn-out. Our fast-paced lifestyle makes each of us vulnerable.

Reconditioning Therapy

While I was in college, I was required to read *Man's Search For Meaning* by Dr. Viktor Frankl. Dr. Frankl, from the Viennese school of psychotherapy, was the originator of the concept of *Logotherapy*. He coined the phrase after the Greek word *logos*, which he interprets as *meaning*. His therapy involved helping people find meaning in life. He believed that healing could take place if people had a significant reason for living.

Dr. Frankl's thoughts and therapy have carried weight and held quite a bit of critique through the years because he based his theories on his experience and observations while in the horrors of a Nazi concentration camp. He noticed that the ones who survived in his study were not, necessarily, those who were the biggest, healthiest, or strongest physically, but those who had a reason for living; those who carried hope.

It was interesting that Dr. Frankl used the Greek word *logos* in his concept of logotherapy. I have always translated *logos* as *word*. As we have been stating in this entire work, the proper *word* is absolutely vital for health or supernatural operations. Establishing our life on the right word is the key to survival and success. Not every word therapy is good for us. The word therapy from the Word of God will work best at bringing healing and health.

If what I have been saying about words having an affect upon our lives, and being powerful change agents is true, it makes sense that God's Word can have a therapeutic affect upon us in a special sense. I believe this from experience.

What I discovered, mostly by accident, is that God has placed a particular section of therapeutic word helps in the Bible just for these down times in our life. They are there for many reasons but they are useful and practical for restoring a damaged or depressed heart.

I am referring to the Psalms. This body of 150 songs provides a unique therapy base for heart restoration. Understanding how they work in this matter is important.

First, they are a part of the authorized Word of God. Jesus validated them as legitimate, prophetic, and divine. He quoted from the Psalms.

Secondly, they are messages, or songs, from the heart and for the heart. They have historical and prophetical implications, but they are heart messages originally set to music for even greater penetration into the heart.

Thirdly, the Psalms touch on just about every human emotion and can be relevant for us today.

Fourthly, the pattern of many of the Psalms moves from a low position to a high position. They start off in the pit, where we often find ourselves, and they move to the mountaintop, where we need to be. This is a unique feature that you find nowhere else in the Scriptures. They have *movement* designed to carry you from one place to another.

Fifthly, the Psalms have a *conditioning* characteristic about them. Repetition and meditation in reading the Psalms builds a strong base for our emotions.

Note the success conditioning formula in Psalm 1:

"Blessed is the man who does not walk in the counsel of the wicked or stand in the way of sinners or sit in the seat of mockers. But his delight is in the law of the Lord and on his law he meditates day and night. He is like a tree planted by streams of water, which yields its fruit in season and whose leaf does not wither. Whatever he does prospers" (Psalm 1:1-3, NIV).

Notice in Psalm 13 the movement from despair in verse one: "How long, O Lord? Will you forget me forever? How long will you hide your face from me?" to the positive faith statement of verses 5,6, "But I trust in your unfailing love; my heart rejoices in your salvation. I will sing to the Lord, for he has been good to me."

The movement from pit to pinnacle is an important reconditioning device. As we read this material our heart relates to it in the pit but then follows it up and up until, unaware of what is actually happening, a positive impression is made. This type of therapeutic device is scattered throughout the book of Psalms. Positive faith statements are there as well. Planting them in our mind and heart will do much good.

I remember reading about a well-known Bible scholar from England. It seems that he, too, went off into a deep hole of depression. It was reported that the main remedy in his recovery was his wife reading the Psalms to him every day. He recovered to serve the Lord again.

I know that the Psalms helped me. I believe that they can help you too. Read them again and again. Let them form and transform your thoughts. Some of them will not be readily understood and you may feel that they are unrelated to your situation, but keep reading them and meditating on them daily. You will find that they will be like vitamins to give you strength. God will use them to recondition a worn or damaged heart.

Along with my daily reading of the Psalms I would read from the book of Proverbs. I found that these ancient snippets of wisdom had a timeless characteristic about them. They hold true today and are much needed in marriage, family life, finances, business, and government.

Again, may I stress that we should not only read and memorize them, but we should allow these nuggets of wisdom to settle into our heart for reconditioning purposes. As the Psalms repair and recondition our heart for a relationship with God, so the Proverbs help recondition and repair our mind, heart, and actions in relationship with man. The Proverbs will help condition our heart so that we can discern the word and will of God as we operate in the context of the world.

In the parable of the soils, Jesus intimated that the soil condition was of utmost importance. Seed would not, or could not, take root if the soil had not been conditioned. Most gardeners and farmers know the importance of plowing, cultivating, fertilizing, and conditioning soil before applying seed. It is the same with our heart.

A Commonsense Prescription For A Chaotic World

Stress, pressure, burnout, depression, and lack of inner peace will be around for a long time. They are not going to be relics of the past. In fact, these maladies will increase as we approach the end of time.

"There will be signs in the sun, moon and stars. On the earth, nations will be in anguish and perplexity at the roaring and tossing of the sea. Men will faint from terror, apprehensive of what is coming on the world, for the heavenly bodies will be shaken" (Luke 21:25-26, NIV).

But, for the believer in Jesus Christ, whose foundation word is the Word of God, there is hope. There is a bright spot in our future because we are living by a better *word*.

Oftentimes, when Jesus would heal a desperate soul, He would tell the person, "Your faith has saved you. Go in peace." When He spoke to the wind storm and crashing waves he said, "Peace, be still." He is called the "Prince of Peace."

Jesus said,

"Come to me, all you who are weary and burdened, and I will give you rest. Take my yoke upon you and learn from me, for I am gentle and humble in heart, and you will find rest for your souls" (Matthew 11:28-29, NIV).

The writer of Hebrews says,

"There remains therefore a rest for the people of God" (Hebrews 4:9, NKJV).

Yes, the promises are sure for the people of God. We have hope of rest and peace. We also have the opportunity for balance and harmony now when we operate from the right word.

Dr. Wayne Oates, in his book, *Your Right To Rest*, said:

"Have you ever noticed that the busiest and most active organ in your body as far as physical exertion is concerned is your heart? It beats 70-75 times a minute, varying somewhat in older and very young persons. This amounts to about 36,000,000 beats a year! Yet you must realize that these beats are always happening on an exertion-rest rhythm. The rhythm of the heart is of greatest importance. The heart cycle of rhythm is timed from the end of one heart contraction to the end of the next contraction. The rhythm consists of an exertion and contraction, called the *systole*, and a period of rest, called the *diastole*. In other words, this fearfully and wonderfully made organ rests half the time in rhythm with its exertion phase of the other half of the time. This delicate balance is found in the healthy heart.

The work-rest rhythm of the heart is more than just an analogy, a metaphor, or a parable of the very nature of life itself. Concretely and actually it is a working example of the way life works, the way we were created. We can ignore and desecrate this basic rhythm of rest and work, and we will pay the price for it in disease, disorder, and misery. Or we can attune ourselves to the inherent rhythm of life and reap the benefits of having driven and maintained ourselves according to the design of the Creator and Ruler of life, the everlasting God" [Wayne Oates, *Your Right To Rest* (Philadelphia, PA: The Westminster Press, 1984), p.2].

Maintenance Of The Temple

"Do you not know that your body is a temple of the Holy Spirit, who is in you, whom you have received from God? You are not your own; you were bought at a price. Therefore honor God with your body" (1 Corinthians 6:19-20, NIV).

The body is important. It houses the most important aspect of our being; our heart. Jesus taught that the physical was secondary in importance even though He went around healing all manner of sicknesses. Thus, we must emphasize the inward, spiritual without neglecting the outward, physical.

There is a huge emphasis on the physical today and more information on diet, exercise, and health than ever before. But what we need is a common sense approach to connecting physical health and spiritual health. After all, is it not spurious for us to think that we can abuse our body, neglect our health, not eat properly, become couch potatoes, forget exercise, remain over-weight, then pray for a miracle of healing when something goes wrong? We get close to mocking our Maker when we do this.

The "Psyche" Key

There are two spheres in which we operate; the *psyche* (mind, soul, heart) and the *soma* (physical body). "Psychosomatic" is a term, for example, which refers to physical ailments or bodily ills brought on by the mind or way of thinking. Most all of our study in this material has dealt with the psyche and how it operates, especially, our heart. We will not deal much with it here.

Nevertheless, our way of thinking is a definite key in gaining physical health. If your thinking is not healthy, your body will suffer as well. We have already shown how that our positive or negative thoughts affect us. We know that stresses of mind and emotional negativism can trigger certain glands and poisons that cause bodily disturbance. What we think and how we think affects us physically.

The body is fed by food that travels by way of a complex blood system. The psyche is fed by words (external, internal, dreams, thoughts) that travel by way of a complex spiritual/electrical system. If you allow poison words to enter your psyche or you allow poison food to enter your body you will get sick and can even die.

What you think affects your physical health. If you think positive, health, hope, love, faith, and magnanimous thoughts you will have a foot up on good health. If you think negative, sick, despair, hate, fear, and diminishing thoughts you will be aiding ill health.

As I have tried to state previously, you can begin to take control of your life by force-feeding your psyche or implanting words on your heart. Begin to say it and speak it even if it is not a true reality in your physical, outward, experience. Say it anyway. Force-feed your soul with God's words. Read the psalms over and over again. Read the gospels again and again to get the life and works of Jesus planted in your mind. Just as your body is to be fed good food for good health, so you are to feed your psyche—your head and your heart—good word food for good health. The health of your physical body begins here. "As a man thinketh, so is he" (Proverbs 23:7).

The "Soma" Key

As the psyche is fed by words that travel a complex spiritual/electrical circuit so the body, or *soma*, is fed by food that travels a complex blood circuit. Your health is dependent to a great degree upon what you eat; what you put into your bloodstream. Thus, we need to deal with some practical aspects of the body. Again, I approach this, not from a medical or even scientific standpoint or make claims based in this regard except where I can quote an authority. My approach is a practical, Biblical, and experiential approach.

Sometime back I decided to take a look at the exercise program of Jesus. It was simple; He walked. The lack of walking has become a curse on our motor driven society. We have become flabby couch potatoes here in the United States. Or, we have gone insane over exercise equipment. I believe that walking could, very well be, the best form of consistent exercise.

While I attended seminary during the seventies, Dr. Kenneth Cooper and his clinic in Dallas, became world famous for the concept of jogging to improve one's cardiovascular performance. Twenty-five years later, and about the same time I was deciding that walking was best for me, they came out with a new report. The report stated that there was as much or more benefit in proper walking as there was in jogging. Walking was also less stressful on joints and cartilage than jogging.

Walking should be long enough and fast enough that it gets the lungs to breathing and the heart pumping. It is also good to walk or exercise until you perspire. In so doing, you clean the lungs, circulate the blood that carries food and oxygen to all parts of the body, and you clean poisons out of your system through the sweat glands. It should be done regularly. Our body needs other forms of exercise, as well, if for no other reason than to burn the poisons and toxins out of our muscles. A government report came out in the spring of 2002 showing that seven out of ten adults had no regular exercise routine. If we really believe that our bodies, as believers in Jesus, are the "temple of the Holy Spirit," we should seriously consider the temple's upkeep! It is a poor witness and a contrary "word" to let our soma or our psyche go to pot.

We not only need proper exercise to prevent atrophy but we need various forms of rest to prevent burnout. We need the long periods of rest each night that we get from sleep. We need to get away on a good vacation and rest our minds from everyday stresses. A good vacation is one that allows your heart rate and blood pressure to subside, and your electrical nerve circuit to calm down. It may take the first few days of a good vacation to begin to unwind.

God established a six day work week with a day of rest, reflection, and worship. He made this one of His Ten Commandments. When Israel failed to keep this commandment, they were punished by being defeated and held captive by a foreign nation for the same length of time they had violated the command. God takes this concept seriously.

How we have violated this command today! I can remember as a boy when all the businesses would close up on Saturday evening and not open until Monday morning. There was even an ordinance, called a "Blue Law," for this very purpose. Now, one of the busiest shopping days is Sunday. I am amazed when I drive by the malls on Sunday and see the parking lots full of cars and busy shoppers. Sunday has also become a big sports day with spectators filling the stands for huge sporting events.

Can we be in line for a judgment from God? It is possible. Every time we think we know best and exchange our word for the undeniable Word of God, we are in for trouble. Man was not made to run without rest, reflection, and response to His maker.

If you don't want to take the clear admonition from Scripture, there are a host of books and seminars out there that will help you get back on track and avoid depression or burnout.

The Minirth-Meier Clinic gives seven principles for escaping burnout:

1. Use time wisely.
2. Keep priorities straight
3. Relax more.
4. Realize I am someone in Christ.
5. Watch perfectionistic tendencies.
6. Look at the true meaning of life.
7. If truly suicidal, make immediate arrangements for hospitalization [Frank Minirth: The Minirth—Meier Clinic, *How To Beat Burnout*, p.17].

Some people have a heart wreck and never recover. But for the believer in Jesus Christ, there is hope. Even Isaiah made it plain.

"You will keep in perfect peace him whose mind is steadfast, because he trusts in you. Trust in the Lord forever, for the Lord, the Lord, is the Rock eternal" (Isaiah 26:3-4, NIV).

15

Power Principles And Positive Word Dynamics

Coach Dillard used to give us pep talks. I still remember some of his snippets of wisdom. One of which was designed to enforce the *never give up concept*; "winners never quit—quitters never win."

The saying could be applied to many areas of life, including the spiritual life. I am not talking about earning our way into heaven or earning salvation. Salvation is offered as a free gift in the finished work of Jesus Christ. Our benefit is a result of His work and effort. But, is there effort in the spiritual life of a believer after the initial decision to accept Jesus Christ? Is there an effort in living the Christian life? Is there effort in getting a word on our heart and acting upon this word by faith? Absolutely!

As in any area of life, there are pointers and techniques that we can use to gain an advantage. This is why we go to school. This is why we work with someone in a mentoring program. This is why we buy books and *how to* manuals on everything from raising earthworms for fun and profit to investing in the stock market. If we learn the secrets or techniques we can prosper better and quicker with less effort. It is the same in the Christian experience. The Bible calls it *discipleship*.

In the next few pages I am going to give you some tried and true tips on *how to* get a word on your heart and *how to* act on it by faith. These are simple but powerful tips that I wish someone had shared with me in the beginning of my pilgrimage.

Focusing The Vision

The Word of God forbade the followers of Jehoveh from consorting with *psychics, seers, or fortune tellers* for visionary purposes. I would say the same thing to those today who call the *Psychic Hotline* to get a *reading*. Leave the psychics alone!

But, in a good sense, the concept of having a dream or *seeing* a desire in one's heart is an excellent thing. God wants to grant us the desires of our heart. But we have a part to play. That is, we must focus upon the desire, goal, or dream.

Focus will not happen if there is not an object, a desire, an imagination, a dream, or a word with which we connect. Mental visualization and other sensory perception is very important. Jesus said, "If you believe in your heart and doubt not." How can one *see* in the heart without visualizing mentally?

Did you ever wonder why God established a tabernacle in the Old Testament days with colored tapestry, gold articles, cherubim, altars of brass, altars of gold, and an object called the *Ark of the Covenant*? Maybe it is the same reason he forbade idols and images of foreign gods. What we look at and worship every day becomes imprinted upon our heart and then only a belief step away from materialization. Why do you think God gave us five ways of sensing our material world? Image, pictures, forms, smell, design, sound, and even taste affect us mentally. Why do you think that advertisers spend billions of dollars on beautiful artwork, ads, and commercials? They are in the heart imaging business!

Walk into a teenager's bedroom and look around. What they listen to on the radio and CD player and what they have in the way of posters constantly before them on the walls is what is being imprinted on their heart. The lyrics of music are really three minute sermons or messages oiled with musical notes designed to slip into the subconscious heart.

Walk into someone's home. The magazines lying around are usually what is being envisioned and imprinted on their heart. A lady's home decor will reflect the magazines she reads and the associations she maintains. If she reads *Southern Living* or *House Beautiful* or *Home and Garden* she will reflect that imaged decor in her own home.

If the man is a hunter you will usually find *Field and Stream, Guns and Ammo*, or hunter equipment catalogs. If the man is interested in automobiles or motorcycles you will usually find magazines that reflect the same in his heart.

But instead of letting someone else impress a vision or image upon your heart, you can begin to take the initiative and work it for your best interest. Jesus told us to do this very thing (Mark 11:24). He told us to believe in our heart. And His emphasis was not on limiting our desire.

Begin to visualize your desire. The secret is seeing it in your heart before you have it in your hand. Most people want to see it in their hand first. But it does not work that way. Keep that desired image before you. This is the first step and will often find its fulfillment in time. Remember, Jesus put no boundaries upon it and said, "What things soever ye desire."

I used to think that words or phrases were enough. But the subconscious heart more readily responds to images and pictures. It does not have to process pictures as it does words. Thus, it is easier to imprint images. If you write a word or hear a word you process an image, not a word. If someone says, "bird," your mind does not think of the letters b-i-r-d, unless you are studying a foreign language and don't know the vocabulary. Your mind naturally races to relate to a bird image—a picture of a bluebird or an eagle in flight. When a child first learns to read it is usually by picture association. There are many foreign language courses that use picture association to teach the language and vocabulary. Our heart more easily reads a word picture.

Our oldest son used to tape a card to the dash or visor of his car and on his bathroom mirror with his book sales goals. I wonder if this had anything to do with him becoming one of the top salesmen and recruiters for the Southwestern Company? I wonder if it had anything to do with him reaching record-breaking sales goals? I wonder if it had anything to do with him being inducted into the company's Hall of Fame? What do you think?

If you don't ever begin to visualize and believe your desires they probably will fizzle. But when you focus in on a desire, concentrate on it day and night, come to the place of believing its materialization, you are stimulating other powerful and helpful elements.

Like the natural mind scientists, we too agree, that focus and concentration upon a desire has power. The Psalmist said it thusly:

"Trust in the Lord and do good.... Delight yourself in the Lord and he will give you the desires of your heart. Commit your way to the Lord; trust in him and he will do this" (Psalm 37:3-5, NIV).

God told Joshua, the Israelite General,

"...do not turn from it (His word) to the right or to the left, that you may be successful wherever you go. Do not let this Book of the Law depart from your mouth; meditate on it day and night, so that you may be careful to do everything written in it. Then you will be prosperous and successful" (Joshua 1:7-8, NIV, parentheses mine).

Again, Jesus said:

"Therefore I tell you, whatever you ask for in prayer, believe that you have received it, and it will be yours" (Mark 11:24, NIV).

Notice all the common words and phrases for concentration: "commit," "trust," "do not turn from it," "meditate on it day and night," "believe that you have received it and it will be yours."

As we mentioned before, the heart is a receptor. Words or images are impressed upon it. It is most often safe to say that if you can capture and hold, in clear focus, a desire upon your heart, a desire image in clear fashion, for a long enough period of time, without doubt, it is likely to materialize in the real world. I believe that this was exactly what Jesus was referring to in Mark 11:24: "…believe that you have received it, and it will be yours."

Can you define your dreams, goals, and heart desires in a succinct fashion? Are they clear or do you vacillate from day to day? Have you come to a clear faith-focus concentration that believes within your heart before you see it in material form?

When you begin daily to make this desire a part of your life—when you live with it night and day—when you begin to see it and believe it before you have it in hand—you have just connected with a powerful tool for fulfillment.

The Simple Power Of Persistence

It seems to me that *persistence* could be one of the most important concepts for seeing the fruit of a vision or desire. Persistence is a practical tool that can be used to achieve goals. Even if you do not possess much faith (or so you think), through persistence, faith will be brought to the surface and exposed. It doesn't take a genius to have persistence. Anyone can determine to set a course, stick with it, and see marvelous results.

The Bible gives several illustrations of persistence—most of them in the context of prayer or in the experience of those seeking after a heart's desire.

Abraham persisted in his petition in regard to the destruction of Sodom. Jacob persisted in wrestling with the angel. He told the angel, "I will not let you go until you bless me." The angel blessed him! The prophets persisted in their praying for their people. Elijah, the Old Testament prophet, fell on his face and prayed seven times for a rain cloud to come. It came. Jesus told the parable of a man who came at midnight knocking on his friend's door seeking bread for guests. The neighbor gave in to the man's persistence. Jesus spoke of a little diminutive widow who kept pleading her case before an unjust and wicked judge until she wore him down and he granted her request. Then there was the Canaanite lady that kept following Jesus, persistently looking to him for aid. She got it. Jesus marveled also at those men who persisted in tearing off the roof of a house to let their invalid buddy down to Him for healing. Or consider the woman with an issue of blood who persistently crawled through the crowd to touch the hem of His garment.

These all had the common denominator of persistence which manifested true faith from the heart. They all succeeded.

Texas Christian University told my wife that there were no more scholarships available. Since both of us were in school and living on a meager income, this scholarship became essential if she was to stay in school. But, persistently, she continued knocking on the Dean's office door until she not only won a full scholarship but a job in the Dean's office!

The persistent dripping of water droplets can wear away stone. The persistence of anyone toward anything can achieve marvelous results. When it is employed in our equation it carries a double blessing from God.

One will notice also that persistence is on man's side of the equation. This, again, strikes against the notion of those who want to disavow what we teach. One just cannot lay this whole issue on the sovereignty of God. It is obvious that man has a part to play in God's scheme of things.

"Ask and it will be given to you; seek and you will find; knock and the door will be opened to you. For everyone who asks receives; he who seeks finds; and to him who knocks, the door will be opened" (Jesus, Luke 11:9-10, NIV).

Jesus made these statements in the context of prayer. They were recorded in two gospels. They must have been important for Jesus not only to make the statements, but to also illustrate them with parables and truths from everyday life.

There is a negative and positive, a right and wrong approach, to using persistence. A person can show persistence with a stubborn and belligerent attitude and not be operating in a right way. But, in our basic application, persistence reveals faith. Thus, it attracts God's favor. Faith pleases God (Hebrews 11:6). It also attracts the aid and help of initially unknown sources. It shows forth a focus and concentration necessary for fulfilling dreams. It even implies a predisposition toward some word on the heart. Persistence is a great tool. If you don't understand anything else that we have talked about, please try to understand and use persistence. It will reward you nicely.

The Mystery Of Attraction And Return

There is something that few people can ever tell you and something that God will usually not reveal to you—how it is to be accomplished! I don't really understand why the *how* is left out except that maybe God demands we walk by faith instead of sight. Many times when we have a dream or desire we do not see the help needed to see it materialize. But, so often, I have seen an *attraction* go to work on our behalf when we step out by faith.

My wife and I have been married thirty years. In these years we have purchased four different houses for our family. In each of the first three purchases we did not have a down payment, yet it was provided. In each of the first three purchases we did not know how we were going to pay for it, yet we have seen it come in. The last house we purchased had an even greater story attached to it regarding this mystery. Today we are debt free with no house payment. I attribute much of it to the mystery of attraction and return.

This principle behind the mystery of attraction and return states that when you have a dream or desire, or a word from God on your heart, and you step out by faith, you trigger a mysterious force of attraction. If you stay focused, determined, and persisitent, you will begin to attract to you those persons and things that will aid you in the accomplishment of your goals and desires. I don't understand how or why it works, but it does work. I have read about it, observed it in others, and experienced it in my own life. I have seen it in business, politics, and religion. It has been used for good and for evil. But it is a real entity and surely exists in a universal way. This mystery played a definite part in the purchases of our houses and in many other ventures.

My desire, concentration, and faith toward a goal as a young boy, of being an accomplished basketball player produced a greater benefit. It inspired others around me so that a corporate team goal was envisioned of winning the State Championship. And that is exactly what happened. The *law of attraction and return* was allowed to work.

My desire to establish a gospel radio broadcast to foreign countries was started without any request, plea for help, or begging for funds. In fact, I told my partner that we would tell no one except God. Yet, people who didn't even know of its existence or needs, gave money that allowed us to keep it going. They were attracted for some reason.

One of our sons has remarked several times that doors just seem to open for him—important people just seem to cross his path—circumstances just seem to play in his hand. We have talked about this phenomenon several times. I think it is because he tries to operate by faith from a word on his heart. He takes action with focus and persistence. He doesn't lead a charmed life. He works hard—believes—focuses—persists. Like a magnet, he is drawn to situations and situations are drawn to him.

The writer of Proverbs says: "Without a vision, the people perish."

The word "perish" here means *to be without clothing; naked.*

You will wither up without hope, dreams, desire, or vision. God honors desire and vision because He gets to work with you in the area that most pleases

Him—heart faith! Develop your desire in the proper way and you will set in motion a mysterious law of attraction and return that will provide aid for you in the accomplishment of these goals. Whether God provides it or it just happens, I don't know. I just know it works.

Jesus said: "Give, and it will be given to you. A good measure, pressed down, shaken together and running over, will be poured into your lap. For with the measure you use, it will be measured to you" (Luke 6:38, NIV).

Here again is a universal law. The businessman who gives good product or service will receive profit. The entertainer who gives good performances will usually see another engagement. The mother that gives the second-mile love to her children will probably be blessed by her grandchildren. There are exceptions but the principle usually holds true. On the other hand, if you are greedy, stingy, and selfish you will have only what you can keep temporarily—sometimes less!

When you get God's word on your heart and become a person who believes in His provision and you begin giving as unto Him—you trigger *the law of giving and receiving*. He opens the windows of heaven to you. Notice also how He incorporates *the law of attraction and return* here as well: "…shall men give unto your bosom" (KJV), or "…will be poured into your lap" (NIV).

I take you again to the Old Testament and to the prophet Malachi as God speaks through him to the people of Israel.

"Will a man rob God? Yet you rob me. But you ask, 'How do we rob you?' In tithes and offerings. You are under a curse—the whole nation of you—because you are robbing me. Bring the whole tithe into the storehouse, that there may be food in my house. Test me in this, says the Lord Almighty, and see if I will not throw open the floodgates of heaven and pour out so much blessing that you will not have room enough for it" (Malachi 3:8-10, NIV).

God honors giving, especially in the sense that it is connected to faith. Jesus told the disciples that the little old lady who gave just a few coins would live on in honor because she gave all she had. The implication was that she gave by faith from her heart.

Since my earliest recollections I have been a regular tither (giving 10% to the Lord's work from my salary and income). I remember as a preschool child going to Sunday School and putting coins into an old Welch's Grape jar with a slot in the lid. As an adolescent boy I mowed lawns for the neighbors. I remember tithing from my earnings. My wife and I gave tithes and special offerings when we were living on a meager existence while going to school. My family and I have given more than the tithe through the years. I believe in giving.

Again, I do not consider it coincidence when we purchase four acres by faith, build a family house, live in it for fifteen years, and have someone come along and offer us three times what it is worth on the residential market. Nor do I believe that it is coincidence that we have raised four healthy and prosperous children. Neither do I believe that it is coincidence that monies have been provided for every mission trip or endeavor I have ever undertaken. I tend to think that these results are the evidence of the principles I have been telling you about! The *law of giving and receiving* works because it is one of God's laws. As such, it is not only valuable for the here and now, but for eternity. You can't out give God!

I have always marveled at the down-and-outer, the homeless, the person who can't make ends meet, the one always behind in payments, the bankrupt person. There have been many beggars through the years who have come to me personally or to our church door for a handout. In questioning them a little, I have discovered that in nearly every single case, they had not been *giving*. They had violated one of God's most basic laws—*the law of giving*.

One of my favorite Old Testament promises goes as follows,

"The steps of a good man are ordered by the Lord: and he delighteth in his way. Though he fall, he shall not be utterly cast down: for the Lord upholdeth him with his hand. I have been young, and now am old; yet have I not seen the righteous forsaken, nor his seed begging bread. He is ever merciful, and lendeth; and his seed is blessed" (Psalm 37:23-26).

Jesus said: "But seek first his kingdom and his righteousness, and all these things will be given to you as well" (Matthew 6:33, NIV).

You must have your priorities straight if you want the full blessing of God. But try this law. Prove God with it!

"Test me in this, says the Lord Almighty, and see if I will not throw open the floodgates of heaven and pour out so much blessing that you will not have room enough for it."

"Don't be deceived, my dear brothers. Every good and perfect gift is from above, coming down from the Father of the heavenly lights, who does not change like shifting shadows" (James 1:16-17, NIV).

The Importance Of A Spiritual Journal

Do you think that NASA scientists just one day went out to a warehouse and built a moon rocket? It took years of combined goals, dreams, plans, calculations, notes, trial and error, and the application of WORDS—positive word dynamics. Men went to the moon on the basis of some word or words. Edison brought us the light bulb based upon a word. Henry Ford produced the automobile in assembly line fashion as a result of a word or words. I can guarantee you that they did not just go out on a whim or a fancy and make these things happen. They kept notes, records, test results, documents, and goal charts. They produced on the basis of a word or words.

Best selling books by famous authors have been written about goal setting. I have read some of these and count them worthy of consideration. But the principle is not complicated. Just keep a clearly defined WORD before you. Sing it. Pray it. Proclaim it. Write it. Breathe it. Think it. Meditate on it. Keep it before you until it becomes a part of you. It must become absorbed into your heart without doubt before it will ever produce. You and your heart's desire must become one. Do whatever it takes to keep it before you constantly.

A trucker carrying valuable cargo is required to keep a "log book." An airline pilot is required to keep a "log" of the flight. Those who watched "Star Trek" will remember Captain Kirk beginning the show with "Captain's log…," and then giving a futuristic date and description of some aspect of the journey. The sixty-six books of the Bible are a record; a log of a journey. Yet few people on a once-in-a-lifetime journey are keeping a "log" of that valuable journey. Your life is unique. No one in all of history has lived your life in your allotted time. You should keep a log book.

I don't know when or where or why I started keeping a "spiritual journal" but I have been writing in one for nearly a quarter of a century. It is one of the most valuable files I have in my library. I would encourage anyone to keep one. It is very important. Let me tell you why.

After thirty years in full time Christian ministry I can look back over the decades and study my self; my inner thoughts. I can see where I was emotionally and spiritually at a particular time in my life. I can see what I was praying about. I can see answers to prayer. I can observe the burdens or joys I was experiencing at the time. With perfect twenty-twenty hindsight I can examine my start to see how far I have come. I can examine my progress or lack of it. I can see where I have failed or succeeded. I can compare. I can see how God was at work and sometimes what He was trying to accomplish.

No one in the whole world can write a manual for your life. You have to write it as you go along. It is your unique record. A spiritual journal gives valuable insight into your past and into your present life as well.

Everyone has goals. Some just seem to never realize it. Some never define their goals. Some aim at nothing and wind up hitting it!

If you have dreams or goals you also ought to have some way of tracking them, defining them, and even changing them. If you are serious about the teachings of this book, if you want to see dreams come true and wonderful things take place, you need to keep a record. A spiritual journal records your prayer requests, your goals, your dreams, and the "desires of your heart."

I was thumbing through one of my first journals the other day and ran across a section dated August 12, 1974. I was praying for an air conditioner for our hot apartment in Fort Worth, Texas. I was also beseeching God in behalf of my sister. I was praying for God to provide a place of work and monetary income. I was praying generally for our families. In the margin I noted answers to these prayers and the approximate date they were answered.

Do you have specific prayer requests and goals? God is more inclined to answer specific requests—not general ones. Can you go back over twenty-five years and show somebody, on paper, what you were praying for and how God supernaturally answered those prayers? If not, why not?

This is a great way of testifying to the power of God in a practical way. Yet, most people go along on the greatest journey and never keep a "Captain's Log!" If you cannot write your goals down and define them specifically, you probably will not achieve them.

Everything hinges on a word of some kind. A spiritual journal helps you define the word of your heart. It helps you express autographically the words of your heart. It helps you see the words of your heart so that you can adjust them and define them.

It also helps you get a word upon your heart that has not been there. When you see a word that you have written which forms an image in your mind, you are on your way to the fulfillment of that word.

As I just mentioned, in one section from my journal, I was praying specifically for an air-conditioner. Within a matter of days a man gave us two large window units. What if I had not written down the request? Certainly, one does not have to write it down, but it helps. You define specifically, on paper, your desire.

Oftentimes we give up asking and praying just moments before the answer comes. Why? Because we have lumped our request into a general mental pile and we forget about it, we neglect it, we lose heart sight of it, and we don't have a clear way of keeping it before us.

You must be specific! A cloudy, foggy, mind, and heart just will not get it. A double-minded man should not expect a thing! You have not, sometimes, because you can't ask specifically from a word on your heart. A spiritual journal defines the word of your heart and for your heart.

16

Using Powerwords For Personal Success And Blessing

The concepts in this material are about *words*, the *heart*, and *faith action*. Much of the application is universal—anyone can use them with good results. Our desire has been to motivate people to use them in regard to the Kingdom of God and a devotion to Jesus Christ as Lord and Savior. The basic theme has been repeated over and over again. It says, **Get God's word on your heart—Act on this word by faith—You will see a wonderful result.**

Now allow me to introduce to you what I call a *powerword*. This concept involves our theme and has to do with application of a word on our heart, acted on by faith, for practical results. Rather than waiting on some unknown word to fall upon our heart, it is the diligent and determined effort to apply a word to our heart. It is the woman who crawled through the crowd to touch the hem of Jesus' garment. It is the centurion who sought out Jesus to heal his servant. It is the diligence of the Canaanite woman who followed Jesus pleading for Him to heal her demon possessed daughter. It is the determination of Esther to have an audience before the King even if she perish. It is Hannah, pleading her cause before God for a child. It is those people in the parables of Jesus that sought for the desire of their heart; the widow pleading persistently before the unjust judge until he grants her request; the man banging on the door of his neighbor at midnight for bread until he receives it; the man who searches for his lost sheep until he finds it.

The *powerword* concept is about diligently searching for a word and applying that word by faith action to practical situations and needs of life. It is not passive. It is proactive. It is about individual initiative. It is about cooperating with God and the principles Jesus taught for wonderful results.

There are times in our life when we become so desperate that we set our face like flint to a goal and it becomes reality. In most of these cases, whether we realize it or not, we employ a powerword. I have been saying that many of the principles that we connect with for success and blessing are universal in nature. They work for anyone in all sorts of situations. They will even work for the ignorant, uneducated, and immature. But this ought to give us hope and encouragement. Let me give you a page out of my personal life's pilgrimage to drive home the point.

What I Learned As A Boy

My adolescent days were challenging days. I was anemic, sickly, and weak. Yet, like most other teens and pre-teens, I wanted to be accepted by my peers. It seemed that this challenge was always before me.

It came to an embarrassing head one day in gym class. It was the day we were going to be tested on certain physical events. President Kennedy had been promoting physical fitness and the schools were cooperating in supporting the President's program.

We all formed a line in the gym that day in front of Coach Dillard, the school's only coach. Standing in front of us was also a crude support with a bar going across for doing pull-ups. Coach Dillard was going to test us on how many pull-ups we could do. When I realized what we were going to do, I headed for the end of the line. I was so skinny and weak that I was afraid that I would not be able to even hang on to the bar, much less, do an actual pull-up.

The boys jumped up, one at a time, grabbed the bar, and did as many pull-ups as possible in front of the coach who recorded the number. Finally, the line disappeared and it was just me and a little red-headed boy named Johnny.

Johnny worked with his family on a goat-milk farm, milked goats, and did chores every day. He was little but strong. He jumped up and began to do pull-ups like someone eating ice cream and cookies—no problem! Finally, Coach Dillard, in his usual gruff voice said, "That's enough." Johnny jumped down and left with a smile. Then it was my turn.

I dreaded it but had to do it. I jumped up and grabbed the bar. The friction began to burn the palms of my hands. My fingers began to slip. I began to try to do a pull-up—just one. Everyone else had done several but my goal was one. I struggled, strained, and grunted. My arms were quivering and the sweat had popped out on my forehead. But, try as I might, I could not do even one. My chin almost touched the bar, but I could not pull up over the bar. I dropped to the floor. Coach Dillard just shook his head with disgust. Several of the other boys snickered. I was ashamed.

I went home that afternoon and went to my room. I took out my comic books, got up on my bed and began to try to distract myself from the hurt and humiliation in gym class. One of the comics was turned on its face. On the back were several advertisements. There were ads for ant farms, X-ray glasses, and one that caught my eye—it was the, now famous, Charles Atlas, body-building ad. The ad showed a bully kicking sand on a ninety pound weakling and a swimsuit clad muscle man named Charles Atlas. He was advertising his body-building technique of isometric tension exercises. I was captivated because the skinny weakling was me! Charles Atlas was the image I wanted to be.

It was that night that I made a commitment—to myself and to God. I asked for God's help that night. Whether He burned a word desire into my heart or not—I am not sure. All I know is that something happened. A word desire, a spark of possibility, a hope came alive in me.

For the next year I would focus on this new word—this new vision and hope of my heart. I would do whatever it took to be stronger and healthier than ever in my life. My goal was to be able to do more pull-ups at next year's test than any of the other boys. I did not realize it at the time, but I had connected with a *powerword*.

I built a pull-up bar and hung it in the oak tree behind our house. I did pull-ups every day. I did push-ups in my bedroom every day. No one, not even the school, had any barbells or weights so I made me a barbell out of a pipe and two coffee cans filled with concrete. I lifted them every day. I tried to cut down on candy bars and colas. I started to get stronger.

At night I would rehearse my dream, desire, and goal in my head. I would pray for God's help. I would go to sleep with this word emblazoned in my head and on my heart.

The next year rolled around. Coach Dillard set up his pull-up bar and the boys lined up. I got in the back of the line again. This time I had a smile on my face and faith in my heart instead of fear. The line dwindled. Johnny was in front of me again. And again, he did so many that the coach finally grumbled, "That's enough." Then it was my turn.

With confidence and poise I leaped to the bar, firmed my grip, and began doing pull-ups. I did as many as Johnny had done and one more for good measure. No one really knows how many Johnny could have completed but it didn't matter. The look on Coach Dillard's face and the silence of the other boys standing around spoke volumes of victory to a young boy who had acted by faith on a word on his heart and had seen a marvelous result!

Like most of us, I didn't know that I was using a *powerword*. It was not until I looked back from my understanding now that I was able to put the puzzle together. This ought to tell us something. It ought to tell us that it is simple and not complicated. A child can do it.

That reminds me, Jesus said, "I tell you the truth, unless you change and become like little children, you will never enter the kingdom of heaven" (Matthew 18:3, NIV).

Powerwords For Dreams And Goals

I cannot tell you where I stumbled upon this concept of using a *powerword*. Someone once said that "necessity is the mother of invention." Maybe my need cried out so strongly that God had mercy upon me and gave it to me in my early days. For I cannot ever remember reading any positive thinking books or "how to" personal improvement books. One book that made an impact upon my life was the Bible—specifically verses like Psalm 37:4-5:

"Delight yourself also in the LORD, And He shall give you the desires of your heart. Commit your way to the LORD, Trust also in Him, And He shall bring it to pass."

Another book that inspired me was the biography of Bob Cousey; all star hall of fame guard for the world champion Boston Celtics. I remember carrying around a small paperback version of the "rags to riches" story of a boy in humble beginnings who made it big.

The "Cooz," as he would later be known, was a skinny, six foot one inch, one hundred and seventy-five pound kid who grew up in the ghetto of Manhattan's East Side. Through adversity, he plowed his way on up through high school, college, and on into the ranks of the NBA and became a superstar during the 1950's. Though small in stature, compared to the other NBA players, he would, through goal setting and determination achieve greatness and go down as a legend. He was called "Mr. Basketball," and the "Houdini of the Hardwood" and won the admiration of fans everywhere. His story must have inspired me because I applied his goal-achieving, *powerword* technique in my own life.

Basketball was about the only organized sport in the small town where I lived as a boy. It was something the men talked about down at the barber shop. Those who played well were the respected warriors of the town. I dreamed of being a great basketball player. This wasn't easy for a child that had little encouragement about sports. No one in my family had ever played organized school sports. It wasn't easy for a boy that was weak and anemic. It wasn't easy for an adolescent that the coach publicly ridiculed and made jokes about. But it became an obsession. My hurt, anger, and frustration turned into a powerful obsession—a desire from my heart.

The obsession translated on into a goal—a dream—a *powerword*. With the word of hope in my mind and heart I would dedicate myself to hard work and persistence. I would push myself when no one was around. I prayed and dreamed at night. I would take a board and scrape the snow off my dirt court in freezing temperatures in order to practice. In the summer I would come in muddy as the sweat mixed with the dust from my back-yard court. Again, without realizing it, I was operating by a *powerword*. I was activating a word on my heart.

Two years later my team and I would be poised to win the district championship. This was the only way a team in our small town with a population of 625 could get to the State Tournament. And we won! We lost only one regular season game by one point in over-time that year and went on to win the coveted State Championship; something that had been done only once in our school's history. I made "All-State" team honors and "The Most Valuable Player" in the district tournament. I wasn't the greatest player that had ever lived. But everything is relative and I had achieved a dream that had been based upon a *powerword* goal within my little world of "B" school competition.

The fruit of my *powerword* tasted sweet the day our cars rolled into town. People were waiting for us on the outskirts of the town and escorted us in a victory parade into town and around the town square. Horns were honking and people were waving. *Powerword* victories are sweet! My dream had come true. But what is strange is that it was, in a way, almost anti-climactic. For I had seen it years earlier in my backyard, in my mind, and in my heart.

One important element of success is to see it before you see it, hear it before you hear it, and get it before you get it. The old gold prospector is rich while standing outside a dirt hole even though holding only a few dollars worth of gold in his hand because he has the whole mine in his heart! I stood in my back yard and held the championship trophy too,...in my heart. You will know when a prayer has been answered when you stand holding the trophy and, somehow, you are not really surprised!

God answers prayers. He grants us the desires of our heart. Dreams do come true. I confess that I don't know all there is to know about the mystery of the heart or how it works. I just know it works. It worked for me as a boy and as a man. It can work for you too!

Powerwords For Monetary Provisions

Our son had a dream of going to a major college. He worked hard and became a high school honor student. Finally he narrowed the colleges down to one of the best but one of the most expensive schools in the country!

He was accepted and awarded about one half of the total cost for the first year. We continued to fill out papers and to seek after grants. We still had a financial hill to climb. He didn't have the money. Mom and Dad didn't have the money.

One night he came home and we talked (He had been taking my course, incidentally). And we talked about the situation. He mentioned several other choice schools where he could receive a full scholarship. He asked me how a person could know for sure about what school to attend.

I asked him what *word* he had on his heart. He told me that he really had never had any other word than this one school on his heart. My suggestion to him was to forget the rest, pack his bags, and head toward his favorite college, regardless of cost. The key is to get a clear word on your heart and act by faith on that word. He agreed.

The very next day, in an unexpected phone conversation, confirmation came. At that moment an assurance was given that our son would be attending his choice university. The man on the phone told us not to worry that he would see to it that the tuition was covered.

Just like that! A prayer was answered. A word was activated. A word was confirmed. Within days a $10,000 check, without obligation, with no strings attached, was given to apply to the tuition! Call it coincidence if you will. I don't, unless you understand that coincidence is the coinciding of two events—two words coming together in agreement!

We had not asked for money from any human source. We had only prayed and acted upon a word by faith. When the bags started to be packed was the moment the money started to be released!

What is interesting is that just about five days before I was taking my daily walk and prayer time. I had the strangest, warmest, sensation that a prayer had been answered—a word had been confirmed. I sensed that it was something big. I told my wife about it and my associate at the church. I couldn't tell them what it was exactly, yet something had come. I received it in my heart before I received it in my hand. I saw it before I saw it. I heard it before I heard it. I couldn't quite make it out at the time but I knew it had arrived.

When my wife called the office to tell me the great news I was not surprised. I was thankful and rejoicing but not surprised. If you are surprised when it arrives you probably have not previously received it in your heart or you were blind to see it on your heart. I knew that this was that!

It was a joy to see our son graduate from Vanderbilt University because it was the fruit of a word on the heart that had been acted on by faith. We had applied a *powerword*—activated it by faith—a wonderful result ensued.

As I have shared before, you and I have the privilege of sharing in the result of a word. I believe this. But few people seem to understand how practical or important a word can be. Let me show you how it worked for me in regard to house finances.

The entry in my spiritual notebook on April 13, 1993 read, *God will pay off our house note.*

This entry was in regard to the total pay-off of a house note with an amortized balance of nearly $87,000 with eighteen years remaining on an interest-bearing note. It was a faith statement—a goal—a *powerword*.

The entry on March 22, 1995 (two years later) read, *Had warm feeling yesterday while walking dog and praying. It was the sensation that a prayer had been answered!*

Then note the joyous entry on January 1, 1996, *Our house note is paid off!*

Unknown to us, a relative had been setting aside, what was to be inheritance money and had been applying the maximum amount to the house note for the exact time period of the prayer notes! The waiver began the same time as the prayer request was noted.

And again, I do not consider this to be coincidence. Rather, I believe that it is the result of an answer to prayer.

Although I have logged other similar but lesser results, let it be noted that this was a major one. The amount literally waived was about $60,000. If the amortized monthly note had been paid out over the next eighteen years it would have amounted to $190,000! Yet, thirty-two months from the time specific prayer began to be made the answer came.

My spiritual notebook reveals acquisitions ranging from tools, household items, automobiles, medical bill payoffs, houses, physical healings, and money for mission projects. I have physical, documented, and dated evidence, surpassing mere coincidence, that the principles taught herein have validity.

Does God answer prayer? Is this all coincidence? Did a word, a prayer, a specified request have an affect? Remember the definition of coincidence and…you decide!

17

Using Powerwords For Personal Success And Blessing (continued)

It wasn't but about a year after our house note was paid off that a commercial developer came by offering us three times what our property was worth on the residential market. For us, it was a huge sum of money, and an opportunity to move to a nice piece of property and a beautiful house. We were excited at the prospects but there were certain obstacles to overcome first. The process would take about two and a half years. Plans would have to be approved by the County Commission, the City Council, and the Office of Planning and Development. The property would have to be rezoned from agricultural to commercial. It was a long tedious process that wore us all down a bit.

Finally, after two long years, we had worked through all the hurdles except one; a final meeting with the County Commission. The process had seen a couple of failures already including a recommendation by the planning department *not* recommending the development. It was a tense day. The meeting would make or break the project and make or break our chance to sell at commercial value.

That morning, during my regular meeting with our staff, I voiced my concern about the meeting downtown and asked for prayer. I was also asking God to give me a word on which I could pray. Suddenly, a Scripture verse came into my mind that I had not read in a long time. I was able to see it and quote it, which I did for the staff. I had never purposely memorized it and I couldn't even remember where it was found in the Bible. But it said,

"The king's heart is in the hand of the Lord, as the rivers of water: he turneth it whithersoever he will."

I quoted it exactly even getting the "withersoever" of the King James Version in there. It seemed that God was giving me this verse as a *word* on which to pray.

I asked our associate pastor if he knew where it was found in the Bible. He turned right to Proverbs 21:1 and there it was. I had quoted it exactly.

I took this word with me to the meeting down town. I was trusting that God could turn the hearts of those "kings" sitting up there on their little judgment thrones.

Finally they came to our project on the agenda. The engineer from the planning department recommended against it again. Our developer spoke. There were a few questions and comments then a vote was taken. The voice vote was so close that they had to call the roll individually. Our developer and our neighbors were anxiously waiting and praying.

I began to look at each commissioner and pray Proverbs 21:1 toward them. Just as I finished, the roll was called to reveal that the development had barely passed. Was it coincidence that these judges ruled against their own planning engineer in our favor? Or, was it the power of God to change the heart of these rulers as a result of faith on a word?

Fifteen years earlier, as I was clearing this property, I had knelt by a fallen pine tree in prayer. I asked for God's help as I didn't know how we were going to afford to build our house. Then I gave the property and the problem to God. He was faithful to work with us from start to finish.

To me, in my own homespun way, a miracle is the supernatural God intervening into the natural and commonplace world of ours to bring about a marvelous result. Call our experiences miracles or coincidences, I see them as the supernatural and loving God intervening in our natural life and world to reflect glory back unto Himself. It becomes wonderful for us when we find ourselves to be a part or a by-product of the occurrence. In this situation, God had given me a *powerword* to speak and pray. I simply lined up with it by prayer and speech and God was free to turn the king's hearts. But what if I had not sought for a word or activated the word by faith and speech? The vote could easily have gone another direction.

You say, "I don't believe in this word on your heart junk. It is just coincidence!" Maybe so, but I prefer to think that God is more pleased with those who try than those who do not.

Get a word from God. Act on this word by faith. A wonderful result will follow.

Powerwords For Great Adventures

As a boy, I grew up in an isolated village and the small-town atmosphere of north central Arkansas. Seldom did I ever venture out of state. When I entered the ministry I began to dream of going to far away places—Africa, Europe, South America, and the islands of the Caribbean for missionary and evangelistic work.

One day I decided to begin praying specifically for places I wanted to go. I put two huge wall maps up in my office; one of the world and the other of the United States. I would begin to develop a word, a desire, a burden, whatever you want to call it, for a specific place. Then I would pin-point that place. I would look at it every day on the map. I would pray for it, give it as a request to God, and think about it often. Several times a day I would look up from my desk at the place on the map.

Without much effort in seeking outside support, with little money, and mostly by this method I have visited every place I pin-pointed. I have been to Europe, Africa, South America, Canada, and the islands of the Caribbean. I would also begin to pray and seek for a word to speak in regard to these areas and areas of the United States. It developed. Before I knew it, the funds, the plans, and the ability was formed in place for the fulfillment of these dreams.

I have, literally, with my body, and with my voice per radio broadcast, traveled around the world. It began in my study with a desire and a word that became directed toward a specific goal.

My teenage boys and I have had several "great adventures;" everything from starting businesses, boating, and camping. The last one was a trek across the northwest United States, camping in the wilderness, trout fishing in Canada, and hiking into beauty made by the hand of God. When we started *praying* for it we had limited funds, no plane fares, no vehicle, and no equipment. But we approached it by faith and a word. We could not see how it was to be accomplished but we proceeded as if it was going to happen.

An unbelievable plan came together. The *law of attraction* kicked in and a man loaned us his nearly new recreational vehicle. In one place he paid our boat rental expense, motel bill, and food. A wonderful couple heard of the trip and wanted to give my wife and daughter plane tickets. Thus, they were able to meet up with us in Portland for an extended vacation. Other friends wanted us to stay with them in their luxury home overlooking beautiful Gig Harbor. A family that we had never met before in our life insisted that we stay in their new "cabin" with whirlpool bath and luxury accommodations while giving us free guided fishing trips around in the area of Glacier National Park. They even provided free home-cooked meals. It was great. We saw moose, bear, elk, and other game. We camped in the genuine wilderness. We fished in crystal clear water for trout. It was something we had always dreamed of doing.

What I am telling you is this, there is no way that a boy from the hills of Arkansas, and a preacher of modest means, could travel on great adventures or missionary journeys around the world. Yet, it has happened. Each time I started with nothing but a word on my heart that I acted on by faith. Maybe God was released to act in my behalf.

May I challenge you to stop saying "I can't." Rather, start getting your desire out of your heart and on the table. Enable a *powerword*. Certain "laws" will kick in and it will only be a matter of time. Use that time to plan. It can become a reality and you should be ready.

Powerwords For Foreign Missions

I heard a sermon once regarding the story of Abraham, Isaac, and the sacrificial ram (Genesis 22). The preacher brought out that while Abraham and his son were going up one side of the mountain in obedience to God for the purpose of sacrifice, the ram was coming up the other side by obedience. It was only when they met at the top that the physical provision of the sacrifice was fulfilled. The angel held Abraham's hand, pointed to the ram caught in the bush, and the boy's life was spared. It is my contention that the act of faith on the word of God was instrumental in allowing the provision to be released. Abraham was operating by a *powerword* that God had given him previously.

A similar principle was applied once in my life. Some years ago, in one of my pastorates, I was presented with the opportunity to go to Africa on a mission trip. Another pastor who had planned to go for over a year had to cancel at the last minute. I only had a couple of months to raise the money, get the passport, and take the vaccinations.

It was a miracle operation in itself as to how everything fell into place for me. But what I want to tell you about is my friend Charles.

Charles was a young carpenter and member of our church. I had been discipling him in one of our programs. One night while we were out on an evangelistic visit I told him about my plans to go to Africa. For some *strange* reason I felt impressed to ask Charles to go with me.

This was really unusual when you consider that neither one of us had the money to go, and Charles was a quiet personality like me. As far as I know, he was not accustomed to speaking before an audience and had participated very little in the activities of our church.

I was pleasantly surprised when, after a few days, Charles told me he was going. He too, had received a word on his heart and was acting on it by faith.

So we began the process of preparation. Passports were secured. Bags were packed. But the money was short. Not only had I submitted to go at the last minute but I had invited another person to go along which doubled the donations needed. Both of us were forced to act by faith (not conscious or sight).

Finally, my money was secured. But the day of departure was arriving with my friend's account still deficient.

To make a long story short, Charles packed and headed to the airport—still short of money. He kept walking toward the plane by faith.

Literally, at the last minute, Charles was handed the full amount needed for the trip. Unknown to him, an elderly lady had provided his funds for the Africa mission!

Charles ended up preaching the gospel to large crowds while there in Malawi, Africa. He then came back to his hometown, packed his whole family up and headed to the foreign mission field. He has been serving God now for many years as a career missionary in the Middle East.

The point is, he received an unusual word on his heart, and acted on it by faith. God was released to act on his behalf in unseen and unknown ways. He had tapped into God's miracle provision pool; the treasure house of his heart.

A stranger thing about it was that about a year earlier, our music director was joking with Charles and actually said, "Charles, you will probably end up as a missionary in Jordan!" But it certainly turned out to be neither coincidence or joke, but a prophetic *powerword*. Charles became an effective and successful career missionary in…Jordan! Words have power when we act upon them from our heart.

Powerwords For Health And Healing

I know that when someone mentions healing there are those who slam the book closed, pull the shutters, lock the doors and hide. But if we believe in God and in the power of prayer, it seems reasonable that, in some situations, out-of-the-ordinary occurrences can take place. God still can heal people and do marvelous things in our midst. I am not one of those who confines the miracles and mighty acts of God only to the first century. Neither am I one that thinks there is a miracle around every corner for every person.

Years ago I pastored in a little mountain town that had only one doctor and no hospital. The clinic closed in the afternoon and the doctor lived a long way out of town. The hospital was in the next town about thirty minutes away.

This all became critical one night when our first born son was about two years old. For during the night he began to cough and bark like a seal. His trachea began to close off due to an allergic reaction. He began to have difficulty breathing. A fever had also developed and was raging.

Our first reaction was one of fear. Was he going to die? Could we get to the doctor or to the hospital on time?

Then, like a gentle feather floating to the ground, a word landed on my heart. I sensed a strong impression to kneel down, place my hands on my son's head, and pray for the fever to cease.

My first concern as a loving father had manifested itself in fear. But I am glad that I had the sense and the faith to operate differently.

Sharon and I knelt by our son. I placed my hands on his head and prayed. In a matter of minutes the fever subsided, the barking cough quieted, the breathing passage opened and my son drifted off to a restful night of sleep.

Call it coincidence if you like, but I prefer to think that the concepts we have been talking about were applied with good results. I have discovered that when something like this happens that it was often preceded by a *powerword*. The word that I sensed in this situation was a *powerword*. It was a word on my heart acted on by faith with powerful results.

Once I was in a home witnessing the gospel to a family. One of the children kept fidgeting and distracting the mother.

Finally, the mother said, "Oh please excuse my son. His ears are bothering him again."

I asked about his ear problem.

She said, "Oh goodness, we've been to the doctors, taken medicine, had tubes put in his ears and he still gets infections. His ears hurt and are always draining. This drainage runs down the side of his face and neck and really bothers him, especially in front of his classmates at school. I just don't know what to do."

A word, an impression, came on my heart as clear as a verbal word. And I knew it. The word was to put my hands on his ears and pray for healing. Now, I am not normally given to this type of public action and I do not practice openly placing my hands on someone as do the more charismatic types on television. And, I had never done this before. But, it sure seemed to be the clear word on my heart. So, I asked the mother if I could pray for him. She agreed.

I put my hands over the boy's ears and prayed a simple prayer.

Some weeks later I met the mother. She was rejoicing. For the first time, in all her son's life, he had no ear problems. The drainage had stopped. He was not embarrassed at school. We thanked the Lord. It is good when you act by faith on a word given to your heart.

Was it just coincidence? Maybe it was the coinciding and lining up of God's word on my heart and my activation by faith. If so, it was a *powerword*.

Please let me assure you that I do not consider myself a *faith healer*. I have no televised healing services. People are not *slain in the spirit* at my touch. We do not have healing services in our church where people get in line to be healed. I do not consider myself to be anything special. In fact, I often suffer with feelings of failure and inadequacies like everyone else. But one of my main points for this book is that God's word is not discriminating. Anyone can apply the universal principles and Biblical truths. It is true that there are certain spiritual gifts given to the body of Christ, and to certain individuals, along these lines. But, my point is that there are some common principles that anyone can use—especially believers in Jesus Christ.

Sometimes we need to apply a *powerword* to heal ourselves of a bad habit. Many of the problems in our personal lives comes from negative or fear engravings that have been etched on our subconscious hearts. The thing we must do is to erase or cover over the negative fear induced engravings and replace them with positive, God-based, faith-induced etchings. This is not easy and usually takes time and effort. The key principle involves volitionally and continuously suggesting or imprinting to your subconscious heart the new *word* or message.

Habits are simply repeated verbal or outward concepts that have become imprinted upon the fertile soil of the subconscious heart. "I did it out of habit," is the common reply. In other words the heart reflected back into action what the head had habitually and repetitiously suggested to the heart. Thus a habit was *formed*. This same habit can be erased and a new one re-formed in its place. But it may take time and effort.

When you understand how the head and heart work you will be able to break bad habits and form good ones. Simply begin by continuously, daily, imprinting the new *word* to your subconscious heart. Keep notes with you, around your house, at work, and in your automobile with the positive faith statement and desire that you are expecting written in simple statements. If possible, use a Scripture verse as your *powerword* change agent. Daily, and often two or three times a day, read, and repeat the statement. It is a prayer; a desire; a dream; a *word* to imprint. Pray it. Sing it. Think it. Sleep it. Focus on this new *word* until it is imprinted without wavering or doubt upon your subconscious. Ask God to help you. In time it will germinate, grow, and bear fruit. The fruit is the materialization, the actualization, the realization of that which, in the beginning, was only a seed dream. But it got planted. If we will take care of the planting, God will often see to the production.

Dreams and desires originate from the heart or can be applied to the heart. But this does not mean that they will materialize. It is only when we mix them with faith action that they have the potential to become reality. When we line them up with God's will, turn them into a *powerword*, and impress them by faith upon the subconscious heart they take root and eventually have the capability of production. Remember the points of our thesis: Get a word on your heart. Act on this word by faith. A wonderful result will follow.

18

Word Dynamics And Family Concerns

There are certain institutions that have a tremendous impact upon our lives; marriage, the home, school, church, and government. As we look at each one of these we find less than perfect models. Each area has its own set of modern day problems. So often it is the result of building the institution on the wrong word.

We find that our homes are crumbling before our very eyes. The states are starting to pass "same sex marriage laws." Children are growing up without the traditional identity many of us have known. Divorce rates are high. More and more, couples are choosing to live together rather than commit to marriage vows. The home has cracks in its foundation.

Many of the school systems are in trouble. The public school system in the Memphis, Tennessee city system, close to where I live, is constantly in the news. Many of the individual schools are about to be taken over by the state of Tennessee because they do not meet proper standards. We are constantly being taxed with a purpose of helping our children only to see the children failing on test scores. Schools in the adjoining state of Mississippi often come in near the bottom of all schools in the United States. Many children graduate with hardly the ability to read and write. Gang violence is on the rise. Teachers are threatened and have to deal with unruly, rebellious, and even dangerous students in the classroom. Drugs are bought and sold on campuses around the country. Guns are found in backpacks and lockers. The foundation of our schools has cracked.

The church, in general, and the impact it had in the beginning of our country, is losing its power and appeal. Attendance is on the decline. In the post-modern relativistic mindset of our world today, more and more people are feeling less and less of a need for organized religion. Scandals of a sexual or financial matter have driven the wedge even deeper. The church, religious leaders, pastors, and Christians in general are the fodder for jokes on late-night T.V. and sitcoms. The church, as the true body of believers in Christ, has diminished in influence since the days when our country was young and men feared God. In many respects, the church has grown more lethargic, liberal, and licentious. The recent scandals in the Catholic church regarding priests and child abuse have weakened the view many had of Roman Catholicism. Lazy, liberal-minded leaders of most protestant denominations have set missions, evangelism, and the proclamation of the Gospel on a low level of importance and priority. With more and more Biblical ignorance prevailing in the pew, is there any wonder that the church is weak. The foundations have cracked.

The government, at most every level, shows varying degrees of waste and malfeasance. Partisan politics wins the day to keep their man in office regardless of his or her morals or values. The courts of the land have single-handedly become more than interpreters of the law—they now take it upon themselves to create it, overriding the original intent of the constitution. The Judaeo-Christian ethic, that our country was built upon, has taken a back seat. The foundation of our government has ever-widening cracks in moral judgment, organization structure, and meted out justice.

The Powerword Concept And the Family

Dr. James Dobson, the founder of *Focus on the Family*, was the featured speaker at the 2001 Southern Baptist Convention. Dobson, citing George Barna said, "Research is showing that individuals only have a 6 percent chance of accepting Christ once they pass their 18th birthday. If the family collapses, then the soil in which the seed of the gospel is planted will turn acidic."

Dobson went on to say that the latest U.S. Census reveals "the dam has broken" in regards to the family. He said households with unmarried partners have increased 72 percent, single mothers have increased 25 percent, single fathers have increased 62 percent, and for the first time ever, the nuclear family has fallen below 25 percent among all American households. In addition, Dobson noted that 70 percent of all African American children are born out of wedlock.

Dobson described the statistics as shocking but added that most Americans have responded to the news with a yawn and "there's hardly been a peep from Washington."

One report gave the following statistics regarding the absence of fathers.

"The United States is now the world's leader in fatherless families. Tonight, almost 40 percent of America's children will go to sleep in a house where their biological father does not live.

Three out of four teenage suicides occur in households where a parent has been absent, wrote Jean Bethke Elshtain in *The Christian Century*.

Children in disrupted families are nearly twice as likely as those in intact families to drop out of school, according to a research study by Nick Zill of *Child Trends*.

Sixty percent of American rapists, 72 percent of adolescent murderers, and 70 percent of long-term inmates are males who grew up without fathers, according to *Behavioral Sciences and the Law*.

According to former U.S. Attorney General William Barr, the one factor that most closely correlates with crime is not poverty, not employment, and not education. It is the absence of the father in the family (*The National Fatherhood Initiative*).

A recent study published in the *American Journal of Sociology* found a direct statistical link between single parenthood and virtually every major type of crime, including mugging violence against strangers, car theft, and burglary" [*Family Facts* (Birmingham, AL 35259:Alabama Family Alliance, June 1995)].

We live in one of the worst times for the family in America's history. And it seems to be getting worse! What can be done?

I have become burdened in heart and mind as I have contemplated this subject. There are several reasons. First, this malady did not come upon us overnight and it will not go away or subside overnight. Secondly, the fundamental base has been eroded away so that there is little to rebuild upon. Thirdly, the enemies and opposition are so prolific and unrelenting that there seems to be no hope.

Our only hope is to get back to a word in this regard that produces healthy fruit. If the family is to be salvaged as a viable institution, there must be the reestablishing of the Word of God as the basis for structure and function. Not only must we get back to the Word of God as a foundation but the essence of the structure must be promoted and enforced. We must *believe* that God's Word is truth and is the best way for life and health. Otherwise, the corrosion of the wrong word will continue to eat away at this foundational institution.

The shift in thinking must be a drastic repentance—a change of mind with a resultant change of direction. The Biblical family concept must not be seen as archaic and outmoded. It must be seen as the model. We must begin to build on the model given by God.

To put it in practical terms, we must begin to agree (confess) that such things as a father's loving spiritual leadership is paramount, that the mother's role is one of submission and nurturer, that the children are to honor their father and mother in respect. We are to agree with the Word of God that adultery is sin and wrong and is to be avoided. We are to agree and confess that sexuality within the marriage is sacred. We are to promote the Word of God in the home and especially to the children. We are to hold the home and its members in sacred trust.

We have systematically bought into a destructive word that has brought on the disintegration of the home and family. Our only hope is to live by another word. This will not be easy in our society today. But it can be done and there are families that are doing it successfully. It all hangs on a word—the right word. A family will survive only if it builds upon the right word—God's Word.

As a boy, I remember being taught the Bible story where Jesus told about the two men who built houses on different foundations. One man built his house on the sand. The rains and storms came and washed away the foundation and the house came crashing down. The other man built his house upon the rock. The rains and storms came but his house stood.

Notice the word, "built, in the story. Each man, over time, and with expense, built his house. This will be the case if we rebuild the family. It will take time, focus, knowledge, dedication, expense, and determination. Building or rebuilding on the right word is absolutely essential.

Though the television series, *The Waltons*, or *Leave It To Beaver* type families are a vanishing species, there are still families around doing a great job at being a family. And when I say "job," I mean just that. Tough is the soccer mom who can shuttle little uniformed team members, make a hot meal, grocery shop, schedule appointments, and keep the clothes washed in this hectic time of ours. At one time we had four children playing on four different teams at the same time! I know what it is like. I cannot imagine what single parents endure.

But may I make an old fashioned appeal? Let us get back to family pride in a good sense. Begin to put forth a family "word." Build the character of the family name. Let a word about who you are as a family and what you stand for go forth to the community. Build pride in that character word. You will be surprised how many will "read" the word your family name expresses. Fight for one another in a good sense. Brag on your family members. The Scripture says, "A good name is rather to be chosen than silver or gold." A strong family will reflect a strong name and word. Would-be predators will steer clear of a strong family. Proverbs talks about a man who has his quiver full of children will not be afraid to approach the stranger at the gate. There is strength in a family. Why do you think the devil has sought to destroy it?

I read a little wall plaque once that said, "A family that prays together, stays together." How true. Why? Because they are harmonizing around a spiritual word. A word toward a common object has a tendency to galvanize them together. Establish a "family charter"—a powerword by which you live. If it is important for a business corporation to have a corporate charter and by-laws, how much more important is it for a family to have a word to live upon? Maybe this is why many families have gone off course, floundered or ended up shipwrecked. Know at the beginning and beforehand the rules that are established for the marriage relationship, child-rearing, and finances and live by them.

Build together. Set goals together. Work as a team with a united front. In this way, the word of your family testimony will shine like a beacon. Pray for one another daily. Speak a good word about a family member. Make the home a classroom for word development and word expression. When families are disintegrating and falling apart you will have a word of witness for the whole world to observe. Certainly, your family won't be perfect. There is no such thing. But in the genuineness and transparency and reality of it others will see and read your family word.

The Powerword Concept For Marriage

According to the 2000 United States Census data, the nuclear family (father, mother, children) has dropped to less than one fourth of all families in the U.S. for the first time in our history. Over one third of the babies born were born to unmarried mothers. Cohabitation, without being married, rose 1,000 percent from 1960 to 1998.

James Dobson, in his publication, *Focus on the Family*, in light of the 2000 Census results said, "First, they mean that the institution of the family is unraveling at a faster pace than ever. They also indicate that the old taboos against divorce and cohabitation are disappearing, and that the culture is abandoning its commitment to lifelong marriage" [Dr. James Dobson, *Focus on the Family* (8606 Explorer Drive, Colorado Springs, CO 80920: Focus on the Family 2001, Pastor's Edition, August, 2001), vol. 25, p.2].

I read somewhere that the average length of time for marriage today is 9.4 years and that forty to fifty percent of all marriages will end in divorce.

Why the staggering statistics? Again, the marriage union is being built upon a faulty word. As I have stated before, so few couples even seek for a word about who to date or, especially, who to marry. Then "vows," or words, are exchanged but are not kept and a philosophy, or word, of relationship is not kept. The word of emotions, "love," feelings, and Hollywood hype will not make a marriage last. A commitment, based on the Word of God, and His word on our heart, is the only viable base for a strong marriage. God takes vows seriously. They are a covenant between Himself and the marriage partners. When divorce takes place, a covenant is broken, not only between man and wife, but between man, wife, and God. His blessing is not on divorce.

"You weep and wail because he no longer pays attention to your offerings or accepts them with pleasure from your hands. You ask, 'Why?' It is because the Lord is acting as the witness between you and the wife of your youth, because you have broken faith with her, though she is your partner, the wife of your marriage covenant.

Has not the Lord made them one? In flesh and spirit they are his. And why one? Because he was seeking godly offspring. So guard yourself in your spirit, and do not break faith with the wife of your youth.

'I hate divorce,' says the Lord God of Israel....So guard yourself in your spirit, and do not break faith" (Malachi 2:13-16).

The unique thing about marriage in the Christian sense is the binding of three areas with a *word*: body, soul, and spirit. The two become one as they commune physically, soulishly, and with the indwelling Spirit of God. If communication between any one of these three areas breaks down, the relationship will get weak. Hollywood says that the physical part is the most important. The soap operas proclaim it and the toothpaste companies use it. Sex sells! But if that is the major level of communication then divorce is predictable. God intended husband-wife communication to be on multiple levels with the spirit first, the soul second, and the flesh last. The word from Hollywood is that the flesh is first (appearance), the soul is second (emotions, feelings), and the spirit, especially the Spirit of God, is not even considered for the most part.

The marriage partners must connect spiritually. Usually this involves building their life around and upon the Bible. But it also includes prayer. It involves individual spiritual growth and corporate spiritual growth. It involves the Word of God as the hub of their existence as a couple. Take this aspect away and the union is weakened. Young couples must get in the Word and in prayer or the relationship will be in jeopardy as it will be influenced and guided by a wrong word.

The marriage partners must learn to allow the Word of God and prayer with God to temper their soul; their mind, their thinking, their attitude, their emotions, and their desires. In getting their spiritual life on the right word so their soulish part will began to respond to a right word. This will affect such things as fear, selfishness, lust, love, kindness, goals, compassion, and a host of other by-products of our psyche-soul makeup.

The marriage of male and female is a unique combination created by God. The sexual attraction and union is a powerful tool. It is often a complex union as the things that attract the male are not the same as those that stimulate the female. Women and men think differently when it comes to sexual relations. Oftentimes, the husband and wife respond from a previously implanted word, even from a childhood experience, in regard to sex. If it is a wrong word it can cause a host of problems. Both partners should seek to build on a healthy word regarding sex just as they build on a healthy word regarding health, finances, or family.

The three areas of body, soul, and spirit must be built upon a right and good word or there will be cracks in the foundation of the marriage. The cracks could grow so large that divorce ensues. Since nearly half the marriages in the U.S. end in divorce, I must assume that these areas have not been firmly established upon a right and good word—a word from God—God's Word.

Each of these vital areas has its own set of complexities. There are, however, many good resources, books, tapes, and conferences that deal with them. It is not our purpose here to delve deeply into those complexities. But, in reality, the issue is simple when you consider that it is all about a word. Just determine to keep in mind that there is a word involved in the marriage relationship. The charter of the marriage has to do with the vows made at the wedding. The by-laws of the marriage have to do with the individual commitments to various principles by each of the partners. Keep to the charter of the marriage if it is based upon a good word. Keep to the by-laws and principles if they are based on good words. Remember that we respond in certain ways because of a word. Remember that we are building upon some word—receiving some word—giving forth some word. Don't lose track of the word. Work on the word!

Building on the right word is vital for success in any area. Until we decide to get back to and line up with the Word of God, degeneration of the home, the family, marriage, and relationships will continue.

19

Word Dynamics And Family Concerns (continued)

The Powerword Concept For Parenting And Children

Child rearing today is a challenging task. Even in solid homes where both parents are together and trying to live a clean life, the children are bombarded by words from outside sources; television, videos, music, and printed material.

Parents in any situation must be about the constant business of putting forth a right and good word toward the child. These little human sponges will pick up on the slightest discrepancy. They quickly discern if there is a disagreement between parents concerning discipline. They know when a parent is not being real and it affects them.

In a contrasting and positive way they can also *read* the parent's sincerity and love. If a parent will be transparent and genuine before them on a daily basis, the child can learn a good "word" as well. The child is a mobile receiving station. Plant a good word in a child and it will sprout forth with fruit. Children are fertile word gardens. Even a gentle touch communicates in a big way to a child. What a parent says or does not say communicates to a child. The way a parent acts or doesn't act communicates to a child.

The key to child rearing is found in the Bible. In fact, it is the Bible! God told the Israelite parents to teach their children in the home and on the way. They were told to communicate the laws and precepts to the children in every way possible. Just as the home is to be built upon the right word, so a child is to be built upon the right word.

"Train a child in the way he should go, and when he is old he will not turn from it" (Proverbs 22:6, NIV).

In the Book of Deuteronomy, one finds the following admonition repeated in similar fashion, at least three different times:

"And these words which I command you today shall be in your heart. You shall teach them diligently to your children, and shall talk of them when you sit in your house, when you walk by the way, when you lie down, and when you rise up. You shall bind them as a sign on your hand, and they shall be as frontlets between your eyes. You shall write them on the doorposts of your house and on your gates" (Deuteronomy 6:6-9, NKJV).

The impressionable Israelite children were to be exposed to God's Word wherever they turned. "Shall be in your heart" is key as well as the idea of teaching "diligently." Everywhere the child went around the home and family he would come face to face with God's Word. This was God's method for power-word training in the home. Yes, it required repetition and effort. The same effort is expressed in Paul's admonition to fathers in their responsibility toward children in the home.

"And, ye fathers, provoke not your children to wrath: but bring them up in the nurture and admonition of the Lord" (Ephesians 6:4).

The word *nurture* refers to a disciplined training by chastening where needed. The word *admonition* refers to training by words or to catechize in the things of the Lord. The parents were to implant and impress the words of the Lord upon the impressionable children in their care in the home.

Too often I see parents who are neglecting this important role. Parents often speak to children without meaning what they say, or, at least, not backing it up with action. Too often, I see children speaking words to parents and parents obeying! Little children who rule over parents is a sad sight. Who is in control? What is the controlling word? And what are we teaching when we repeat a command over and over again without backing it up? We are putting forth an untrue word. We are teaching the child that our words are not true—that they don't carry weight and power.

Instability in the home is often the result of parents not living by a word. They don't say what they mean and mean what they say. They don't back up their word with action. They lay down laws that are frivolous and unnecessary and aren't upheld. And if a child gets to where they don't really believe the parent when they lay down the law, what happens when the parent tells the child that they love him. Is he to believe this word without having to believe the other word? Why should he be confident when a positive word dynamic is put forth if he has conditioned himself to reject the negative word dynamic as untrue? A stabile home is a confident and truthful word factory producing confident, truthful, and productive citizens. An unstable home has wrong words strewn throughout cluttered minds producing grownups with a lot of baggage.

Teens And Word Dynamics

Teens pose a special challenge in regard to words. The teen years are the adolescent years of transition. In fact, it is a struggle of transition in regard to words. The teen will test the word of the parents, possibly even the Word of God, and the word that was implanted in their heart. Teens will often even begin to use foreign words that identify them to their peers, their culture, or the world around them. They will stretch the word tether that ties them to the old and test the waters of the word outside their previous world. Parents, if they hope to communicate, must understand this dynamic going on inside their teen.

Hopefully, there has been the nurture and admonition of the teen in such a way that the Word of God has been implanted in their heart. The degree that the parents have been successful in implanting the right word will be the degree of tinsel strength inherent in the word-tether. The invisible tether should be one of a solid and good word; a positive word dynamic. It should be strengthened constantly by prayer.

The parent must begin to give the teen space and yet provide limits. Sometimes those limits will only be the limits of an invisible word that was planted on the heart. The teen will be in a testing mode—receiving and rejecting words—understanding and not understanding words—neglecting or emphasizing certain words. A teenager goes through a real word dynamic whirlwind. The parent must learn to let them grow. They are becoming adults. Conscientious parents should be careful in how they put forth a word on their teenager so as not to generate rebellion. Yet the parent must seek God's wisdom to know what word to put out as a guideline or limit. So much is dependant upon what has been implanted before. Parents cannot be negligent in their word implanting responsibilities in the formative childhood days and hope to have any kind of a strong tether when the adolescent struggles begin.

Words are crucial during the teenage years. The teen will often say things that may seem inappropriate in attitude or actual word. The parent may respond to an immature word without realizing they are talking to children changing into adults. Sometimes it is difficult to determine who is speaking; the child, the teen, or an adult. Sometimes the teen doesn't even realize what is transpiring. It makes for a difficult situation because you never quite have a grip.

In college we were required to read a psychology book that dealt with human relationships, especially between family members. The author said that in each of us is a parent, an adult, and a child. The ideal pattern is parent to parent, adult to adult, and child to child. There are sometimes problems when the lines cross. If you have a husband and wife relationship going on and the wife speaks as a parent to the husband as a child, you will have stress and conflict. If you have a child addressing the parent as a child, you will have conflict. The idea of the author's thesis was that we need to talk parallel when the occasion allows for it; parent to parent, child to child, adult to adult. The thesis breaks down when you get into various situations but it does bring home the point that when parents talk to teens they must discern who it is they are talking to; parent, adult, child, or—teen! The teen may say something childish but by the time the parent responds the adolescent may have morphed into an adult or another parent. Then the sparks will fly! Yes, it is a challenge to raise teens.

Negative word dynamics are at their most volatile peak during the teenage years. Parents must be extremely on their toes so as not to launch off into the battlefield of negative gunfire. It can be disastrous. This is excruciating for concerned parents because positive word dynamics are often snubbed. The teen often rejects any positive word dynamic as prudish, old fashioned, or instructionally unnecessary. Sometimes teens give off the impression that the parents don't know much at all. It is all part of their testing the word.

Parents must not give up during these trying days. They can and should continue to speak positive words and pray for their child. The words we speak have power even though it appears that they are not getting through to the teen. Prayer has power if it is real power based upon a good and proper word. It is the invisible tether that connects us to our child.

An old pastor friend of mine told me about his son one day. He said that his son rebelled during the teenage years, left home, and eventually ended up in the army. The son told him later that when he was in the army and ready to go out boozing it up with his buddies or drinking himself into a stupor with alcohol, or having sex with some strange woman, he would remember. The son said that he could travel all the way to the jungles of Viet Nam but couldn't get away from the words of his mother and father. Their word implanted on his heart kept him in tow.

A word that parents must give forth toward their children and especially their teenagers is the word of assurance. The children must hear and feel and know that there is unconditional love and acceptance for them. They must feel and know that the door is always open—that mom and dad will love them no matter what. God is this way. He loves the prodigal unconditionally.

And speaking of the prodigal—in Jesus' story of the prodigal son, it says that when the boy arrived at the end of himself—in the pigpen of life—he "came to himself." He remembered. A word came up inside him that had been planted there years earlier. He remembered, repented, and returned home. There is hope for our children if they have a word of hope to draw upon—a word that we, as parents, have planted in their heart.

I fear that I am sounding repetitious here, and maybe I am, but the key to all of the problems of home, family, marriage, and parenting is bound up in words that are tied to thoughts and expressed in actions. Simply, we have bought in to and built upon a faulty word. Everything hangs upon a word. To correct this, we must build or rebuild upon a right and good word. And that may take time and energy because it must be impressed upon our heart as well as implanted in our head. It is as simple as that and so vital.

The Powerword Concept For Schools And Teachers

Systems, even empires, rise or fall on the basis of a word or philosophy that people build their lives upon. Historically, this can be observed in one of the greatest empires ever established; the Roman Empire. It has been observed that this great empire went through a certain sequence.

Rome, it is said, was built upon ***strong families***. There were high moral standards in the home with the father as the head of the family unit. In the early republic, the father had legal authority to discipline rebellious members of his family. In fact, the parents were responsible for the children's ***education in the home*** and participated closely with them in the process. As a result, Rome experienced ***prosperity;*** national achievements, victorious armies, wealth, prestige, magnificent building programs, roads, and grand public facilities.

But as Roman families prospered, it became fashionable to hire educated Greeks to care for the children. Godless humanism in the Greek philosophy was soon passed on to the Roman families. The family began to disintegrate; illegitimate children, divorce, and open marriages became vogue. ***Social ills*** began to develop. Government became the big god. By the first century A.D. the father had lost his legal authority. It was delegated to the village, then to the city, then to the state, and finally to the empire. In Rome, citizens complained about housing shortages, soaring rents, congested traffic, polluted air, crime in the streets, and the high cost of living. Unemployment was a perennial problem. To solve it, the government created a multitude of civil service jobs, including building inspectors, health inspectors, and tax collectors.

Like any great institution that builds on a wrong word so there came ***decline and persecution.*** The final act of the Roman Empire was to bring great persecution to Christians. Rome was quite tolerant of all religions except Christianity.

Christianity was banned and Christians were persecuted, burned, and thrown to the lions. Why? Because the very nature of Christianity is intolerant of 'the lie' of Satan which is the basis of every other religion and because Christianity represented a contrary word. They were actually trying to stop the word of Christianity—a word which decentralized the city and the Caesar and emphasized the Kingdom of God and the Lordship of Jesus Christ.

A new word (philosophy) was established for the Roman Empire by those in government leadership. Gradually, the generations received this corrupt word and the result is historically obvious.

When we entrust our children to the public school system or even a private school system, we are volunteering our children to become human "word" sponges in that system for twelve, or more, years. What they are taught and how they are taught becomes vitally important as it is the planting of seeds that will crop up in their life for the rest of their days. When bad words are sown, bad fruit will come forth. Society will go the way the generations are taught.

An example of word replacement has recently been observed in our public education policies. For years, since the founding of our nation, children were taught from basic educational tools as the Bible, the McGuffy reader, and by phonics, even in one-room schools or homes.

With twenty-six letters of the alphabet, forty-four phonic (listening) sounds and seventy phonographs, we are able to efficiently and quickly learn a million different words. In the remarkable concept of teaching reading through phonics, educators are telling us that children can learn to read nearly anything, including the newspaper, by the second grade, and illiterate adults can learn to read in two weeks.

I heard Jeanie Eller, who is called the "First Lady of American Literacy," talking about this one day on the local radio station. She pointed out that close to ninety million adults are illiterate and one half to two thirds of children cannot read. This alarming statistic, she said, was due to a change in educational methods during the last generation. Some years ago the "whole language method" was propounded by certain educators who, she claims, were upset with publishers and were trying to cash in on some of the money spent on national education materials. She called it a "fad" and said that three major research groups have done studies to show it to be a "disaster." As a result, twenty-seven state legislatures have forced their state education system to go back to the phonic philosophy. Mrs. Eller proved, on the Oprah Winfrey show, that illiterate adults could be taught to read in two weeks, not the eight years anticipated by the "whole language method." Ask the one-half of the adult population in America, who can't read properly, if a change in a "word" or "philosophy" did not affect their life!

The compounding of this problem comes when the children have learning difficulties. This has become ever more obvious to me as I observe the children that come through my wife's ministry where they are tested and curriculum is applied for their specific needs. The professional curriculum expert that she works with for testing is having more and more people respond for testing and the list is growing. I told him in one of our conversations that I, personally, do not feel that we have seen the tip of the iceberg. The next generation of children will have even more problems. He agreed. And why? We are building on so many wrong words. The computer age coupled with video and audio proliferation has provided a well-greased vehicle for the transport of "word" more than any time in human history. Everything hangs on a word. God help us to reestablish a right word on which to build. Our dear children, and society at large, are going to suffer if we don't make a gallant attempt.

Parents must begin to speak out to the teachers and the local school boards and hold them accountable for the dissemination of a right and good word toward our children. Private schools, as well as public schools, must constantly be held accountable. What is the basic philosophy of the teacher or teachers who have your children? What is being taught in the textbooks? Does the teacher or teacher propound a bias in the class? What is the bias? There is the subject matter in the class and then there are the little snippets slipped in between the lines of the main subject.

I remember going off to a major university and discovering that teachers often try to get across more than the subject matter of the class. I was taking a general English literature class my freshman year at the university. Midway into the semester, the real bias of the homosexual professor began to surface. Every interpretation of his, in every piece of his selected reading requirements, had to do with sex and especially homosexuality. It was difficult to switch classes at midterm. He had caught us and was pounding his biased word into our formative brains.

One of the best positions we can take in regard to education, schools, classes, and teachers is to know that there is an underlying word floating around somewhere that will be the emphasis or basic philosophy. It may not be in any of the handbooks, and the administrators may deny it, but the real word is in there somewhere. Find it!

Secondly, we can go into any educational situation with our eyes wide open. We can be discerning and even cautious. The words of the institution are going to have affect one way or another. The books and materials presented are going to speak with a certain bias.

Thirdly, we can go in on a strong word foundation. As I stated before, I had an antagonistic atheist speech teacher and a homosexual professor as teachers in college but neither of them swayed me because I was founded on a stronger word. I also had an anthropology teacher that taught evolution, but he didn't convert me either. In fact, I reacted to his position so that I was strengthened more toward a Biblical creation model. But many students are going through the education systems with blind naivety and swallowing everything as the truth.

Fourthly, we ought to go through the educational systems with a confident bias toward a right and true word. If we are not sure, we ought to study and compare with Scriptural truth until we are sure. Then, we ought to take a stand for the truth as we become confident of it even if it means being ostracized or persecuted. The first century Christians did it and the same is incumbent upon us. If we do not, how can we be considered "salt," and "light"? Why are we here if not to enlighten as to the truth?

20

Word Dynamics And Church-State Issues

There was a time in our country when separation of church and state was not an issue as it is interpreted today. It is my opinion that the founding fathers intended to keep government out of the church rather than to keep the church out of the government. And when I say "church" I am referring to the Bible, Jesus Christ, and spiritual-Biblical principles for life. For the last several decades there has been an effort to separate society, at large, from the Judaeo-Christian principles our country was founded upon. There has been an effort to make us totally secularistic.

Those who are trying to rewrite our history are actually trying to establish us upon another "word." The *word* and philosophy of secular humanism and post-modern relativism has pervaded our landscape. We have sown the wind and are reaping the whirlwind. We must get back to another word, maybe the word our country was founded upon? Many, however, want to deny the foundational word that has made our country great. But, observe the truth.

The very purpose of the Pilgrims in 1620 was to establish a government based on the Bible. The New England Charter, signed by King James I, confirmed this goal: "...to advance the enlargement of Christian religion, to the glory of God Almighty...."

The Rhode Island Charter of 1683 affirms the Biblical beginnings: "We submit our persons, lives, and estates unto our Lord Jesus Christ, the King of kings and Lord of lords and to all those perfect and most absolute laws of His given us in His Holy Word."

Those "absolute laws" became the basis of our Declaration of Independence. Our national Constitution established a republic upon the 'absolute laws' of the Bible, not a democracy based on the flimsy philosophies of man.

Our nation's fathers have attested to the connection we have with the principles of the Word of God and even Jesus Christ as Savior and Lord.

Noah Webster said, "The religion which has introduced civil liberty is the religion of Christ and His apostles…to this we owe our free constitutions of government.

…The moral principles and precepts contained in the Scriptures ought to form the basis of all our civil constitutions and laws. All the miseries and evils which men suffer from vice, crime, ambition, injustice, oppression, slavery, and war, proceed from their despising or neglecting the precepts contained in the Bible."

Abraham Lincoln said, "All the good from the Savior of the world is communicated through this Book; but for the Book we could not know right from wrong. All the things desirable to man are contained in it."

Not only was the United States of America founded upon the Word of God but upon a relationship with God. Nowhere is this more evident than in the monuments and building of our Capital in Washington D.C. Observe the truth in the following sampling:

1. Every session of the House and the Senate begins with prayer.

2. Each house has its own chaplain.

3. The eighty-third Congress set aside a small room in the Capitol, just off the rotunda, for the private prayer and meditation of members of Congress. The room is always open when Congress is in session, but it is not open to the public. The room's focal point is a stained glass window showing George Washington kneeling in prayer. Behind him is etched these words from Psalm 16:1: "Preserve me, O God, for in Thee do I put my trust."

4. Inside the rotunda is a picture of the Pilgrims about to embark from Holland on the sister ship of the Mayflower, the Speedwell. The ship's revered chaplain, Brewster, who later joined the Mayflower, has open on his lap the Bible. Very clear are the words, "The New Testament according to our Lord and Savior, Jesus Christ." On the sail is the motto of the Pilgrims, "In God We Trust, God With Us."

5. Above the head of the Chief Justice of the Supreme Court are the Ten Commandments, with the great American eagle protecting them.

6. Engraved on the metal cap on the top of the Washington Monument are the words translated, "Praise be to God." Lining the walls of the stairwell are such Biblical phrases as "Search the Scriptures," "Holiness to the Lord," "Train up a child in the way he should go, and when he is old he will not depart from it."

The founding fathers were not shy in recognizing the Bible, the God of our Bible or their dependency upon Him.

1. Ben Franklin called the first Continental Congress to fall upon their knees in prayer.
2. The Picture of Moses was upon the first coin made in America along with "In God We Trust."
3. There are Scriptures on the walls of the Library of Congress.
4. John Adams said, "Our Constitution was made only for a religious and moral people. It is wholly inadequate for the government of any other."
5. Christopher Columbus' "Book of Prophecy," in the British Museum records: "It was the Lord who put in my mind to sail from Spain to the Indies. I could feel His hand upon me. All who heard my project rejected it with laughter and ridicule against me. There is no question that my inspiration to sail came from the Holy Ghost of God, because He comforted me with a ray of illumination from the Holy Scriptures, encouraging me to sail on till I found the country."
6. Lincoln said: "It is the duty of nations, as well as of men, to own their dependence upon the overruling power of God and to recognize the sublime truth announced in the Holy Scriptures and proven by all history, that those nations only are blessed whose God is the Lord."
7. In our pledge of allegiance are the words: "One nation under God...."
8. There is a famous picture of George Washington in the snow at Valley Forge, on his knees praying.

Our nation was, unquestionably, established on the firm foundation of Scripture—on the Word of God and upon an acknowledgment of Jesus as Lord. The most fundamental concepts of the republic find their roots in the Bible. From the beginning, the basis for law and government in American society was decidedly Biblical.

One cannot deny, even though there are those today who are desperately trying to change it, that America bears the stamp of the Bible, Christian influence, and the Judaeo-Christian work ethic. This impact is evident in the leaders chosen, the laws written, and the changes brought about through the transforming power of Christ in individual lives and corporate experience. America was not formed a nation apart from or without consideration for God, but a nation under God.

In my lifetime I have seen people like Madelyn Murray O'Hare attempt to remove "In God we trust" from off our currency. I have watched people endure the lopsided injustices put upon us by the Civil Liberties Union. We have been yelled at by the ungodly extremist to be tolerant of their views when, in fact, they are intolerant of us, perpetuating an anti-Christian, anti-Bible persecution.

We have seen foolish laws passed by men operating in cowardice or greed from a wrong word to the point that bad is seen as good and good as bad, light is seen as darkness and darkness viewed as light. Our value system has been bombed and a subtle secularistic, hedonistic, post-modern relativistic humanism has crept into our society and schools so that we have a defective moral base for decision making. We don't know what is right any more because we have diminished and destroyed the standard by which right was measured.

Writers and editors of our public school books put a negative and lop-sided slant on the material. Recently, on a television documentary, it was reported that in one history book, a paragraph or two was devoted to George Washington but several pages were given to discussing Marilyn Monroe!

The lop-sided thinking is also pictured in the fact that until recently, it was a $25,000 fine and a felony charge for destroying an eagle's egg yet we could legally protect doctors who perform partial birth abortions. We allowed these murderers to puncture the baby's cranial region with a sharp instrument before it completely exited the womb, causing the baby to die on the spot! Not only has our government and elected leaders sanctioned this murder but the doctors who perform the act are paid to do it! The result since Roe v. Wade has been the murder of millions of innocent lives.

The problem has to do with *a word—a wrong word*. The answer has to do with *a word—a right word*. Everything in life hangs on a word. When society presents a word of violence, promiscuity, sexual deviance, and rebellion, they are going to reap the results of that implanted word. It is as simple as that. We have had more than the "sexual revolution" of the sixties. We have had, what the Bible calls "rebellion" against a word and the author of that life word. We are living in the midst of a society that has rebelled against God and His true Word.

It is my passion and great conviction that our government leaders must understand this concept and help us get back to the right word for life and health. The laws of our land are a "word." The "platform" of a particular political party is a "word." The "character" of the man running for office is a "word." The emphasis that office holders give to certain projects sends forth a "word."

I have watched voters promote a particular candidate because of the color of the skin or gender, or because of what personal gain they were going to get out of it in "pork barrel projects." I have seen friends and family members vote for a particular party when the candidate and platform violated a host of Biblical principles. They voted primarily because their family had always voted that party affiliation. We all have a responsibility about what word we promote.

Legislators and lawmakers can help. Pastors, public school teachers, city councilmen, and school board members can help. We must reestablish a right word or we will perish.

I could go on talking about the ills of our nation and society as a result of building on a wrong word. But, surely you are observant of these very same things, regardless of your political, philosophical, or religious bent. Anyone who watches the news and spends any time just thinking can surmise that there is a problem. It is my desire that every able-minded human consider that the fix might just be contained in the concept of a *right word* activated in the *right way*. Again, this is the key: get a right word and act upon it. You have words and the ability to act upon words.

Nations have been toppled because an emperor's lover relayed confidential information that was whispered in her ear in the bed chamber. Words have power. Words represent potential action. Words conjure up images and stimulate our imagination. Words represent thought. Everything hangs on a word.

Most of us are familiar with a compass. It is a basic navigational tool to detect true north. It is used to help find one's way. If you are a camper lost in the woods or a pilot of an airplane caught in a cloud bank, you will value the basic purpose of an accurate compass.

Our world is lost in the woods of wrong words—in the forest of failed philosophy. We need an accurate compass and we need to know how to use it. There is only one in my opinion. His name is Jesus.

Jesus was hauled into judgment before the magistrates. There He gave a somewhat strange response to Pilot.

"Pilate therefore said to Him, 'Are You a king then?' Jesus answered, 'You say rightly that I am a king. For this cause I was born, and for this cause I have come into the world, that I should bear witness to the truth. Everyone who is of the truth hears My voice.'

Pilate said to Him, 'What is truth?' And when he had said this, he went out again to the Jews, and said to them, 'I find no fault in Him at all'" (John 18:37-38, NKJV).

Jesus is here saying that He is the true and accurate compass. His purpose in coming into this world was to point to the truth. And everyone who uses Him as a life compass and follows the point of His needle of truth, will find their way out of the woods of darkness and danger and on to eternal life. It is, again, tied exclusively to Him and to His word.

"Then Jesus said to those Jews who believed Him, 'If you abide in My word, you are My disciples indeed. And you shall know the truth, and the truth shall make you free.'" (John 8:31-32, NKJV).

Jesus claimed that He was the way, the truth, and the life and no one would get safely to the eternal home apart from Him (John 14:6). He proclaimed Himself to be the compass—the direction to Heaven. We will choose to use Him or we will lose our way. We will choose to abide in His word or we will sink helplessly in the world's word. The world's word cannot give ultimate direction because every man's compass is faulty. "All have sinned and fall short of the glory of God." "No man is righteous—no not one." "All we like sheep have gone astray and turned every man to his own way."

I fear that our world has been using the wrong compass whether out of ignorance or rebellion. A wrong directional word has been chosen because it is read from a faulty inaccurate compass. I fear that we are pictured in the last verse of the last chapter of the Book of Judges which is a terrible history of disaster and defeat for the nation of Israel. There we read the haunting refrain: "In those days there was no king in Israel; everyone did what was right in his own eyes." In other words, they had no compass. They followed their own foolish direction and broken moral-spiritual compass.

The Church

The word "church" conjures up different visions for different people. For our founding fathers it may have been the Church of England. For many throughout the world it would be Roman Catholicism. Others may think of the protestant or evangelical church in which they grew up. It may be the high and lofty, stained glass edifice of a cathedral in which they worshipped or a small country church with a wood frame steeple. The concept of "church" is varied.

Biblically speaking there is the universal church of called-out believers in Jesus Christ and the smaller local congregations. The denominations, schisms, cults, and parachurch groups with different Biblical interpretations came later and were man-designed.

So when I speak of "church" I am referring to the true, Biblically-based, called out believers and followers of Jesus Christ. In this body, both local and universal, are essential and non-essential Bible-based doctrine. Essential Christian doctrine is fixed and inflexible. Non-essential Christian doctrine holds varying interpretations by different believers. We can disagree on the non-essentials and still be Christian but we cannot do so with the essential doctrines. Thus, the "church" should be a body of called out believers in Jesus Christ who hold to essential Christian, Bible-based, doctrine, and principles. They should be a Biblical and spiritually purposed people who are living by a word from the Word of God.

Church influence and attendance, in general, is on a decline according to most pollsters. This is a sad commentary if it is applicable to the true church. For the true church is loved by God, purposed by God, and destined by God. The true church is called the "Bride of Christ" who will rule and reign with Him in the Kingdom to come.

So how are we to think about the church today? First one should realize that there is a true church and a false church. The prophetic book of Revelation speaks of this in regard to the end time. Secondly, we should realize that God has established the church. Yes, man has corrupted it but God designed it, has a plan for it, loves it, and is coming to retrieve it out of the earth. Thirdly, we must see that we have a responsibility in the true church which is the body of Christ on the earth. Therefore, we must be associated with some true church fellowship. We should not, as the Scripture says, forsake the assembling of ourselves together. We are to work in this body and through this body regardless of its imperfections.

We are living in a day when there are more churches and more copies of the Scripture than ever before. We have more radios and televisions broadcasting the gospel and Bible teaching than any time in human history. We have more information regarding Bible subjects than one can imagine. Pollsters are predicting that in the next few decades the great majority of people will be relying on the internet for their Biblical or spiritual information. Things are certainly changing.

But even in the changing environment, there are certain things that we must keep in mind. We must not abandon the fellowship of true believers. We must find a "church home" through which we can be fed the truth from the Bible and through which we can serve. Many today don't see the need to participate in a church service or fellowship. Many of those who do attend church are "church hoppers" going from one church venue to the next hoping that the smorgasbord of attractions will be better at the next fellowship. Maybe we should consider "getting a word on our heart" about what God wants us to do? Sometimes, God will lead us to a place were we can be fed and nurtured. Sometimes God may lead us to a place where we do more ministering than being ministered to. But in our self-focused, "me generation" this is not always a consideration. Sometimes people move to a local fellowship because the "kids feel more comfortable there." Sometimes they move because "friends" are there. These may be legitimate reasons but they may not be the best. The best way to move is to get a word from God, regardless of how you feel or what the children desire, and act by faith upon it. I have seen people make tragic mistakes because they did not go by God's directive word or their heart. Find a church that holds to essential Christian doctrine and preaches and teaches the Word of God, a church fellowship that is mission-minded and evangelistically motivated, and expresses the love of Jesus. A good church fellowship is important. You will not find any that are perfect because they are all made up of imperfect people on a journey of faith.

The true church is a body of believers that is involved in God's Word and in His words. We are commissioned to go into all the world preaching and teaching His word with the goal of baptizing and making disciples. (The Great Commission, Matthew 28:19-20). Who else has this responsibility? We have a "word" commission. God desires to use His church first and foremost to dispense His Word and words. Yes, the church is important along with every true member-believer that helps form her body worldwide.

God has established the church and sanctions proper civil government as institutions for our benefit. It is true that throughout history both have been abused and have been abusers. When either have gone wrong it is because of basing their decisions and actions upon a faulty word. Believers should be proactive in trying to steer both back on course to a good and sound word. And you say, "Who am I? I have no influence or voice." This is faulty thinking. Your words have power and influence. You can sow good words and cause change. There have been a host of individuals through history that have changed the course of society and even the world. Martin Luther was just one man, yet when he tacked his ninety-five theses (words!) to the castle church door in 1517, he started a revolution that helped pull the church back on course and the world out of the Dark Ages. And again, his method had to do with words—just words on a piece of paper nailed to the church door. Amazing! Words have power!

21

Word Dynamics And Important Life Decisions

The Bible records that Solomon was given a two-pronged gift from God: wisdom and riches. People and rulers from around the known world came to hear his wisdom. He also amassed great wealth. But, the wisest of all men, a man who knew the anointing of God, a man who was a "success," failed miserably in regard to keeping and doing the word of God on his heart. The Bible records that he deliberately married seven hundred foreign wives and took unto himself three hundred concubines. This was in direct violation of God's command not to intermarry with the heathen nations. As a result, his kingdom was torn in two and a black mark stricken across his legacy.

It is interesting to note that Solomon's problem was a *word* problem and a *heart* problem. The wisest man in the world acted on a right word and wisdom and wealth came to him. The wisest man in the world acted on a wrong word and his legacy was marred for ever.

"As Solomon grew old, his wives turned his heart after other gods, and his heart was not fully devoted to the Lord his God, as the heart of David his father had been....The Lord became angry with Solomon because his heart had turned away form the Lord, the God of Israel, who had appeared to him twice. Although he had forbidden Solomon to follow other gods, Solomon did not keep the Lord's command" (1 Kings 11:4, 9-10, NIV).

If the wisest man in the world can make bad choices it follows that we are probably vulnerable as well. Oftentimes these decisions occur at critical places along our life path and require wise choices—action on the right word. Yet, like Solomon, we fail to choose the right word and make the best decision. Three of the most important decisions in life are often the most neglected when it comes to acting upon a wise word from our heart. They are: "With whom will I spend my life?" "What am I going to do as a vocation?" "Where am I going to spend eternity?"

"With Whom Will I Spend My Life?"

I took an unscientific, on the spot, poll once in one of our Sunday morning worship services. I asked how many married people in the audience prayed about, sought for a word about, or sought God's will about the person they had married. I could count the number of couples who raised their hand on the fingers of one of my hands. Ninety plus per cent of those in attendance had never even thought to consider God's word or will in regard to one of the most important and influential decisions of their life! The decision of who one marries should not be built upon emotions or even "love." This important decision should be based upon our word on our heart that lines up with God's word on our heart. So many things are affected by the marriage union of two people; children, heritage, influence in the community, social values, Christian witness, schools, church, and country.

I have taken the same poll at other times. The same has held true in most every case. The tragedy is felt when we come to realize that the polls were taken in a church congregation! If so few believers are not considering a heart word from God, what is it like in the world? Statistics are telling us: half the people who marry are divorced in a matter of years, the illegitimacy rate for babies is going through the roof, the number of single mothers is increasing, and people living together outside of marriage is at its highest level ever. Many are buying in to an unsound word from the world.

I have come to the place in my thinking and observation that the American way of "dating" is not the best approach leading up to one of the greatest decisions we will ever make. But, it is the standard method of pre-marriage in our culture. The disastrous results we are seeing should cause believers, especially, to consider some options that include a word other than that from the world, the flesh, and Hollywood. Parents should pray about and try to get a word on their heart about a particular person that desires to see or date their child. Every young person should pray about and try to get a word about anyone they see or date. Two people who are "dating" should pray together regularly on their dates and constantly seek God's word about the relationship.

If two people are contemplating marriage, they should spend time every day, separately, making sure that the word on their heart is lining up with the word of God. If there is any doubt or misalignment then call off the relationship. Marriage is one of the most important decisions anyone will ever make. It can make you or break you. It can cause joy and blessing or misery and cursing. God can give you a clear word on this matter and the ensuing marriage will begin and be built in confidence, strength, and blessing.

"What Am I Going To Do As A Vocation?"

The second decision that has life-long consequences, has two parts. First, there is the decision regarding education. Whether it is training to serve hamburgers at the local fast food outlet, training at a vocational-technical school, a two-year junior college, the military, or a major university, a person will usually be required to have some kind of education. Many times the high school graduate doesn't know what he or she wants to do in life. Often, students will expose themselves to education that will have nothing to do with what they end up doing in life. Others will expose themselves to damaging philosophy that will color their decisions for the rest of their life. Many graduates go to a college because it is their ticket to fun and freedom.

Education has to do with words. The words of the institution will influence and train the minds of those who expose themselves to their curriculum. In other words, where one goes to school makes a great difference in the life of that person. But how few try to align their word or heart's desire with the word and will of God? Very few, I suspect.

My wife's father commented once that he went to the university to study agriculture science and learned how to grow carrots, then he spent the rest of his life in real estate and construction! I graduated from the university with a degree in Public Administration, having studied business, political science, and government administration. I have been a pastor for nearly thirty years! But, regarding college, I never knew to try to line up any word. I just stumbled along, doing what I thought best or wanted to do! I never prayed about it or sought God's will or word as to where to attend.

My unscientific poll revealed the same result in this case. Only a handful of people in a large congregation of believers had ever sought a word on where to go to school or what to do in life as a vocation.

Statistics have revealed that most people are not happy with their job and can't wait to change or retire. Job dissatisfaction is high. Why? Maybe it has to do with alignment or misalignment of a word?

We should seek alignment before we strike out on our education leg or our vocation leg. But what if you are seeking to change jobs or careers? The principle is the same. Determine the desire of your heart. Get a clear heart word. Seek alignment with the word of God. When the two words are in alignment, act by faith. A wonderful result will follow. But do not have fear or doubt. This will short-circuit the power.

The point we are making here is simple. The problem with most people is that they do not know to use a word on the heart concept and they don't include God and His word. God likes to be included! He has promised that when you include Him and line up with His word, He will be free to act on your behalf. Most people simply don't consider or include God!

Jesus said that the Father has the very hairs of our head numbered, and is more concerned about us than He is His animals and plants. If this is the case, do you not think that God would be concerned about three of the most important decisions anyone will ever make? He is not only concerned, but will aid you in getting the right conclusion and results of your decisions.

"Where Am I Going To Spend Eternity?"

This is THE most important decision of our life. Yet, so many people are operating under no word or a false word in this regard. Whatever you have to do to get to the true word and act upon it in this matter is the most important thing any one of us can do.

The greatest treasure for any individual is the miracle of salvation. Man is "dead" in trespasses and sins. He is separated from the life of God. Yet, God offers new life and forgiveness of sin through the finished work of Jesus Christ; His death, resurrection, and exaltation.

If you are willing, God will save you from your sins and a life built upon a wrong word. He will save you from the wrong word put upon you by your forefather, Adam, even though you had nothing to do with it. He will save you from the wrong words you have received and expressed, for which you ARE responsible. Apply the principles we have mentioned in this book. You will mine much greater riches than physical healing or monetary gain. Listen and respond.

"'The word is near you; it is in your mouth and in your heart,' that is, the word of faith we are proclaiming: that if you confess with your mouth, 'Jesus is Lord,' and believe in your heart that God raised him from the dead, you will be saved. For it is with your heart that you believe and are justified, and it is with your mouth that you confess and are saved. As the Scripture says, 'Anyone who trusts in him will never be put to shame'" (Romans 10:9,10, NIV).

I remember making this wonderful transaction. I was only ten. I had not been that regular in church, but I was a "good little boy." I had not committed any great violation of the laws of the land. Yet, the Holy Spirit had convicted me of my sinful condition and I came under a terrible burden of being lost and headed for hell. Somehow, even though no one ever sat down and witnessed to me in a formal sense, the word of the gospel of Jesus reached my ignorant little brain, in the midst of my conviction, and I cried out to God.

To the best of my memory, it was a Friday night. The family and I had gone to bed. It was dark. I lay there staring up at the ceiling. I could take it no longer. I began to cry. Tears wet my pillow.

"Dear God, I don't want to go to hell. I want to go to heaven. Please forgive me of my sins and save me. Jesus, I believe you died on the cross for me and were raised from the dead. Please come into my life and save me and forgive me."

That night—that moment—the God of the universe responded to the unorthodox prayer of a child. He saved me from my sin. He forgave me. He gave me a home in heaven. He made me a "joint heir with Christ." He redeemed me. He loved me with an everlasting love. He became my Father and my Savior. The blood of Jesus Christ covered all of my sin. He gave me eternal life. Isn't it amazing!

An ignorant little boy, that knew so very little about the Bible, God, or the plan of salvation, lined up his words with the words and promises of God and the greatest miracle of all time took place! The Scripture was true: "For whosoever shall call upon the name of the Lord shall be saved" (Romans 10:13).

I am not quite so ignorant now or infantile in my thinking. I have had time to evaluate the crude connection I made with God. Was it real? Could it have been emotions? Could I have been mistaken? Would God save such an unlearned child? After forty years of contemplation—after formal theological education in a master's degree program—after reading and studying the Scriptures—after proclaiming the truths of Scripture for over thirty years—after counseling others regarding the way of salvation—after writing books and tracts on the way of salvation—after delivering over 5,000 messages on Bible texts—after leading my own children to salvation in Christ—I give you a confident and resounding YES! It was real, not because I was educated or knowledgeable of the Scripture way of salvation, or because I was a "good little boy," but because of the grace and love of God.

"For it is by grace you have been saved, through faith—and this not from yourselves, it is the gift of God—not by works, so that no one can boast" (Ephesians 2:8-9, NIV).

Salvation is the greatest miracle for several reasons. First, it would be easier for Holy God to save a plant or a rock than a human. Humans are born with a bias against God—a rebellion against the word of God for their life. Plants and rocks do not have this same resistance. Man, from his conception in the womb, has a built in resistance to God. He is at "enmity against God and is not subject to the laws of God" (Romans 8:7).

Secondly, Holy God has to enter into the realm of man's unholiness (our sinful heart) in order to commune with us, convict us of sin, or deposit His word on our heart. This presents a conflict as Holy God cannot cohabit with sin.

Thirdly, this is a great miracle because man is "dead in trespasses and sins" (Ephesians 2:1). How can a dead man hear the word in order to act by faith upon it? How can a dead man, if he could hear, respond? Dead means dead. Dead men do not respond because they can't respond. They are dead. A primary characteristic of being dead is being inanimate and lifeless.

But, in God's plan of mercy, grace, and the finished work of Jesus Christ, dead men hear and respond. Holy God inhabits the unholy. He gives forth His word and allows men to line up with it for eternal life. Is it a miracle? Absolutely! It is the greatest miracle of all!

You, dear friend, have the capability of lining up with the miracle word of salvation on your heart. It is not about education, experience, or knowledge. In fact, sometimes, these tend to get in the way. It is not about age, gender, or where you were born. It is not about religion, church, or man's creeds. It is about a word—lining up with a word. Everything hangs on a word, even, and especially, our salvation.

Make sure that you are lined up with the true word of salvation. Life is too short and eternity is too long to be misaligned with such an important concept. Believe in your heart. Activate with your confession.

Get God's word on your heart. Act on this word by faith. God will be free to work in your behalf for wonderful blessings…even the miracle of salvation!

Below is a simple gospel outline or plan of salvation. See if you understand or line up with the Scripture as presented.

1. **Understand and believe that God loves you.** "For God so loved the world, that he gave his only begotten Son, that whosoever believeth in him should not perish, but have everlasting life" (John 3:16). "But God demonstrates His own love toward us, in that while we were still sinners, Christ died for us" (Romans 5:8, NKJV).

2. **Understand and believe that all are sinners.** "For all have sinned, and come short of the glory of God (Romans 3:23). "As it is written, There is none righteous, no, not one" (Romans 3:10).

3. **Understand and believe that God has a remedy for sin.** "For the wages of sin is death; but the gift of God is eternal life through Jesus Christ our Lord (Romans 6:23). "But as many as received him, to them gave he power to become the sons of God, even to them that believe on his name" (John 1:12). "For I delivered unto you first of all that which I also received, how that Christ died for our sins according to the scriptures; And that he was buried, and that he rose again the third day according to the scriptures" (1 Corinthians 15:3-4).

4. **Understand and believe that God's remedy is available for you.** "For whosoever shall call upon the name of the Lord shall be saved" (Romans 10:13). "That if you confess with your mouth the Lord Jesus, and believe in your heart that God has raised Him from the dead, you will be saved" (Romans 10:9, NKJV).

5. **Understand and believe that God's gift of salvation, eternal life, and forgiveness is available and offered but not automatic—one must repent (turn from self and sin) and turn to someone (Jesus Christ alone).** "For by grace you have been saved through faith, and that not of yourselves; it is the gift of God, not of works, lest anyone should boast" (Ephesians 2:8-9, NKJV). "But as many as received him, to them gave he power to become the sons of God, even to them that believe on his name" (John 1:12).

6. **Understand and believe that God's Word is true.** "Most assuredly, I say to you, he who hears My word and believes in Him who sent Me has everlasting life, and shall not come into judgment, but has passed from death into life" (John 5:24, NKJV).

If you will receive these words into your heart, confess or agree with them outwardly, and activate them by faith, you will line up with the promises of God as based on the finished work of the Lord Jesus Christ. You will experience salvation, forgiveness, and eternal life. In other words, get these words on your heart, act on them by faith, and see the miracle of salvation!

Maybe you would like to pray a prayer similar to the one I pray with people nearly every week:

"Lord Jesus, I confess that I am a sinner. But I believe that you died on the cross for me and were raised from the dead to give me eternal life and forgiveness. I ask you to forgive me of my sins and come into my life. I turn from my sin and my self and I turn to you as the only way of salvation. I confess you as my Lord and Savior. I thank you and praise you for your gift. Amen."

This life is too short and eternity too long to miss out on the answer to the most important question—"Where am I going to spend eternity?" Get into the Bible, the Word of God. Pray often. Find a good church home and get involved. Grow in your relationship with Jesus Christ and become a witness for Him. Get God's word on your heart—act on this word by faith—God will be free to provide for you a most wonderful result!

22

Word Dynamics And The Believer's Unique Relationship To God

In this section I want to reveal the bias that accompanies a believer in Jesus Christ. This chapter is a little different than all the rest in that moves away from our pragmatic theme to deal with the "why"—why do the ungodly seem to prosper—why do the righteous bear thorns in their side. For if we do not reason through the "why" we will give up and throw in the towel. My hope is to help you understand why there are universal overlaps, why there seems to be a discrepancy, and why it is important to approach this concept as a believer in Jesus.

The Bible indicates that it rains on the just and the unjust. The rain is a universal element in creation. The sun shines on the whole earth. It is universal. There are many things not exclusive to a particular people. The air we breathe is universal. Any mammal can freely partake of oxygen. It is universal. Some things are exclusive and selective. Other things are general and universal. The elements that we have been driving at in this book are universal and non-exclusive although some will self-exclude them in ignorance or fear. The head is universal. Most everyone has a mind; an objective thinker. The heart is universal. Most every human has a subconscious heart. Words are universal elements limited only by ignorance of their meaning. Faith is universal in that all humans have to exercise some kind of faith about many different things in order just to exist in the world. God so loves His creation that he allows even His enemies to enjoy His universal blessings. The wicked can even temporarily prosper over the righteous. God is no respecter of persons.

In Christendom and even in Judaism there has been confusion arising from this issue. The Jews of Jesus' day tended to believe that a rich and prosperous person showed he was under the favor of God—he was blessed of God. But if a tower fell and crushed some folks, those people were seen as sinners and cursed by

God. Jesus was even addressed regarding a blind person. They asked, "Who sinned, this man or his parents?" Jesus was quick to point out that the consequences one found himself in were not necessarily the judgment or the blessing of God—"Neither this man sinned or his parents." Conversely, some of the richest people in Jesus' day were wicked and evil rulers. Again, some of the most righteous were poverty stricken. Even Jesus was relatively poor, not even owning his own home or many possessions.

This contrary thinking has persisted up to the present time and is often manifested in the basic theology of radio and television preachers and teachers. We hear of their riches. We see the large diamond and gold rings on their fingers. We hear of them owning mansions and driving expensive luxury cars. They seem to attract riches like a magnet. Their auditoriums are full and over-flowing with people clamoring to get in to hear them. They always have a "world-wide ministry." And the message that is sent to the common people is—"I am 'blessed' because I have faith and God's favor is upon me." The subconscious ulterior message that we receive is—"I am not blessed. Therefore, God must not favor me or I must not have enough faith."

A church can give off this same theological aroma. If a church is wealthy and able to build grand buildings with a smorgasbord of ministries it must be because the favor and blessing of God is upon them! The poor church must not be doing something right. They must not really love God or have faith, otherwise, He would have blessed them with riches.

I find that the problem involves two issues. First, there is the issue of universal truths. Anyone, yes, anyone can plug into the concepts I am addressing here in this material. Bill Gates, the richest man in the world had a mind that he filled with knowledge. He pursued a dream (a word) upon his heart about building computers for the whole universe. Then he and some other men acted by faith on that word on their heart and the rest is history. But it does not mean that God was in it. It does not mean that Bill Gates is a committed follower of Jesus Christ. It does not mean that he shares any of his enormous profits with a single gospel effort or missionary project to proclaim the name of Jesus. It could simply mean that he plugged into these universal truths and saw the result.

The second issue involves time and eternity. So many people have only one limited concept of time and space—this present time and space. The Bible speaks of another arena that is not time as we know it and is not limited to the space that we know. It indicates that we are on a very limited time-space continuum, a straight line, if you will, that has a beginning and an ending. The more I study the Bible, the more I realize that it is designed as a manual for living in eternity as well as living in this time. The Bible's perspective on our time here is somewhat shocking to us. It speaks of this time as just a vapor that appears for a short time and then vanishes away. It speaks of numbered days; three score and ten. It speaks of a thousand years as one day and one day as a thousand years in God's sight. Jesus said it was better to cut off your hand or pluck out your eye and live maimed in this life rather than miss out on eternal life. The faithful believers mentioned in Hebrews 11 went through all kinds of tortures and yet looked for a new dwelling whose builder and maker is God. Most of the Apostles of Jesus died horrible deaths because of this new perspective on eternal life.

So here's my point—this is not all there is my friend! To live only for the here and now is a sad mistake. To look around and see some prospering and you floundering and make an assumption about value, worth, or ability is a false assumption. Yes, we can all operate in the universal truths because they are universal! Anyone can use them. Even Jesus pointed this out to His bewildered disciples. We really don't understand God's plan for mankind until we understand the concept of eternity and our relationship to it.

Now, with that in mind let me get to the bias. That is, even though the truths mentioned in this book are universal, they had an original intent. It goes all the way back to the Garden of Eden. It follows through in God's chosen people, the Jews. It was manifested in the Lord Jesus Christ as the New Adam. And it was intended to be used by believers in Jesus Christ especially. I realize how narrow-minded, exclusive, and prejudicial this may seem in our relativistic and all-inclusive world today, but any serious student of the Bible can uncover it for themselves.

Yes, the Bible indicates that true believers in Jesus Christ have a unique relationship with God as His children. Peter tells us that we are God's "peculiar treasure" or "special possession." This reference was to the King's special little box of "keepsakes"—special little treasures that he would put no price upon. They may not have meant much to others but were sentimentally valuable to the king. We are God's special keepsakes. We are called "joint heirs" with Jesus Christ—subject to the vast treasuries and possessions at His disposal. Along with this, the Bible indicates that we are joint rulers with Jesus and will rule with Him during His thousand year reign on the earth after His return. But possibly, the most unique relationship position is that of the "Bride of Christ." We have been bought by the precious blood of Christ on the basis of His shed blood for our sins and will be made pure in righteousness as His worthy wife. Yes, true believers have a unique position and relationship with God.

What Happened?

The problem we have today in understanding the theme of this material can be traced all the way back to the Garden of Eden. It was there that we see man in full measure enjoying God's creation. But the thief enters upon the scene and throws in a monkey wrench. Man is tempted. He succumbs and the pure relationship he had with God is broken. Before the "fall of man" there was the perfect operation of "word." God communed with man in the garden. There was no problem in knowing God's word or His will. The head and heart were clear. Faith was not necessary and fear was unknown. Then sin entered and so death and corruption passed upon every man and every descendant of man. The head was corrupted so that man could not think purely. The heart was corrupted so that man could not believe purely. The body was corrupted so that man could not live in the eternal perspective of God.

But God had a plan—a plan of redemption and reclamation. His plan would involve His word (a covenant), a nation (the Jews), a savior (Jesus), a new word (the new covenant or testament in the blood of Jesus) and all who would believe on Him (believers). It would involve present reality in the things we have been emphasizing; the head, the heart, a word, and faith action. It would involve a future state; the Millennial Kingdom to come and the eternal rule following the earthly rule. It would involve universal principles that anyone could use but it would be designed as a preparation room for something greater to come. Man would be judged on the decisions he made and upon the words he chose to live upon, use, think, and speak. Every idle word would be judged.

Reclaiming The Promised Land

God promised a certain land to His people Israel. It was labeled, *The Promised Land*. Everyone was happy about that until spies were sent in to spy it out. The spies returned with a report that verified the promise of God that it would be a land of abundant fruit; a land flowing with milk and honey. But there was a catch—the cities had formidable walls—the inhabitants fierce—and giants! Ten of the twelve spies were so overcome with the obstacles, they voted to turn back, and tried to get the whole nation to turn back. God was not pleased.

Could it be that the spiritual promise land that the Lord has given to us is also a formidable land with obstacles and even giants? Could it also be that many have turned and gone to safer ground because of fear and intimidation? Somehow, I feel that this is precisely what many in the Christian life have done in regard to the things of the supernatural and spirit world. We have abandoned an area approved, sanctioned, and authorized by God. We have fled in fear, leaving the bounty to wicked inhabitants and giants of all stripes. And, since they inhabit the land, we assume that it is rightfully and exclusively theirs. I probably stand in the unsafe minority like Joshua and Caleb, the only two spies that wanted to go forward, but I feel compelled that we should trust God and move ahead.

When the Israelites activated God's word by faith, and expressed it by moving forward, powerful things started to happen. The waters of the Jordan parted, the walls of Jericho fell, and enemies were routed in complete victory. These mighty things happened because Joshua and the other leaders received a word from God on their heart and acted on it by faith. Nothing but death was recorded for those who tucked tail and ran.

The true follower of Jesus Christ is often cast upon the horns of a dilemma. The believer in Jesus and the Bible sees and knows about faith, words, the heart, belief, prayer, power, moving mountains, and miracles. At least, they will tell you that they side with these things. But then, they do not seem to operate in them, are ignorant of them for daily life, or are afraid of them.

While the believer in Jesus and the Bible is trying to decide where they stand in practicality to the spiritual issues, the mind scientists, psychologists, shrinks, positive thinkers, and wealth building *giants* propound their doctrine in every form of media and are accepted with the acclaim of a celebrity out to help humankind become better and richer.

Oftentimes, the prayer services in the local church are powerless and peopleless. Maybe, we have lost the practical and powerful insight into real prayer or we simply don't believe that it works. We wouldn't ever say that, mind you, but it could be what we really believe.

Pollsters and statisticians like George Barna, have told us that 68% of churches across the country from every denomination are either stagnated or in decline. Have we lost our power?

The dilemma for the believer is that the world thinkers have stolen the thunder. Success motivation seminars and books on how to think your way to success are sold out while the church auditoriums are emptying out. Somehow, believers have to sort through the verbiage, and media hype, and get at the truth, and use it.

Although he confessed to not knowing how it worked, A. Conan Doyle, creator of Sherlock Holmes, and for many years a member of the British Society for Psychic Research, declared that he believed there was a constructive and destructive power in thought alone which was akin to the "faith that can move mountains."

The business minds took the principles of moving mountains to a new level during the sixties with an array of "success formulas." Just listen to some of the most popular titles: *The Success System That Never Fails*, *Success Through A Positive Mental Attitude*, *Think And Grow Rich*, and *The Magic Of Thinking Big*.

"Dr. Maxwell Maltz, author of Psycho-Cybernetics, spelled out the dilemma a few years back. In 1969, at a time when his book on success had already sold 5 million copies, Dr. Maltz was speaking to a group in Dallas. Following the speech, he fielded questions from the audience. The question came, 'Are spiritual-cybernetics the same as psycho-cybernetics?'

'Certainly not,' Dr. Maltz replied. 'The churches certainly seem to like my book. It teaches a great many things they teach—but mine is practical, everyday living which does not, incidentally, fit perfectly with religious concepts' (*Dallas Times-Herald*, Oct. 2, 1969)" [William Cook, *Success, Motivation, and the Scriptures* (Nashville, TN: Broadman Press, 1974), p. 3].

William James, the father of American psychology, said that the greatest discovery of the nineteenth century was not in the realm of physical science. The greatest discovery was the power of the subconscious touched by faith. He said that in every human being is that limitless reservoir of power which can overcome any problem in the world.

In a similar philosophy as William James, Dr. Joseph Murphy, wrote,

"Scientific prayer is the harmonious interaction of the conscious and subconscious levels of mind scientifically directed for a specific purpose. This book will teach you the scientific way to tap the realm of infinite power within you enabling you to get what you really want in life." [Joseph Murphy, *The Power of Your Subconscious Mind* (Englewood Cliffs, NJ: Prentice—Hall, Inc., 1963), p. 7].

Pat Robertson of the *700 Club* fame, countered the metaphysical mind scientists in his book, *The Secret Kingdom*:

"That which the writers of the many 'success' books call 'positive mental attitude,' or PMA, is indeed important. Because our minds are the agents our spirits use in influencing the world around us, it is patently clear that negative attitudes can vitiate our most valiant attempts. Conversely, positive thinking will more often than not lead to successful action.

Unfortunately, such people as Napoleon Hill, who wrote *Think and Grow Rich*, have gleaned only a few of the truths of the kingdom of God. They try to gain the kingdom without submitting themselves to the King.

Some of the metaphysical principles of the kingdom, taken by themselves, can produce fantastic temporal benefits. But without the lordship of Jesus, these benefits are both transitory and harmful. In fact, many of the advocates of mind over matter ultimately end in hellish spiritism" [Pat Robertson and Bob Slosser, *The Secret Kingdom* (Nashville, TN: Thomas Nelson Publishers, 1982), p. 69].

Dr. Bill Cook sums it all up, from the Christian perspective, in his book, *Success, Motivation, and the Scriptures*:

"In our current situation, proponents of success and proponents of the spiritual life have fought to a standoff. On the one hand, there is the success-bug who has never figured out how to maintain his success-image and still be spiritual. So he concludes, wrongfully, that his is the only team really in the ball game. On the other end of the field is the individual who views his relationship with God as being of prime importance. He is suspicious of accepting new ideas about success and motivation until he is sure they do not rob him of what he already has. So the life of maximum achievement God intended never seems to bounce in his direction.

As in any standoff, both sides lose....it need not be that way—that the individual who correctly assimilates success, motivation, and the truths of Scripture is in for fantastic excitement and achievement" (William Cook, *Success, Motivation, and the Scriptures*, p. 4).

Aware Of The Enemies

If a believer in Jesus Christ is going to operate in the metaphysical, or the somewhat intangible world of the non-physical, he or she must become aware. There is the obvious awareness of words, subconscious heart, and faith. But, there is also the need to be aware of the unseen spirit world. Not only should the Christian be aware but should be armed and ready for warfare.

"Finally, be strong in the Lord and in his mighty power. Put on the full armor of God so that you can take your stand against the devil's schemes. For our struggle is not against flesh and blood, but against the rulers, against the authorities, against the powers of this dark world and against the spiritual forces of evil in the heavenly realms. Therefore, put on the full armor of God, so that when the day of evil comes, you may be able to stand your ground, and after you have done everything, to stand" (Ephesians 6:10-13, NIV).

The Bible plainly tells us that there are evil spirits that operate with man, for man, or against man. Jesus spoke to demons and cast them out. He believed in the devil. He gave His disciples authority to cast out demons. The Bible says that we not only war against our own flesh, the world system, but also, the devil and evil spirits.

Richard W. De Haan, well-known and respected Bible expositor, wrote:

"Are you aware that evil spirit beings operating through men in positions of authority and influence are the real motivators in human society? Yes, that is exactly what the Bible teaches! Perhaps this concept seems strange to you, almost like an outmoded superstition, but the Bible definitely states that Satan is the 'god of this age' (2 Corinthians 4:4), and that he is the leader of a well-organized army of beings invisible to men but very active among them" [Richard DeHann, *Satan, Satanism And Witchcraft*, (Grand Rapids, Michigan 49506: Zondervan Publishing House, 1972), p. 41].

The believer should also be aware that these evil spirits work with our mind, our heart, and words. Just as the Holy Spirit can implant a word in our mind, so can an evil spirit.

C. S. Lovett, in his practical little book, *Dealing With The Devil*, wrote:

"The Spirit of God and the spirit of Satan have equal access to the unconscious portion of our minds. They can quicken material already on deposit or that which is newly arriving by the senses and send it into the thought-life in the form of a suggestion. Man is free to respond to these suggestions or refuse them. Therefore, it is the Christian's responsibility to decide whether the Holy Spirit or the unholy spirit will dominate his life" [C.S. Lovett, *Dealing With The Devil* (Baldwin Park, California: Personal Christianity, 1967), p. 114].

Black Magic, White Magic, Or Biblical Faith?

Again, before the true believer in Jesus can walk the straight and narrow and live in Biblical orthodoxy, he must be made keenly aware of his surroundings and the path before him. If we are to be defensive against the enemy, we must know the enemy. This is not always the case in Christian circles. The hidden dagger of untruth has stabbed many a naïve soul.

Such is the case with much of the psycho mind-science of the day. Many call it *white magic*.

"White magic is declared by its practitioners to be in direct opposition to black magic. Whereas black magic includes an open allegiance with the powers of darkness, in white magic, the name of God is invoked, and Biblical phrases are utilized. Most people who practice it, however, have no understanding of the basic doctrines of the Christian faith. Some possibly are endowed with an unexplainable psychic power, and their desire to use it was not totally selfish at the beginning. But many find very soon that they become enslaved to a yearning for self-exaltation. The Radio Bible Class has received letters from a number of people who, for a time, had engaged in a 'healing ministry' of this kind, but who abandoned it because it led to a gradual departure from God. Although some cult leaders and those classified as healers are no doubt psychically endowed people, they are using the name of God and Christ in a manner that violates the Lord's will.

...Dr. Merrill F. Unger sums up the distinction between religious white magic and Biblical faith and prayer as follows:

'In Biblical faith, trust is placed solely in the Lord Jesus. In white magic it is deflected to someone else (the human agent) or to something else (one's own faith, etc.). In the Biblical prayer of faith, the praying person subjects himself to the will of God. In white magic the help of God is demanded under the assumption that exercising such power is in accordance with God's will. In white magic the Christian markings are mere decorations that camouflage the magical means for knowledge or power (Merrill F. Unger, *Demons in the World Today*, p. 86)" (Richard DeHann, *Satan, Satanism And Witchcraft*, pp. 109-110).

Israel sent twelve spies in to check out the Promised Land. Ten out of the twelve came back and said there were giants in the land and that they would have to turn back. Two of the spies, Joshua and Caleb asserted that their God was bigger than the giants and that they should proceed ahead. The majority ruled the day and the people of Israel wandered in the wilderness until the unbelieving generation died off. Could it be that the majority rules our day as well? We cannot be afraid to move forward by genuine faith and relevant Biblical orthodoxy to possess what God says belongs to us. Yes, there are giants, enemies, and obstacles. But if God has given us a word, we can act by faith on it and see His power unleashed for awesome results.

23

Word Dynamics And The Believer's Unique Relationship To God (continued)

A Call For Biblical Soundness And Application

The Christian lives in the arena of evil spirits; principalities and powers of the air. We war against the world, the flesh, and the devil. But, not only should we be aware, we should be able to defend our selves and live victoriously. The warfare is real. The believer will live defeated unless he knows the enemy and how to fight him.

"For though we live in the world, we do not wage war as the world does. The weapons we fight with are not the weapons of the world. On the contrary, they have divine power to tear down strongholds. We demolish arguments and every pretension that sets itself up against the knowledge of God, and we take captive every thought to make it obedient to Christ" (2 Corinthians 10:3-5, NIV).

There are three important issues that the believer must come to grips with: awareness, armament, and attack. It is not enough to just be aware of elements in the unseen spirit world. We must arm ourselves in a defensive position as we are engaged in a spiritual warfare and need defensive measures for survival. But, thirdly, we have the ability, granted to us in the Scriptures, and by the Lord Jesus, Himself, to exercise authority. Many do not feel up to this, but it is available, nevertheless, and it is by means of our heart words expressed. Notice the action words in the following Scriptures.

"Submit yourselves, then, to God. Resist the devil, and he will flee from you" (James 4:7, NIV).

"Take the helmet of salvation and the sword of the Spirit, which is the word of God" (Ephesians 6:17, NIV).

Yes, we are given power and privilege and are urged to stand strong.

"Finally, my bretheren, be strong in the Lord, and in the power of his might. Put on the whole armour of God, that ye may be able to stand against the wiles of the devil" (Ephesians 6:10-11).

One of my respected seminary professors, Dr. Curtis Vaughn wrote:

"In military strategy the failure to estimate properly the strength and capabilities of an enemy is a tragic mistake. In the Christian confrontation it is not only tragic but inexcusable, for we are clearly warned both of the nature of the conflict and of the formidable character of the enemy. 'We wrestle not against flesh and blood.' We are engaged in a life-and-death struggle, not against a frail human enemy but against the supernatural forces of evil. The word translated 'we wrestle' suggests hand-to-hand combat and thus magnifies the personal nature of the encounter" [Curtis Vaughn, *Ephesians: A study Guide Commentary* (Grand Rapids, Michigan 49506: Zondervan Publishing House, 1977), p. 126].

We can exercise words against the evil spirits that encroach upon us. Words have power. Let us get aware, get armored, and use the "sword of the Spirit," which is the "Word of God" against the enemy.

"So with resisting Satan. We do it. The name of Jesus is our authority for doing so. The Holy Spirit is our strength. The Word of God is our weapon. The shed blood of Christ is our guarantee of victory. Satan is already a defeated enemy on the basis of that blood" (C.S. Lovett, *Dealing With The Devil*, p. 140).

We can never rest, however. The proliferation of false word proponents will be a thing of the present and the future.

"But there were also false prophets among the people, just as there will be false teachers among you. They will secretly introduce destructive heresies, even denying the sovereign Lord who bought them—bringing swift destruction on themselves. Many will follow their shameful ways and will bring the way of truth into disrepute. In their greed these teachers will exploit you with stories they have made up" (2 Peter 2:1-3, NIV).

"For such men are false apostles, deceitful workmen, masquerading as apostles of Christ. And no wonder, for Satan himself masquerades as an angel of light" (2 Corinthians 11:13-14).

It is wonderful to know that we have powerful, authorized, capabilities. Our words are powerful tools for offense or defense. Let us be aware and be wise and know that the believer has a unique relationship with inherent power not promised to any other.

The World's Word Or The Word Of Truth

One of the most important passages in the Bible is the longest recorded prayer of Jesus—the high priestly prayer He uttered for His disciples just before He went to Calvary. It is recorded in John 17. In this passage Jesus keeps speaking of the "world" and how the disciples are left in the world and how the world hates them. He counteracts the concept of the "world" with His "word." He identifies His "word" with truth.

Here is the issue as it relates to us. The "world" is a system that carries its own philosophy or "word." Jesus came to reveal the truth or the true "word" from the perspective of the Father and eternal life. The world's "word" came into direct conflict with the eternal "word" of truth. The result was the crucifixion of Jesus and the persecution of His followers.

This is precisely the problem we are faced with today. Our post-modern relativistic, humanistic, atheistic world is putting forth its "word." The eternal "word" of truth and the living "word" (Jesus) are coming under attack. It is a battle of words.

This is nothing new. We have a classic example of it in the story of Daniel. He and his brethren were captured when Jerusalem fell and were transported to Babylonian captivity. Being the best and the brightest they were afforded room in the palace. The design was to indoctrinate them with a new word—the word of Babylonian philosophy. They were dressed in Babylonian clothing. They lived among Babylonian nobles. They were pressured to eat the Babylonian food and worship the Babylonian gods. They, however, were strong men of God. They lived by another word—the word of their God. This, of course, did not sit well with the King. Daniel was sentenced to the lion's den and his Hebrew brothers were sentenced to the fiery furnace.

What we see in this Old Testament story and in the prayer of Jesus is a truth smacking us in the face today. It is a battle between "word" systems; belief systems; philosophical systems. It is a battle between the world's word and God's word.

So can it be done? Can we live in the world's system and remain true to God's word? Can we be in the world but not of the world? Can we operate with a word on our heart by faith to see wonderful results? The answer is "yes."

Understanding The Difference

There is great confusion and misunderstanding regarding this issue by people on both sides; believers and unbelievers alike. The natural man uses the principles and sees success and prosperity apart from any recognizable relationship with God. In fact, wicked men use these principles and often see wonderful riches come their way. Faithful believers and "good" folks operate in the same principles but see poverty and pain. What is going on? How could the Jewish and Roman magistrates and rulers of Jesus' day live in splendor and riches while the disciples lived in poverty and ended up tortured to death? How can the ungodly prosper and the righteous perish? Don't the principles work across the board?

Yes, very definitely, the principles work across the board. But there is something else at work here for the true believer in Jesus Christ. First, there is an *eternal purpose* at work. Secondly, there is an *eternal perspective* to keep in mind. Thirdly, there is *eternal preparation* to consider.

Sometimes God may not allow them to work in our time frame for a very important reason. God has an eternal purpose in mind for the believer. That purpose involves purging for greater service. It involves preparation in the fires of tests and trials. It involves purging away the dross so that the Master will have a vessel of great value. As believers we should be careful about shedding tears and harboring sorrows. God has a purpose for us if we are truly His.

We may have trouble seeing God's purpose because of the earthly cloud we are under. We must seek to develop an eternal perspective. That is, see our pilgrimage as temporary, like those mentioned in Hebrews 11 who suffered without an earthly answer but who cast their sight to eternity and trusted God. One of my favorite passages is Psalm 37:1-11:

"Do not fret because of evildoers, nor be envious of the workers of iniquity. For they shall soon be cut down like the grass, and wither as the green herb. Trust in the LORD, and do good; dwell in the land, and feed on His faithfulness. Delight yourself also in the LORD, and He shall give you the desires of your heart. Commit your way to the LORD, trust also in Him, and He shall bring it to pass. He shall bring forth your righteousness as the light, and your justice as the noonday. Rest in the LORD, and wait patiently for Him; do not fret because of him who prospers in his way, because of the man who brings wicked schemes to pass. Cease from anger, and forsake wrath; do not fret—it only causes harm. For evildoers shall be cut off; but those who wait on the LORD, they shall inherit the earth. For yet a little while and the wicked shall be no more; indeed, you will look carefully for his place, But it shall be no more. But the meek shall inherit the earth, and shall delight themselves in the abundance of peace" (NKJV).

Did you notice, in this passage, how many times the author talks about the wicked being "cut off"? The believer must develop an eternal perspective. This life is not all there is. The believer is living for a whole different dimension. But unless we begin to see the difference we will mope around like so many others who have no hope.

Thirdly, the believer is in a preparation mode. Everything that happens to us now in this earthly dimension is a preparation for a dimension to come. Even in so-called "failure" we are being tested and purified for that which is to come. We are being prepared, as the Bride of Christ, for presentation to Him and rulership with Him. Everything that happens to us now will be part and parcel of that which is to come. I cannot say this for the unbeliever. It could be that much of, if not all of, that which is a part of the unbeliever's life will be wasted and burned like wood, hay, and stubble. What a shame if this is true! All the suffering, all the tests, all the hardship, and all the trials of the unbeliever are for naught in the eternal perspective. Not so for the believer. Maybe this is why James would proclaim:

"My brethren, count it all joy when you fall into various trials, knowing that the testing of your faith produces patience. But let patience have its perfect work, that you may be perfect and complete, lacking nothing" (James 1:2-4, NKJV).

It is so very important that we see the believer bias in the Word of God lest we get confused or discouraged. Believers are special. Believers are on a journey. Nothing about the believer's life will be wasted; no tear, no sorrow, no test, no hidden act of kindness. But the believer must see the eternal aspect of his or her relationship with God. We have an eternal purpose. We have an eternal perspective. And we are involved in an eternal preparation.

It is so very important that we, as believers, understand the issue of words. We shall be judged for every idle word that we speak. We shall be judged for how we have received words and used words. And how shall we rule in the Millennial Kingdom along with Christ if not by words and thoughts? A large part of our preparation and testing here upon the earth is in regard to how we think, how we speak, and how we believe. And these areas all involve words.

We should also continually recognize that the principles outlined in this book and in our theme are universal in nature. This is vitally important, both to understand the capability of secular man in his natural capabilities and also in the believer's life in the realm of the Biblical and spiritual.

Word Dynamics And The Believer's Unique Relationship To God (continued)

In the area of universal truths, Jesus said, "whosoever." We need to see this literally. If we do, it will clear up a lot of confusion. Yes, He meant Jews, Christians, Muslims, Buddhists, Nazis, agnostics, atheists, mind science practitioners, witch-doctors, the good, the bad, and the ugly. When He said, "Whosoever shall say unto this mountain…," He meant whosoever!

Secondly, Jesus said, "whatsoever." "Whatsoever you shall ask for in prayer…." When He said, "whatsoever," He meant whatsoever! He did not put the same limitations we want to put on it. Invariably, He left out the parameters.

Jesus recognized that a word, any word, is a universal element that has freedom to be used and applied. It can be a good word or a damaging word. He even pointed out that our words have binding and loosing power, and that we would be judged by our words. He showed us that words could come from outside sources, or from within. He revealed, without question, for anyone who will see, that words are a universal element.

Jesus, as well as other New Testament writers, tell us plainly that the heart is a universal element able to be influenced from within or from without—by good or by evil. They teach us that we have power to harden our heart or cultivate a receptive heart. The heart is a universal element not exclusive to Christians. Every human being has a heart.

Jesus, as well as other New Testament writers, tell us plainly that faith is a universal element able to be used by all kinds of people—Roman centurions, widows, Jews, Christians, agnostics, mind scientists, and yes, atheists too! It is not exclusive to followers of Jesus. Anyone can use faith. It is a universal element.

Now, if Jesus put no parameters on these items, why should we? Could it be because we are ignorant of them from a Biblical perspective? Could it be because we do not want to be identified with the metaphysical, mind science, new-age, success-motivation crowd? Could it be that we want to confine these elements only to the Lord Jesus or His disciples? Aren't we afraid of being seen as a little weird—a little too spiritual, or superstitious?

In so many ways, believers in Jesus Christ shirk their responsibilities to the one they call Lord. It has been stated that only about 4% of Christians ever share their faith and that only about 11% think that it is important or a priority! Most believers I have ever known in the local church have never shared the gospel or any kind of verbal witness for the Lord Jesus. If a local church can get 10% of those attending (the percentage would be even less for the whole church roll) to come out for organized evangelism or witness training or visitation of any kind, they are usually doing well. It is sad.

The same can be said of believers operating in the principles we are driving at in this material. How many really pray from a word on their heart? How many even know to get a word from God on their heart from which to pray? How many know that a clear, clean, and uncluttered heart is vitally important and why? How many pull the trigger of faith from a word on their heart and allow God to work?

An awakening is needed. Just as in the days of Isaiah and Jesus, so there are those among us who have eyes to see but see not and ears to hear but hear not. We need a new understanding of these concepts. We need an application, not just in the religious or church realm, but in practical every day living. We need to be driving toward accomplishing great and mighty things for ourselves and for the glory of God. We Christians, above all else, need to be operating in these spiritual truths and elements with the utmost integrity. The world is watching. I fear that we look like wimps that have hunkered down in the back seat. But for those willing to apply the principles, God is willing to respond.

Dr. Gregory Frizzell wrote in his book, *Returning To Holiness*:

"In spite of today's staggering moral decline, there are growing signs God is mightily touching His people. A rising number of believers and churches are seeing miraculous moves of God's Spirit. In fact, some churches are experiencing things so incredible only God can explain what is happening!" [Gregory Frizzell, *Returning To Holiness* (Memphis, TN: The Master Design, 2000), p. 3].

In the Bible book of Acts we have the account of the coming of the Holy Spirit, the preaching of Peter, three thousand people repenting and turning to Christ for salvation, and mighty signs and wonders being performed. The church was born and God smiled.

Through the next 1,970 years we have seen the ebb and flow of Christianity. The church has come through persecution and ease, exaltation and demise, expansion and decline, worldliness and revival. Whenever the church was in a revived state there were characteristic signs and wonders—mighty powers manifested by the believers—strength in faith—results from prayer. The people cleansed their heart and aligned themselves with the word of God. They acted by faith on the aligned word on their heart and God responded. Evaluate the main characters and leaders in any one of the *Great Awakenings* of history and you will find that they operated by the principles we are outlining in this material.

A Final Summation Of God's Intent For Word Dynamics

Even though this concept of our thesis is simple and not necessarily easy, it is powerful. To prove my point I want to illustrate the use of this concept by three examples; from an Old Testament prophet, from the life of Jesus, and from a Scripture verse most everyone refers to in regard to salvation.

The first illustration has to do with Elijah the prophet in a contest with the prophets of Baal on Mount Carmel to prove the one true God. The test had to do with calling fire down from heaven to consume a sacrifice on the stone altar. The prophets of Baal went first. They prayed fervently all day and nothing happened. Then the lone prophet Elijah walked up, prayed a simple and short prayer and fire fell in torrents and consumed the sacrifice, the water that had been poured upon it, and the stones!

I maintain that Elijah, as opposed to the false prophets, discovered the secret. How do I know? Just listen to his brief pre-fire prayer.

"Lord God...let it be known this day that thou art God in Israel, and that I am thy servant, and that I have done all these things ***at thy word***" (1 Kings 18:36, bold italics mine for emphasis).

Did you get it? Maybe not, but listen on. Remember, in the Bible, when Lazarus died and lay in the tomb for four days? Remember how the sisters were fuming because Jesus wasn't around to heal him from his sickness unto death?

The Scripture records that Jesus was out in the countryside with His disciples and knew that Lazarus had died. When news finally came to him he went to the grieving sisters and to the tomb. With majesty and confidence he stood before the tomb getting ready to call his friend from the dead. But wait. The protests come.

"'But Lord,' said Martha, the sister of the dead man, 'by this time there is a bad odor, for he has been there four days'" (John 11:39, NIV).

Jesus did not waver but mildly rebuked sister Martha. Then he asked for the stone to be removed. Before he called for Lazarus to come forth out of the grave he offered a simple prayer, much like that of Elijah.

"Father, I thank you that you have heard me. I knew that you always hear me, but I said this for the benefit of the people standing here, that they may believe that you sent me" (John 11:41-42, NIV).

Did you notice the past tense? Jesus came to the tomb confidently, like Elijah had approached the stone altar, because He had received this *Lazarus resurrection word* on His heart prior to coming to the tomb. He simply acted upon the word on His heart by faith and a wondrous result took place.

I maintain to you that both Jesus and Elijah operated in confidence, authority, and faith because they acted from a word that the Father placed on their heart. Listen, again, to what Jesus says in John's Gospel.

"Jesus gave them this answer: 'I tell you the truth, the Son can do nothing by himself; he can do only what he sees his Father doing, because whatever the Father does the Son also does'" (John 5:19, NIV).

Are you getting it? Maybe, but you are saying that it only applies to two of the greatest miracle workers the world has ever known. Not so, I say. Let me show you how it applied to you if you know salvation in Jesus Christ.

Most of us who are Bible reading believers are familiar with Paul's letter to the Romans. In 10:8-10 it says,

"But what does it say? 'The word is near you; it is in your mouth and in your heart,' that is, the word of faith we are proclaiming: that if you confess with your mouth, 'Jesus is Lord,' and believe in your heart that God raised him from the dead, you will be saved. For it is with your heart that you believe and are justified, and it is with your mouth that you confess and are saved" (NIV).

Did you see it? Here you have every element in our simple little concept. A man receives God's word on his heart. He acts on that word by faith. The wondrous miracle of salvation takes place.

I know what you are still saying, "Well, that was Elijah and Jesus. That was salvation. It doesn't apply to me in everyday life for everyday things."

This is where we have steered the train off the track and tried to run it down a dirt road. This is what I want to shout from the rooftop. It is not just for the few—but for you—every day—and in every way! Jesus said it so plainly:

"The thief comes only to steal and kill and destroy; I have come that they may have life, and have it to the full" (John 10:10, NIV).

The concept is repeated from Genesis to Revelation. It is used by prophets, priests, and kings. It is used by Jesus and His disciples. But it was also used by widow ladies, fishermen, single moms, soldiers, and common people alike. It is for you and me in every day affairs.

The question remains, are we, as believers, going to shirk our responsibilities and leave the wonderful truths of Jesus with the shrinks and secular positive thinkers? Not only will we shirk our responsibilities in doing so but we will miss the wonderful opportunity of mining the treasures of our heart and blessings from the Father's storehouse. It is high time that we get a word (preferably God's word) on our heart, act on this word by faith, and see a wonderful result. There are latent word dynamics sitting out there with your name on them just waiting to be used. It is just possible that, of all the people in the universe, you are the only one who can employ them. What are you waiting for? Get a word on your heart—act on that word by faith—see a wonderful result!

Word Dynamics Summary Points

1. A *word* is anything that communicates.
2. Everything hangs upon a word.
3. Words are universal elements and can be used by anyone.
4. Words are powerful change agents.
5. Our world stands affected by negative and harmful words.
6. We stand affected by negative and harmful words.
7. We can change ourselves or others with our words.
8. We possess a *head* and a *heart*; a conscious and subconscious.
9. The head and heart have different functions.
10. Words planted on the heart have powerful potential.
11. *Faith* is the activator of heart words.
12. Faith is *universal* and can be used by anyone.
13. Knowing the right word in order to act upon it by faith is the key to success and blessing.
14. Knowledge of the right word is often difficult but can be discerned with effort.
15. Knowledge of God's word is the key to knowing His will.
16. Knowledge of God's will is the basis for acting upon the best word for eternal success and blessing.

17. We receive many word seeds sown toward our heart. Only a few get planted because of opposition, i.e. *the parable of the soils.*

18. God has an abundant seed storehouse that He is willing to share with us.

19. There are factors that enhance the operation of heart words; order, alignment, agreement, forgiveness, focus, clarity, purity of mind.

20. *Prayer* is powerful when understood and connected with proper word dynamics.

21. Real prayer is getting a word from God on our heart in clarity and acting upon it by faith.

22. Foul, offensive, distracting, and damaging words are flooding our world and our minds.

23. All of us will have to give account for every idle word that is thought or spoken.

24. The believer in Jesus Christ has a responsibility to think proper words and speak proper words.

25. The spoken word is God's power tool for our use.

26. The use of *positive word dynamics* can change our life and those around us.

27. Negative, untrue, and harmful words should be identified and rejected.

28. The believer in Jesus Christ has authority to reject negative, untrue, and harmful words.

29. We all can manipulate our heart for success and blessing by *autoimplanting* words to our head and to our heart.

30. Our heart can become damaged by the reception or implanting of negative words.

31. Our heart can be repaired with a therapeutic application of positive words, thoughts, and especially Scripture words.

32. We can employ certain techniques that help establish a positive word dynamic in our life; focusing the vision, persistence, giving and receiving, "powerwords," and by keeping a spiritual journal.

33. *Powerwords* are positive word reinforcement statements in clear and concise terms that spell out our desire or dream.

34. Powerwords can be used for success and blessings, dreams and goals, monetary provision, great adventures, health and healing.

35. Powerwords can be used as positive change agents in the important institutions of our life; the family, marriage, parenting, school, church, and government.

36. The powerword concept can and should be applied to the important decisions of our life; *choosing our life mate, choosing our life vocation, and choosing eternal life.*

37. The believer in Jesus Christ has a unique relationship to God and a unique privilege as His children regarding word dynamics.

38. The believer in Jesus Christ has a unique privilege of knowing and applying powerwords from the Word of God; the Bible.

39. The believer in Jesus Christ faces a battle between the *world's word* and *God's word*; the word of truth (John 17).

40. There is an obvious *inequity* between the godly and the ungodly in regard to success and blessing.

41. To understand the apparent inequity, one must understand the universal nature of the word, heart, and faith.

42. To understand the apparent inequity, one must understand the difference in *temporal* and *eternal* and God's plan and design in each.

43. The believer in Jesus Christ lives not only for this temporal time and dimension but for the eternal time and dimension and its success and blessing.

44. The words that we think, speak, and act upon now have impact, not only for now but for eternity.

A Word Dynamics Action Inventory

Try to answer the following questions as honestly as possible. They are designed to awaken in you an awareness of where you are in regard to understanding our theme and motivating you to sharpen up your life direction and purpose.

1. What is the theme of this book?

2. Name the critical elements involved in the theme; the H_____, the H_____, a W_____, and F_____.

3. Evaluate the word or words you live by now to determine if they are good and positive or bad and negative. Write out your findings in a brief paragraph.

4. List three negative word dynamics from your past that have affected you through the years.

5. List three positive word dynamics from your past that have influenced you today for success and blessing.

6. Name an achievement in your life that was directly related to an implantation or autoimplantation that you acted upon by faith to see a good result.

7. I chose my education or life vocation as a result of faith action on a clear word on my heart (yes) (no).

8. I chose my life mate as a result of faith action on a clear word on my heart (yes) (no).

9. I chose my eternal destination as a result of faith action on a clear word from God's Word on my heart (yes) (no).

10. I see clearly the distinction between the world's word (philosophy) and God's word of truth (yes) (no).

11. State in one succinct sentence your life goal or purpose.

12. This goal has the elements of a heart word and persistent faith action (yes) (no).

13. List three negative word dynamics that come from your speech or action that need correcting.

14. The major areas of my life (marriage, family, health, job, school, parenting, leadership, etc.) function by clear and stated words (vows, covenants, contracts, by-laws, expectations, moral principles, etc.) (yes) (no) (partially).

15. List the top three areas in your life that you feel need the most attention for clear and positive word dynamics.

16. I often allow fear to suppress my faith action (yes) (no).

17. I have a time for Bible reading and meditation on the Scriptures and prayer (regularly) (seldom) (never).

18. Have you ever received a word on your heart and acted on it by faith?

19. Name one instance where you are convinced that God answered your prayer.

20. In the past I have been (obedient) (disobedient) to God's word on my heart.

If you had trouble answering the yes/no questions or if you came up empty on some of the listing statements it could indicate that you do not fully understand the concepts or that your life is not fully purposed for success and blessing God's way. You may need to read the book through again to gain an understanding of the concepts in order to apply them to your life. Your goal is to move beyond understanding of the theme and concepts to actual implementation in daily life. Your goal is to have inner eyes that see, inner ears that hear, a heart that receives a word, and faith that acts to see a wonderful result.

About The Author

Jerry Smith, B.S., M.Div, D.D., is a graduate of the University of Arkansas and Southwestern Baptist Theological Seminary. He has served as the pastor of five churches in the United States and participated in missionary projects in Europe, Africa, South America, and the West Indies. He is the founder and President of Jerry Smith Ministries, Inc., a non-profit evangelistic and missionary organization started in 1978. He is the author of numerous books on the Christian life and has spoken to over 5,000 different audiences since 1973. He and his wife, Sharon, have been married since 1972 and have three sons and a daughter.

Contact Information

www.jerrysmithministries.com

or

www.jerrysmith.org

0-595-30931-3